CLOSING THE LITERACY GAP IN AMERICAN BUSINESS

CLOSING THE LITERACY GAP IN AMERICAN BUSINESS

A Guide for Trainers and Human Resource Specialists

Edward E. Gordon, Judith A. Ponticell
and Ronald R. Morgan

QUORUM BOOKS
New York • Westport, Connecticut • London

Library of Congress Cataloging-in-Publication Data

Gordon, Edward E.
    Closing the literacy gap in American business : a guide for
trainers and human resource specialists / Edward E. Gordon, Judith
A. Ponticell, and Ronald R. Morgan.
        p.   cm.
    Includes bibliographical references and index.
    ISBN 0-89930-621-7 (alk. paper)
    1. Functional literacy—United States.   2. Employees—Training of—
United States.   3. Literacy programs—United States.
4. Individualized reading instruction—Case studies.   I. Ponticell,
Judith A.   II. Morgan, Ronald R.   III. Title.
LC151.G67   1991
418'.00715—dc20   91-22016

British Library Cataloguing in Publication Data is available.

Library of Congress Catalog Card Number: 91-22016
ISBN: 0-89930-621-7

First published in 1991

Quorum Books, One Madison Avenue, New York, NY 10010
An imprint of Greenwood Publishing Group, Inc.

Printed in the United States of America

The paper used in this book complies with the Permanent Paper Standard issued
by the National Information Standards Organization (Z39.48-1984).

10 9 8 7 6 5 4 3 2 1

To the thousands of
volunteers, tutors,
teachers and trainers
who have helped America's adults
improve their workplace literacy

Contents

Tables and Figures

Preface

For over two decades, we have had the opportunity to help workers and managers who lacked basic literacy skills. The information presented in this book is based on actual case studies and test data taken from a broad and diversified cross section of American business employees, including hourly workers in the factory, warehouse or office, as well as supervisors, managers and even executives in the boardroom. Companies and workers requested help in basic reading and math, managerial business writing and grammar, foreign languages, English as a Second Language (ESL) and sometimes speed-reading. Many of these employees had already experienced numerous failures and frustrations with traditional educational services and training programs. In most instances, corporations and/or individuals came to us as a last resort in an attempt to end years of personal hardship, discrimination and frustration or declining corporate competitiveness.

It has been of considerable interest to us watching the evolution of these work-related education-training issues. Before 1980, many corporations vehemently rejected any notion of housing an educational program within their organizations. However, more and more workers at all levels lacked essential literacy skills to efficiently perform on the job. By 1984, we were in contact with businesses requesting "tutors" for their employees in many skill areas because of past training program failures.

Since the early 1980s, public rhetoric about the problems of workplace literacy has increased but has led to little corporate action. Judith Ponticell and Ronald Morgan have worked with me to prepare this guidebook for people in commerce and industry who are concerned about the Work Force Education crisis. The majority of human resource and training and development managers remain uninformed regarding these multiple problems and their solutions. We intend to help close this information gap by reviewing what approaches work, for which audience and why. Our goal is to energize the business community into immediate action toward a systemic and structural change in training and development that includes Work Force Education programs.

The development of adult literacy is only a small part of our story. America must find a way to dramatically improve the education of its entire work force. Today our country needs employees with much higher educational abilities than in past generations. Limiting this discussion to "basic skills" or "literacy" is totally insufficient for America to remain globally competitive in the industrial or service economic sectors. We have developed Work Force Education™ as a new paradigm that encompasses twenty-first-century educational and training standards. There is much more conceptually to Work Force Education than acquiring better reading, math, writing and thinking skills. Instead of seeing this issue as a "technical problem" to be solved, managers must understand Work Force Education as part of a broader work-team "empowerment process." Work Force Education for the twenty-first century has the potential to become the linchpin of modern productivity, corporate innovation and renewed employee personal commitment.

Shortly before this book's publication, U.S. Labor Secretary Lynn Martin's Commission on Achieving Necessary Skills (SCANS) called for educators to begin phasing in the teaching of these complex skills required for the contemporary workplace. During the decade of the 1990s the authors envision Work Force Education as a process that will encourage school and business training programs to work in concert toward this goal. The alternative of economic stagnation now faces many businesses and their employees.

In what follows we will first outline the nature of this human resource development issue and briefly trace the history of literacy in the United States. A cross section of current basic-skill educational/training programs for the adult worker will then be examined, and how they can be best used in employee training. The focus will then shift to why so many adults, after receiving this training, still fail to learn the skills and application abilities required for their successful performance on the job.

A literacy training approach, the Individualized Instructional Programs™ (IIP), was developed by the authors to satisfy these requirements. The essential components of the IIP will be described in great detail. Why does this program succeed? Who are the types of workers best suited for its use? A summary of numerous case studies will illustrate the utility of using the IIP with both hourly workers and managers in the workplace. IIP alternative training formats will describe the benefits of potential applications that use Human Resource Development (HRD) trainers, volunteer company tutors or educators.

We will then examine how to successfully involve senior management in the development of a corporate Work Force Education policy. How will you manage a company task force that identifies needs of and solutions for this issue throughout the organization?

A comparison will then be made with how the international business community is now addressing the Work Force Education issue. We will see that this is an almost universal problem among the industrialized nations, and not a uniquely American business issue.

Finally, we will consider those Work Force Education trends that we expect will develop and persist into the twenty-first century. It is our view that American businesses will become much more closely associated with the local education process, guaranteeing an up-to-date, skilled, educated, competitive work force. Our concluding remarks lay out a "game plan" for HR managers as they establish a company, in-house Work Force Education program.

We have all heard the numerous doomsayers' accounts that time is running out for the American worker to preserve a trend-setting place in the world economy. Corporate America must face the reality of the diminished capacity of the public schools to support a work ethic of thinking, problem-solving, creative employees. In this book we have developed the case for Work Force Education as a viable short-term solution for the ever expanding education gap encountered by American business. Most of us will agree that the restructuring of U.S. elementary and secondary education is long overdue. An education revolution for the twenty-first-century work force is the only acceptable long-term solution. The business community can no longer passively wait for that long-term political change. Together we must adopt a Work Force Education plan that preserves our economic system and reenergizes America as a competitive world power.

Acknowledgments

The authors' material for this book was literally 23 years in the making. Without the close collaboration of Judith Ponticell and Ronald Morgan, I would never have coherently reviewed the mountain of information and research that is the foundation of this guide to workplace literacy education. Judy has helped me consider the data of over 7,000 individuals who have been tutored by our program. Her expertise in empirical research methodology, statistics and curriculum provided a fundamental base for our insights into how to best formulate Work Force Education programs for business. Ron provided the other important focal point for our joint collaboration, by relating the concept of how adults learn to the issue of literacy programs for the workplace.

Many other individuals helped to make this a "user friendly" guide, through their personal interviews with the authors or their contribution of materials. We wish to acknowledge the following: Dave Cox, Manager, Corporate Literacy Program, IBM, Chicago; Susan Hooker, Corporate Training and Development, Motorola; Patricia Garcia, Human Resources Development Institute, AFL-CIO; Charles O'Malley, Executive Assistant to the Secretary for Private Education under U.S. Secretaries of Education Bell, Bennett and Cavazos; Richard Nolan, Director General, Canadian National Literacy Secretariat; Peggy Luce, Director, Job Development, Chicago Association of Commerce and Industry; Dave Speights, Editor, *Report on Literacy Programs*; Paul Jurmo, *Business Council for Effective Literacy*; Julia Bauer, The Rockefeller Foundation; Day Piercy, Council on Urban Affairs; Suzane Knell, Illinois Literacy Resource Development Center; Leonard Lund, Conference Board; Constance Coleman, Job Corps Region V; Eunice N. Askov, Director, Institute for the

Study of Adult Literacy, Pennsylvania State University; Dominick M. Maino, Illinois College of Optometry; Lawrence M. Rudner, Director, ERIC Clearinghouse on Tests and Measurement; Doris Scott Baker, Best University, Inland Steel; Phillip Benning, Human Resource Manager, Clorox, Chicago; Larry Sharp, Human Resources Manager, Quaker Oats; and Keith Ervin, Education Director, Midwest Region, International Ladies Garment Workers Union, among many others.

We wish particularly to thank Professor Hans A. Schieser of DePaul University for his invaluable counsel and information regarding European education and job-training programs. Elaine H. Gordon, Instruction Librarian, DePaul University, contributed her masterful manuscript editing, research and pertinent criticism. Sandra Gula-Gleason's accurate word processing and formatting of our endless chapter revisions were essential in producing our final ideas clearly and concisely for the reader. We also wish to thank the managers and staff of Imperial Corporate Training and Development for supporting our field research and offering many valuable suggestions. However, for any errors or shortcomings found in this book, the authors take sole responsibility.

CLOSING THE LITERACY
GAP IN AMERICAN
BUSINESS

The Broken Cog in the American Economic Machine

The applicants that we do get are ridiculous. They can't read, they can't write . . . they can't do fractions and can't figure out how many inches there are in a ruler.[1]

President of the Illinois
Manufacturer's Association

The U.S. Department of Education reports an upsurge in the number of adult workers who function below the twelfth-grade skill level, which is now recognized as the twenty-first-century functional literacy standard. It will not surprise many human resource executives that today many adults fail to meet this standard. In the United States, 30 percent of unskilled, 29 percent of semiskilled and 11 percent of all managerial, professional and technical employees are functionally illiterate.[2]

In what has been the closest to a national survey on adult literacy, the Census Bureau and U.S. Department of Education tested a national random sample of 3,400 adults over 20 years of age. They found that one in eight Americans cannot read. Eight percent were from rural areas, 41 percent in large cities and 51 percent from small towns and the suburbs. English-speaking whites composed the largest nonreading group, 41 percent; blacks, 22 percent; Spanish-speakers, 22 percent; and all other non-English-speakers, 15 percent. The age groups of these illiterates were: 20 to 39, 40 percent; 40 to 59, 28 percent; and over 60 years of age, 32 percent.[3]

From a practical standpoint today (1991), 1 in 20 adults cannot read newspaper headlines, and 3 in 20 have trouble reading the sports page. For every 20 people, 4 fail to completely comprehend wire-service stories. Up to 8 in 20 adults have great difficulty reading manuals, safety directions and even product labels. Many of these adults fail to understand they even have a reading problem until it shows up at work.[4]

Maria's job at a daily newspaper is inserting sections by hand. Recently machines began doing the inserting. Maria must operate these machines but has difficulty reading the instructions to operate the new technology. She can read a few words in the instruction manual, but she often fails to understand what they mean. Until now her third-grade education level was adequate in her job. The new technology now requires more.[5]

So why care? Lack of basic skills in the American workplace has led to lower productivity and seriously reduces our capacity to compete internationally. Allen Sinai, the chief economist for the Boston Company of New York, sees this as a major change originating in 1980. Sinai notes, "Literacy, retraining, the ability to work with machines, is now much more important to keeping inflation down and productivity up." According to the U.S. Commerce Department, the U.S. economy reportedly now suffers an estimated $140 to $300 billion annual productivity loss traced directly to adult worker illiteracy.[6]

The enormity of the problem is compounded by the standard used to define *literacy*. If literacy is defined in terms of ability to read simple texts and street signs, then about 27 million adults would be labeled "illiterate." If the standard is higher—the ability to read local newspapers or digest magazines—about 45 million adults are illiterate. But if we define literacy as the ability to read technical manuals or national news magazines, then we might classify 80 million Americans as illiterate.[7]

As this Work Force Education crisis deepens, it has become a major contributing factor in helping the United States to become the world's largest debtor nation ($664 billion in 1989).[8] Without a new approach to education and training which produces a highly skilled and literate workforce, the United States is in danger of becoming a second or third rate economic power.

LITERACY'S WAR STORIES

Many have added their voices to warn us of this broken cog in the American economic machine. The United Nations Educational, Scientific, and Cultural Organization (UNESCO) ranks the United States 49th among the 156 United Nations members in terms of literacy, a drop of 18 places since 1950. The U.N. also reports that the high rate of American illiteracy makes it "the least developed" country of the major Western industrialized nations.[9]

A recent survey by the Human Resources Management Association confirmed this when it reported that 63 percent of the companies surveyed hired workers who lacked basic skills; 92 percent said they still had functionally illiterate employees working for them; 81 percent reported that these employees could not be promoted; and 10 percent reported workplace accidents caused by a lack of reading ability. However, 70 percent of the same companies did not provide any Work Force Education programs to their underskilled employees. Of those that did, 26 percent upgraded the skills of current workers only, not new hires, and 23 percent had employees with limited English abilities.

A joint study by the U.S. Departments of Labor, Education and Commerce contacted 134 small and large businesses. They found that employers were nearly unanimous in lamenting that entry-level workers lack appropriate job skills in reading, writing and math. The International Association for Evaluation of Educational Achievement estimated that 29 percent of high school students drop out before graduation. In addition, 20 percent of those who do graduate do not possess the skills required to function in today's workplace in basic entry-level positions. These same workers fail at problem-solving, teamwork, initiative and adaptability tasks in the office or workshop. Even more disturbing is the fact that 2.3 million Americans—including 1.2 million legal and illegal immigrants, one million high school dropouts and 100,000 refugees—are added to the U.S. pool of the functionally illiterate every year.

From a social welfare standpoint, a direct correlation has been made between the number of functionally illiterate adults beneath the standard necessary for current employment needs and the public money spent in the United States for child welfare and unemployment compensation. One-half of all heads of households cannot read above the eighth-grade level, and one-third of all mothers on welfare perform below the fourth-grade level in basic skills.[10]

Horror stories emerging from corporate human resource departments give broad credence to the Work Force Education crisis. The Midwest-based Campbell-Mithun-Esty Advertising reported that only one applicant in ten met minimum literacy standards for mail-clerk jobs. A New York–based insurance company estimated that 70 percent of dictated correspondence must be redone at least once because of human errors. Swift Textiles of Columbus, Georgia, installed Japanese-made computerized looms that many of its workers simply could not operate. Many employees lacked the basic reading and simple math skills necessary to operate the equipment.

IBM in Austin, Texas, reported that approximately 50 percent of the production work force is functioning at the fifth-grade level or lower in math. Approximately 32 percent read at the fifth-grade level or lower. Computer hardware and software products built at this IBM facility include computer workstations and printed circuit boards. These production programs require workers to be at least on an eleventh-grade competency level or higher.[11]

Motorola reported that 80 percent of all applicants screened nationally fail entry-level tests that require competency in seventh-grade English and fifth-grade math. Robert Galvin, Motorola's founder and Chairman, told an American Society for Training and Development audience that only one Motorola worker in five possesses the necessary Work Force Education skills to meet the quality standards demanded by the "factory of the future" workplace environment. Beyond mastery of basic skills, Motorola's employees will need to learn continuously as the workplace changes, be flexible, and work as members of problem-solving teams.[12]

UNISYS of Pueblo, Colorado, spent $50,000 for color photos that show how to assemble its machines. Employees cannot grasp written directions in company manuals.

An East Coast insurance company authorized a $22.00 payment on a dental claim. The patient was surprised to receive a check for $2,200. The clerk who processed the payment did not understand the meaning of the decimal point.

A Colorado resort hotel lost $1,500 worth of pots and pans in its kitchen. Employees could not correctly read the directions on the dishwashing cleanser.

In 1988 New York Telephone received 117,000 applications for several hundred full-time jobs. After the applicants' basic skills were assessed, only 2,100 individuals qualified for consideration.

Across the continent in Los Angeles, Security Pacific Corporation interviewed thousands for entry-level teller jobs who could not add or subtract well enough to balance their own checkbooks. An executive vice president complained, "I'm almost taking anyone who breathes." This increasing difficulty in hiring educated entry-level workers was confirmed by the *Saratoga Institute Human Resource Effectiveness Report/SHRM* (1990), which cited that the nonexempt cost per hire in 1989 was $803, up from $719 the previous year. This represented a rise of 60 percent since 1987. The report calls the dramatic nonexempt increase a "forerunner of the widely known shortfall of skills in the entry level ranks."[13]

THE CHANGING FACE OF AMERICA

Why do we now face this human resources predicament? The Hudson Institute's *Work Force 2000* reported that between 1955 and 1970, more people at work combined with higher output-per-worker (i.e., productivity) gave America a solid annual economic growth rate of 3 percent. This trend continued with the maturing of the "baby boomers" and with the addition of more women to the job rolls. But this process has ended.[14]

In 1990, labor force growth had fallen from 3 percent to 1 percent each year. Most of those who can work in today's economy are already on the job. Chicago and Illinois illustrate the problem. By the year 2000, the number of entry-level workers in Chicago is expected to decline 23 percent, from 563,000 to 432,000. For all of Illinois, the pool of young workers is projected to shrink to 544,000, a 25 percent reduction.[15]

In addition to a declining population of workers, the United States has begun a substantial demographic shift as women and minority group members make up an even larger percentage of the national work force. Only 9 percent of the growth in the labor force between 1986 and 2000 will be white males. Fifty-six percent will be minorities. By the year 2000, four of every five new workers will be minorities, women and immigrants. Much of this labor pool is now ill-educated or uneducated.[16]

In 1990, there were 7 million fewer people in the U.S. work force between the ages of 18 and 24 than in 1980. Leading human resource experts have suggested some strategies aimed at beating this labor shortage crisis: hire immigrants; hire ex-convicts; hire older workers; hire the handicapped; hire more women; and improve productivity. All of these options will require Work Force Education programs to make them succeed.

As the educational levels decline for an increasing number of new entry-level workers, the majority of new jobs in the 1990s will require some postsecondary education for the first time in history. Only 27 percent of all new jobs will fall into low-skill categories. This compares with 40 percent of jobs today. Jobs that are in the middle of the education skill level today will be the least skilled occupations of the twenty-first century. Technology demands more skills at a time when far too many workers have less personal knowledge to offer.

Even though many companies across America are beginning to experience trouble finding employees to fill certain jobs, there is no dramatic rush to deal with these changes in the work force. Few are using new approaches to train poorly prepared workers. A 1990 Hudson Institute/ Towers Perrin survey of Chicago-area businesses found that only 17 percent provided Work Force Education programs. Many have no plans to institute such policies. "That's astounding. It almost sounds like an ostrich's head-in-the-sand attitude," said David Glueck, vice president of Tower Perrin.[17]

However, several leading companies on workplace issues (e.g., Motorola, Inland Steel, Marriott, Clorox, M&M Mars, IBM, General Mills and others) are encouraging managers to become more sensitive to the Work Force Education issue. They recognize that it is not only the composition of the workplace that has changed but also the nature of work itself. Jobs in the service, information and manufacturing sectors continue to grow more complex while the majority of our schools are now structured to support the agrarian and grunt-labor/basic-skills jobs of the pre-1960s. It is our belief that those organizations that recognize this gap will enjoy a huge advantage over competitors that have not yet begun to address the problem.[18]

EDUCATION THAT FAILS AMERICA

Why have America's schools failed to produce a skilled work force? After almost a decade of efforts directed at school reform and billions spent in additional education dollars, are the public schools doing any better in preparing American youth for work? The National Alliance of Business surveyed 1,200 large U.S. corporations (June 1990) and found that 72 percent thought new employees' math skills had worsened since 1985. Sixty-five percent reported that reading skills had declined over the same period. Only 36 percent were satisfied with the competency of new employees entering the work force.[19]

The Alliance president, William Kolberg, noted: "We are on a collision course with the reality that America is developing a second class work force. Somewhere along the way we lost respect for the skills we now so desperately need in our factories and on the front lines of our service industries." The Alliance's *Work Force Study* (1990) predicts that filling the 82 million jobs that do not require a college degree may become impossible unless the U.S. educational system is changed. By the year 2000, 5 million to 15 million manufacturing jobs will require skills other than those used today, and an equal number of service jobs will be obsolete.[20]

The dilemma posed by the changing nature of work in an information- and service-based economy is made more evident in the curricular goals that will have to be developed to support that change. Public schooling objectives still focus largely on industry-based skills: read, write, count, add, subtract, multiply, divide, spell, punctuate, comprehend and communicate. Success in information technologies and service occupations depends on an entirely different set of skills: diagnose, determine, estimate, obtain information, organize information, identify alternatives, analyze, plan, coordinate, work collaboratively, implement and monitor.[21]

Equally troubling is the disappearance of the vaunted "American work ethic." Dr. Dong Man Cha, Director of Chicago's Language and Math Academy, attended the University of Chicago in the 1960s and returned to America in 1980. He recognized an enormous change in U.S. schooling during his 20-year absence. Discipline, the work ethic, and intellectual standards had virtually disappeared from many classrooms. "I was shocked to find that all those virtues I had associated with America, the very things that had made me want to come here as a boy, were now rapidly vanishing.[22]

Many business, government and educational leaders have established a twelfth-grade reading level as the current standard of "functional literacy." This requires that an individual will read a variety of material written in sophisticated, abstract language. An employee must be able to think critically and solve problems found in a high-tech world. Yet national assessments for both school-age students and young adults out of school (ages 21–25) indicate that only about 40 percent of these individuals achieve this literacy standard. Even more troubling is the fact that less than 20 percent of 17-year-old minority students and young adults ever master these abilities.[23]

How can this be happening? In 1990 the U.S. Department of Education estimated that education spending by federal, state and local government totaled $353 billion. The United States spends comparatively more on higher education, $216 billion, than ten other major industrial nations, including Sweden, Canada, Austria, West Germany, France, Australia, Britain, Holland, Japan and Italy. Historically, federal spending has been limited largely to higher education. But when spending on higher education is removed from comparative data, U.S. spending by state and local government on elementary and high school education falls to the bottom ($137 billion) of the 16 major industrial nations. Only Australia and Ireland invest less in their public elementary and secondary schools relative to the size of their economies than does the United States. As a result many teachers in the United States are poorly paid, and the education profession fails to attract a sufficient number of our best college graduates. By comparison, the Japanese government made a conscious decision during the postwar period to offer entry-level elementary school teachers up to $40,000 a year, the same salary level as a new engineer. This attracted very bright young adults into teaching. The Japanese public holds the teaching profession in far higher esteem than do most Americans. Too many contemporary horror stories abound concerning unmotivated, unprepared U.S. educators. A professor at a large midwestern university told the authors that several teachers enrolled in a postgraduate education course were functionally illiterate. The economics of human resource supply and demand apply as much to the classroom as to the factory or office.[24]

So what? Though America's public schools may have tightened their belts a notch or two, most upper-middle-class parents believe that their children are better-than-average achievers. We all probably suspect that the best students in America, many attending private schools, probably do just as well as the best students in Japan, West Germany or elsewhere. Unfortunately, the Education Testing Service (ETS), which administers the SAT, GRE and other national aptitude tests, refuted this argument in their 1990 report, *A World of Difference*. Using data from the International Association of Educational Achievement, headquartered in the Netherlands, ETS compared the top 1 to 5 percent of students in all of the developed countries. The report noted: "The most able U.S. students scored the lowest of all of these countries in algebra and were among the lowest in calculus. Furthermore, average Japanese students performed higher than the top 5 percent of the U.S. students in college preparatory mathematics."

ETS reported that the United States was the lowest of any country studied in math and science achievement. The algebra test scores of the top 1 percent, our most able students, were lower than that of the top 1 percent of any other country. The top 5 percent in algebra scores were lower than any other country except for Israel.

To drive this point home, ETS related the story of a Japanese semiconductor company that recently opened a plant in the southeastern United States. It had to use college students at the graduate level to perform statistical quality-control functions. These same jobs are performed by high school students in Japan.[25]

But Japan also has its own education concerns. Functional illiteracy among Japanese adults is almost unknown. The Ministry of Education's rigorous standardization of the way children learn basic skills produces dependable workers for the factory of the future. However, the later years of school spent in colleges or universities may fail to educate the original thinkers and leaders that Japanese business needs or the writers, scientists, poets and philosophers that Japanese society demands. It is important to note that more and more Japanese are studying at American universities or their branch campuses in Japan. U.S. higher education is recognized as being among the finest in the world and wonderfully diverse. As already noted, America outspends almost every other industrial country on higher education, with about 48 percent of all American 18-year-olds entering higher education institutions. This compares with 38 percent for Japan.[26] For the most part, the U.S. university scene remains an American education success story. However, American higher education is very uneven. At the top end of the spectrum exist Harvard, Princeton, Yale. At the other end, Miami-Dade Community College reported in 1990 that 25 percent of the top one-fifth of high school students lacked the basic language or math skills for college-level work. Overall, six out of ten Dade public school graduates who entered the college in the fall of 1989 had to take remedial courses in reading, writing and math. What is even more alarming is that 44 percent of students from private schools also failed minimum-skill standards and required remedial courses.[27]

Europeans also are worried that students are often ill-prepared for the workplace. In France, a debate about the "level of attainment" in student basic skills drew attention to its wide variations across the entire country. Britain's skill shortages show no signs of improving. With a school dropout rate of 60 percent, only 15 percent of all British 18-year-olds enter higher education. The average German academic level for the lower half of students is the same as the average for all English schoolchildren. British children in the bottom half of their class are as much as two years behind similar German and Japanese children in math skills.[28]

The MIT Commission on Industrial Productivity concluded in a major study, *Made in America*, that a comparison of cross-national research on education achievement showed American children far behind most other societies in science, math and language skills. This begins at an early age, with students progressively falling further behind as they move through the school years. A progressive failure of elementary and secondary schools in the United States is reflected by the high rates of functional illiteracy, even among workers that graduate from high school. This translates into an education pattern that graduates badly educated young adults with skills that are narrow (weak both in craft skills and higher academic abilities) and therefore susceptible to rapid obsolescence.

American high school vocational education enrolls about 5 million students annually. The MIT study reported that in comparison with vocational education in other nations, that in the United States "has a very disappointing performance and is not generally viewed as a viable pre-employment training system." Most programs are so weak that employers tend to "stigmatize workers" who have participated in high school vocational education.

Any comparison between U.S. schools and their foreign counterparts must be made carefully. But we now know that in many other industrial nations, there is a significant, growing discrepancy between what an average worker's education can produce and what is required by sophisticated technology in a twenty-first-century global economy.[29]

TECHNOLOGY CHANGES PRODUCTION

In the Brookings Institution's study "A Future of Lousy Jobs?," the editor Gary Burthless concludes that America's productivity problem "is not that we are drowning in a sea of lousy jobs, rather we have a surplus of workers whom employers must consider lousy—that is, workers who are relatively unskilled." Our education system produces students full of facts but lacking in thinking, problem solving, and technical skills. As the U.S. trade deficit swells, the pool of academically and technically accomplished workers is shrinking while the number of jobs requiring broad intellectual abilities is ever expanding.[30]

During most of the twentieth century, manufacturers and service companies fine-tuned a production process that broke down each job so that it was performed with minimal formal education or job training. America did not place a high emphasis on the individual employee's work. We narrowly defined tasks and motivated workers to produce more. Our mass-production system was so successful that few questioned its basic assumptions. American industry remained flexible because workers with limited skills became interchangeable. We simultaneously constrained the training of multiskilled workers. "Dumbed-down" jobs have required lower technical-skill levels since the turn of the century (nineteenth to twentieth).

The realities of a high-tech workplace are now in place for many large and small businesses. Alongside complex quality controls, global competition, production work teams, enhanced customer service and other modern business realities, we now know that the current work force is ill-educated to use technology at its fullest potential. Clustered microproduction facilities, automatic guided vehicles and computer-integrated manufacturing represent new programmable automation technologies that need a whole new corporate approach to the practice of human resource development. Computer software can check for spelling in a business letter but cannot proofread for complex meaning and grammar. Robots can assume assembly work from people, but new jobs will require both more technical skills and higher personal education abilities for monitoring and troubleshooting computerized equipment.

With mass production becoming outdated, high-wage nations like the United States will survive as a significant economic power in the twenty-first century only by increasing product quality, offering consumers greater product diversity, speeding up the introduction of new products and creating newer automated manufacturing/industrial/service systems than are operated overseas.[31]

The good news from the U.S. Commerce Department, in a revised look back at the 1980s economy, was that the role of manufacturing had actually grown as a percentage of the GNP. Even though manufacturing employment had fallen, the sector grew through the increased productivity of individual workers until 1989.[32]

The equally bad news from the Labor Department is that those worker productivity gains are now vanishing. Labor costs continued to rise as the economy constricted. Productivity fell 0.8 percent in 1990, compounding a 0.7 percent drop during 1989.[33] The National Center on Education and the Economy, in its 1990 report *America's Choice: High Skills or Low Wages*, concluded that if U.S. productivity continues to decline, either the top 30 percent of America will grow richer while the bottom 70 percent becomes increasingly poor, or the entire population will be threatened with a long-term drastic reduction in its standard of living.

An example of this problem is the need of employees in many types of organizations to apply statistical process control (SPC) technology for quality assurance. Many cannot do the math required, are poor verbal communicators, and have never learned how to conduct an effective meeting. However, all these issues are important for the effective use of statistical process control technology. These new technologies require the ability to search for and retrieve information, work collaboratively to solve problems, make decisions and think creatively. In formal schooling, students are insulated from what they will see and experience in the workplace. Schools, despite the national attention to restructuring, still structure learning as an individual effort (don't talk), as expert-driven (don't question the teacher) and as memorized, fragmented facts (teach to single-answer tests). What is taught in school does not, as yet, prepare workers who can use collaborative problem-solving skills, interpersonal skills, and adaptability to change and ambiguity. The $500 million spent by business on basic skills is only a small part of the $30 billion allocated for formal employee training. With the inception of Work Force Education to deal with growing education and training deficiencies, the National Association of Manufacturers predicts that over the next ten years, formal training budgets will increase to $88 billion annually.[34]

THE WORK FORCE EDUCATION SOLUTION

During the 1980s, more than 40 percent of the 1979 Fortune 500 companies were dropped from that list. The Japanese seemed to "reinvent" the car, taking over 30 percent of the U.S. auto market for themselves. We have all observed the impressive surge of productivity in Korea, Taiwan and Singapore in the international market. Soon a united Europe will emerge as a stronger economic rival.[35] Yet the commitment of most companies to training and development remains grossly inadequate. According to former Labor Secretary William Brock, less that 1 percent of businesses account for 95 percent of all training funding. The companies doing most of these development programs use their money to train managers, not hourly workers.[36]

America is in a race between capital technology and human resource education. Many in business, labor and government feel that the United States is now losing. Chrysler Chairman Lee Iacocca, during an address to the National Association of Manufacturers, said: "It goes without saying that we as manufacturers have a huge stake in education. Would you believe survival? You want to know what Chrysler's most harrowing, private nightmare is? Our nightmare will be finding people capable of running that sophisticated plant in years to come."[37]

In a speech at the City Club of Chicago, Preston Townby, the president of the Conference Board, a New York nonprofit business think tank, revealed that findings from a survey on the American work force confirmed widespread inaction. American employers are well aware of basic skill deficiencies among their workers, but few are willing to do anything about it. Almost half of the surveyed companies say that over 35 percent of their current workers are incapable of doing more complex work. However, few of these companies have a Work Force Education program to address the problem. Most companies do not test for reading or math skills. Indeed, few organizations know how many of their current employees are adequately literate. Twenty percent of these companies have increasing trouble finding qualified literate people for entry-level jobs, but few have any literacy training programs to fill this void. About 14 percent can trace serious work delays and stoppages directly to workers who cannot read, perform math operations, write adequate reports or utilize thinking skills to get the job done.[38]

A Conference Board survey of nearly 600 CEOs suggests that U.S. business may experience a decline in the 1990s. About half of these executives expect that the U.S. GNP will not match the 2.9 percent growth rate of the 1980s. The biggest reasons for this economic decline are, in descending order:

1. health care costs
2. the federal budget
3. the S&L/banking crisis
4. Work Force Education
5. the foreign trade deficit
6. environmental cleanup costs
7. an aging infrastructure
8. slow productivity growth[39]

Some companies have heard and already understand these urgent signals from the work force. Xerox, Motorola, Polaroid, General Motors, Ford and Chrysler are among the few companies that have made a strategic HR commitment to compete nationally and internationally. They know that today every country in the world can buy the same machinery. These companies have confidence in their products but also think their people are important resources worth the investment of additional money and effort. But these corporations remain in the minority, which may propel American literacy and economic productivity in the 1990s into a serious economic-social crisis of monumental proportions. Few small businesses have organized Work Force Education programs. Strategically, this represents a major training gap, considering projections that 85 percent of the work force in the year 2000 will work for firms employing fewer than 200 people.[40]

U.S. business can continue to send skilled labor jobs overseas. During the 1980s, one "home-grown" industry after another conceded to more aggressive and competitive foreign competitors. First went cameras, followed by televisions, tape recorders, stereo equipment and semiconductors. In 1990, Cincinnati Milacron, the last wholly U.S. producer of heavy industrial robots, sold its business to a Swiss firm. Its market share had dwindled from a commanding 75 percent to only 10 percent because of a lack of competitiveness. We can automate to accommodate a low-skilled domestic work force. American business may decide against upgrading its operations in the plant or office and may veto required Work Force Education programs needed by many employees. If most new jobs become low-skill jobs, America will also have chosen low skills and corresponding low wages. We will have settled for lower productivity and a universal lower standard of living for everyone.[41]

For many in American business, the necessity of Work Force Education represents a severe corporate culture crisis. A large metal-container manufacturer allowed a midwestern production plant to dwindle from 4,000 to 1,500 employees. To introduce new technology and make the operation profitable, the plant required extensive remodeling and a Work Force Education program for its employees. However, since senior management had never before offered extensive training for its hourly workers, the alternative decision was made to shut down the plant gradually through attrition over a ten-year period. This resulted in a $200 million loss.

"Job upgrading and lifelong learning are truly new concepts for the American economy," A. William Wiggenhon, the vice president and director of education and training for Motorola, told a congressional subcommittee. "In a competitive global market, they are not merely quality of life issues, but questions of economic survival."[42]

American companies today need well-educated, motivated people throughout their organizations. Training is the key goal in a strategic plan for corporate growth and profitability. But this training is much broader than the question of worker literacy. U.S. business needs workers who can think, read detailed instructions, write clear reports and apply math skills to precision manufacturing or computer programming needs. These workers must be capable of using these educational skills for a variety of jobs—technical, clerical or professional. American executives need to travel abroad and converse in other languages and understand foreign cultures and business practices. We have concluded that until the nation's public schools can provide these prerequisites for the twenty-first-century economy, corporate human resources must vigorously pursue a Work Force Education program. There are few, if any, palatable economic alternatives for America. David Cox, the manager of IBM's literacy programs, believes, "If we don't act and do something . . . I can guarantee you that the social and economic order as we know it today is headed for serious difficulty."[43]

These are the components of the contemporary Work Force Education crisis in America. Conceptually, it is not just teaching reading, math, writing, a foreign language or a technical skill. Work Force Education is a human resource response to twenty-first-century competitive requirements. There is more to be gained than higher levels of literacy and thinking skills for workers. Instead of seeing this as a "technical problem" to be solved, managers must understand Work Force Education as part of a "new work culture" that empowers personal commitment, innovation and productivity.

Before proceeding with our discussion of the available human resource solutions, we will briefly review how American businesses in past generations satisfied their own Work Force Education requirements. We will see how an earlier training and educational transition period was mandatory for nineteenth-century business to secure a properly educated twentieth-century America.

NOTES

Superscript note numbers in this and subsequent chapters direct the reader to publication information for both references cited parenthetically in text as well as to sources for general reading. Readers should be aware that superscript note numbers in many instances cover several paragraphs preceding the appearance of the note.

1. Robin Gareiss, "High Schools Flunking Out in Job Training," *Southtown Economist* 12 (October 1988): 19.

2. Ron Zemke, "Workplace Illiteracy, Shall We Overcome?" *Training* 26 (June 1989): 33–39.

3. Jean-Pierre Vélis, *Through a Glass, Darkly: Functional Illiteracy in Industrialized Countries* (Paris: UNESCO, 1990), 65–66.

4. Marrietta Castle, "Adult Literacy Efforts: Gaining by Losing Control," *Reading Today* 8, no. 4 (February/March 1991): 9.

5. Catherine M. Petrini, "Literacy Programs Make the News," *Training and Development Journal* 45, no. 4 (February 1991): 30.

6. "Productivity Drop Is Biggest Since '81," *Chicago Tribune*, 5 August 1988, sec. 3, p. 3.

7. J. S. Chall, E. Heron, A. Hilferty, "Adult Literacy: New and Enduring Problems," *Phi Delta Kappan* 69, no. 3 (November 1987): 190–96.

8. "U.S., at $663.7 Billion, Deeper in Debt to World," *Chicago Tribune*, sec. 3, pp. 1, 4; Zemke, "Illiteracy," 34, 35.

9. "Fresh Statistics," *Report on Literacy Programs*, 17 May 1990, 77; "Slants and Trends," *Report on Literacy Programs*, 31 May 1990, 81; "Survey: Most Workplace Literacy Problems Remain Undiscovered until Promotion Time," *Report on Literacy Programs*, 28 June 1990, 100.

10. Day Piercy, *Developing Chicago's Workforce: An Adult Literacy Basic Skills Initiative* (Chicago: Chicago Council on Urban Affairs, 1989), 7; "Slants and Trends," *Report on Literacy Programs*, 28 June 1990, 97; "Prisoner Literacy Amendment," *Report on Literacy Programs*, 26 July 1990, 114.

11. Alecia Swasy and Carol Hymorwitz, "The Workplace Revolution," *Wall Street Journal*, 9 February 1990, Education section, 6–7; "How Business Is Joining the Fight against Functional Illiteracy," *Business Week*, 16 April 1984, 94.

12. Robert Galvin, Speech to Region V ASTD Conference, 1 November 1988, Schaumburg, Ill.

13. Julie Amparano Lopez, "System Failure," *Wall Street Journal*, 31 March 1989, 48–49; *Human Resource Management News Weekly* 28 (July 1990): 2; David Lewis, "Colorado Companies Face Growing Gap between Literacy, Technology,"

Rocky Mountain News, 22 January 1991, sec. 1, 1; *The Crisis In American Education* (Schaumburg, Ill.: Motorola, 1991).

14. Arnold Packer, "Preparing Workforce 2000," *Human Capital* 1 (November/December 1989): 34–38.

15. Patrick Reardon, "Big Shortage of Workers Seen in City," *Chicago Tribune*, 25 May 1989, sec. 1, p. 10; Patrick Reardon, "Poorly Educated Put Job-Training Dollars to the Test," *Chicago Tribune*, 5 June 1989, sec. 2, p. 3.

16. George S. Odiorne, "Beating the 1990s Labor Shortage," *Training*, 27, 32–35.

17. Laurie Cohen, "Job Scene Changing, Bosses Aren't," *Chicago Tribune*, 23 July 1990, Sec. 1; p. 4. Arsenio Oloroso, Jr., "Local Companies Not Preparing for Aging of Workforce," *Crain's Chicago Business*, 23 July 1990, 16.

18. *The Bottom Line: Basic Skills in the Workplace* (Washington, D.C.: U.S. Department of Labor, U.S. Department of Education, 1988), 4.

19. Chris Lee, "Literacy Training: A Hidden Need," *Training*, September 1986, 64–71; "Employers Give Job-Seekers a Poor Grade," *Chicago Tribune*, 16 July 1990, Section 1, 3.

20. *National Alliance of Business Work Force Study* (Cleveland, Ohio: North Coast Behavioral Research Group, 1990).

21. M. Cohen, *Restructuring the Education System: Agenda for the 1990s* (New York: Carnegie Corporation, 1988).

22. Ron Grossman, "Bootstrap Academy," *Chicago Tribune*, 16 July 1990, Sec. 5, 5.

23. Jeanne S. Chall, "Policy Implications of Literacy Definition," in *Toward Defining Literacy*, ed. Richard L. Venezky (Newark, Del.: International Reading Association, 1990), 54–61.

24. "Spending on Schools, Pick Your Number," *Economist*, 17 February 1990, 1; "Report: U.S. Trails in Funding Education," *Chicago Tribune*, 16 January 1990, Sec. 1, 8; *Public Elementary and Secondary School Revenues and Current Expenditures for Fiscal Year 1985* (Washington, D.C.: Center for Education Statistics, U.S. Department of Education, Office of Educational Research and Improvement, March 1988); Charlene M. Hoffman, *Federal Support for Education: Fiscal Years 1980 to 1989* (Washington, D.C.: U.S. Department of Education, Office of Educational Research and Improvement, August 1990), iii.

25. Archie E. LaPointe, *A World of Difference* (Princeton, N.J.: Educational Testing Service, 1988); David R. Boldt, "Even America's Best and Brightest Aren't That Good," *Philadelphia Inquirer*, 4 February 1990, 2.

26. "Japan's Schools," *Economist*, 21 April 1990, 3; Norberto Bottani and Isabelle Delfau, "The Search for International Educational Indicators," *OECD Observer*, February 1990, 162–63.

27. Charisse L. Grant, "College Studies: Dade Graduates Lacking Basics," *Miami Herald*, 8 August 1990, 6.

28. "School Brief," *Economist*, 10 March 1990, 10.

29. Michael L. Dertougos, Richard K. Lester, Robert M. Solow, and the MIT Commission on Industrial Productivity, *Made in America* (Cambridge, Mass.: MIT Press, 1989), 82, 85.

30. Gary Burthless, ed. "A Future of Lousy Jobs," Washington, D.C.: The Brookings Institution, 1990.

31. Tom Hundley, "Big 3's Future Rides on Tips from Japan," *Chicago Tribune*,

19 March 1990, sec. 5, p. 7; MIT Commission, *Made in America*, 83; Anthony P. Carnevale, Leila J. Gainer, Ann S. Meltzer, and Shari L. Holland, "The Skills Employers Want," *Training and Development Journal* 42 (October 1988): 23–30; Lawrence Holpp and Richard S. Wellins, "The Role of HRD in World-Class Manufacturing," *Training*, March 1989, 50–55; Zemke, "Illiteracy," 38; Gene Marlowe, "Real U.S. Job Problem Called Bad Workers," *Richmond-Times Dispatch*, 1 April 1990, 12; David C. Rudd, "School Days Never End, Workers, Companies Find," *Chicago Tribune*, 17 February 1989, Sec. 7, 1, 16; Wendy Leopold, "Workers Get New Look at Three R's," *Los Angeles Times*, 13 February 1987 Sec. 1, 1, 22; *America's Choice: High Skills or Low Wages* (Rochester, N.Y.: National Center on Education and the Economy, 1990), 1, 38.

32. Merrill Goozner, "Study Shows No Drop in Manufacturing," *Chicago Tribune*, 5 February 1991, Sec. 3, 1.

33. "Drop in U.S. Worker Productivity Worst in 8 Years," *Chicago Tribune*, 5 February 1991, Sec. 1, 5.

34. *Crisis in American Education. America's Choice: High Skills or Low Wages!* Rochester, New York: National Center on Education and the Economy, 1990.

35. Tom Peters, "U.S. Graduates '80s Far from the Top," *Chicago Tribune*, 8 January 1990, Sec. 4, 8.

36. Gisela Bolte, "Will Americans Work for $5 A Day?" *Time* 136 (23 July 1990): 123.

37. "Workplace Technology Squeezing Out Illiterates," *Chicago Tribune* 4 June 1989, Sec. 7, 11B.

38. Preston Townby, "The Class of '95 Born to Fail?" Speech at the City Club of Chicago, 14 June 1990.

39. Leonard Lund and E. Patrick McGuire, *Literacy in the Work Force* (New York: Conference Board, 1990); "More Work Force Worries," *Report on Literacy Programs*, 2, 24, 29 November 1990, 188.

40. Lynn R. Offermann, Marilyn K. Gowing, "Organizations of the Future," *American Psychologist* 45 (2 February 1990): 96–97.

41. "There Goes Another One," *Time* 136 (September 199)0: 71.

42. John N. Maclean, "Upgrading of American Jobs Pushed," *Chicago Tribune*, 7 March 1987, sec. 4, p. 12.

43. "Training Tomorrow's Work Force," *Chicago Magazine*, January 1990, 129.

2

Adult Literacy:
Past-Present-Future

Society's acceptance of literacy as an essential for daily living has become an almost forgotten basic component of modern American life. Literacy slowly increased with the beginning of the industrial revolution, population growth, and urbanization. However, it is essential to recognize that there has never been an absolute standard for what constitutes "literacy." The level of literacy needed by an adult to profitably function in any specific era is defined by the societal values and requirements of that time. That level of "functional literacy" has constantly changed and will continue to change. To add further confusion, until the beginning of the twentieth century, any accurate measurement of who was literate was problematic at best and qualified by an assortment of historical motives.

Why has the level of American literacy become such a key determinant for our future in the twenty-first century? Part of the answer lies in coming to terms with the ever changing meaning of *literacy*.

A WORKING DEFINITION?

The U.S. Department of Education defines a literate person as one who has completed the sixth grade of school. This is far from adequate. The UNESCO definition is a very elastic one: "A person is literate who can with understanding both read and write a short simple statement on his everyday life." However, what is meant by "understanding" and "short simple statement"? These concepts remain too vague to act as our model.[1]

There are few contemporary absolute standards of literacy. A consensus does not exist on what constitutes literacy or illiteracy. Contemporary

America no longer even equates "schooling" with "literacy." We do know what skills in vocabulary, comprehension, writing and math theoretically are learned at each grade level of elementary school and high school. But it is shortsighted to rest our idea of "a literate person" solely on the achievement of these academic skills. Abstract reasoning ability, and its application to specific tasks, must be added to our definition.[2]

For our purpose of examining Work Force Education, "functional literacy" is best defined as the ability to read, write or compute at the appropriate level to accomplish the kinds of basic and everyday tasks found at home and on the job. Literacy is more than a set of skills; and it is not just a technical ability. When an occupation or daily living standards change, and the individual does not acquire new knowledge and application skills, then that person becomes "functionally illiterate."

Functional literacy in a language means the ability to read and write, to do something with the language. It does not mean that an individual recognizes that language is composed of words or that he or she can identify letters of the alphabet.[3]

Functional literacy in mathematics means the ability to add numbers, solve problems—to perform mathematics. It means the ability not only to recognize numbers, fractions or decimals but also to be aware of the vocational applications of being able to do mathematics.

In this information age, computer literacy requires the ability to do the computing, not just recognize or identify the information or numbers to be loaded into a computer.[4]

Adult literacy in the twenty-first century will require ever higher levels of educational competencies. It will never reach a static state because of ever accelerating technological advances. We must also recognize the human factor. Learning more and more skills for harder job-related tasks is not a natural, inborn process that is easy, automatic or inevitable. Ask any student. Learning is hard work; it takes time and considerable effort.

Literacy is one barometer measuring a society's technical sophistication. In the course of history, there has been a great metamorphosis in the definition of a literate person.

THE LEGACIES OF LITERACY

Before the availability of modern census data, historians counted signatures on documents from church registers or civil court records. They broadly used the ability to sign one's name as a determinant of literacy. Using this data, historians estimated what proportion of the entire population was literate.

Before the twentieth century, only a small fraction of all children went to school. Many were taught at home. In the eighteenth and nineteenth centuries, women were considered literate if they could read. It was then thought essential that women read the Bible and other religious books because of their future role in child rearing. Writing was thought to be a useless and dangerous skill for women, since it was then considered necessary only for business. Society prohibited women from the world of commerce and industry. Since women did not sign documents, but many were able to read, how accurate are the historians' literacy estimates from these early time periods? Another troubling fact in interpreting the historical record is that many male signers of documents never went beyond learning how to sign their names. So in many cases, a signature was the mark of a population that knew how to sign but not always how to read or write. Critics charge that the relationship between the learning of writing and reading skills varied enormously from place to place, from time to time or from group to group.

Keeping all of these possible exceptions in mind, we find that after 1600, the percentage of signers rose sharply in Europe and America. Based on this ability to sign a parish register, male literacy in New England was estimated to be 60 percent, as compared with 40 percent in England. The passage of school attendance laws in New England was a primary reason for this great disparity. Male literacy based on signatures on New England wills showed a steady rise throughout the seventeenth and eighteenth centuries (1650—60%, 1705—70%, 1758—80%, 1795—90%). These rates compared favorably with those of Europe in 1800 (France 54%, England 62%, Scotland 88%).

Beginning with the 1840 U.S. Census, literacy data was based on asking heads of families how many persons in the family over age 20 had the ability to read and write. However, this form of "self-reported literacy" contained many accuracy problems. What it meant to read and write was self-defined and self-assessed by each adult. Sometimes illiterate adults reported themselves as being illiterate in writing but not in reading (thinking this was the lesser evil), thereby further distorting the census numbers reported at the time.

These problems were partially corrected by the 1870 U.S. Census. For the first time, literacy information was gathered on children between the ages of 10 and 19. More important, for the first time a distinction was made between reading literacy and writing literacy. As a result, the 1870 census showed a 25 percent decline in U.S. literacy since 1860. (See Table 2.1.) By 1900 the U.S. Census Bureau defined an "illiterate" as a person 10 years of age or older unable to read and write in a native language.[5]

In the nineteenth-century United States, business and political leaders' linkage of schooling with social progress was a social force behind the continued universal decline of illiteracy. The world of economic and political theory represented by John Locke and Adam Smith, was now joined by Samuel Gompers of the AFL, the industrialist Henry Ford, the scientist Thomas Edison, the "robber baron" Andrew Carnegie and the

Table 2.1
U.S. Illiteracy Rates

| Year | All U.S. | Whites | | All Whites | Blacks |
		Native-born	Foreign-born		
1860	8.3	---	---	---	---
1870	20.0	---	---	11.5	81.4
1880	17.0	8.7	11.8	9.4	---
1890	13.3	6.2	13.1	7.7	57.1
1900	10.7	4.6	12.9	6.2	44.5
1910	7.7	3.0	12.7	5.0	30.4
1920	6.0	2.0	13.1	4.0	22.9
1930	4.3	1.5	9.9	---	17.5
1940	2.9	1.1	9.0	---	11.5
1952	2.5	---	---	1.8	10.2
1959	2.2	---	---	1.6	7.5

Source: 1988 U.S. Census Bureau

politician Theodore Roosevelt. These men saw literacy and education as fostering a better American society. Their view was that education helped create useful, productive members of society. A new relationship existed between the social and economic forces spawned by nineteenth-century U.S. industrialization. Instead of home crafts and agricultural industries, a worker's production was now set by a clock and an imposed production schedule. Literacy through schooling was one of the best mediums discovered by business to perpetuate productive worker values that included punctuality, respect for authority, producing quality work and self-discipline. These were the essential work-ethic demands of a new twentieth-century mass-production urban society.[6]

The impetus for the industrial revolution in America first began, particularly in the textile industry (1790–1830), as a response to a severe shortage of unskilled labor. This necessitated the introduction of labor-saving devices. However, this new technology relied on sophisticated gauging techniques, variable speed control, automatic stop-motion mechanisms and advanced cutting tools. A severe shortage of machinists appeared as industry expanded. As the eighteenth century advanced, even available machinists proved themselves to be increasingly incapable of operating more complex technology. Most machinists until then had relied on rule-of-thumb methods and had neither the mathematical nor the technical knowledge required to mass-produce precision parts.

Industry and the skilled trades responded by establishing "mechanics' institutes" as voluntary organizations that promoted the learning of practical and scientific knowledge. However, the reading and math used by most of these institutes far exceeded the prior school preparation of many workers. Proposals began to appear by mid-century in many trade journals calling for educational reform to bring this instruction into the common school. The *Scientific American* noted in 1859, "We cannot help reflecting, as we write, how many thousands of dollars, and how much wasted brainwork would have been saved to the inventors of this country, if our common schools had paid more attention to the physical and mathematical sciences than they have hitherto done." These "old" ideas sound strikingly familiar to a late-twentieth-century audience.

Moreover, it is interesting to note that education for industrial utility was not enthusiastically shared by all. Many argued that literate workers would place too much pressure on the social system. A well-educated worker might become not only unhappy with his/her job and social standing but also politically critical and restive. Literacy only alienated people from manual labor. The natural social order would be undermined, social mobility overpromoted. Why should business have to pay to educate its workers? This debate went on throughout the nineteenth century and continues into our own time. The American public school won out.

Good, free public schools emerged victorious through an alliance among educators, social reformers and workers' associations. These diverse groups agreed that America's multiplying skilled-machine factories needed workers with greater knowledge and technical skills. They saw public education as largely industrial education. It would provide the functional context for teaching the elements of the mechanical arts and natural sciences needed to work in industry or agriculture. (These were the two chief occupations for most Americans of the time.)

Horace Mann, America's most famous advocate of free public education, often based his arguments on the role of the schools in industrializing America. Mann was from Massachusetts, which might help explain, in part, why that state was the first state not only in starting early industrial production but also in establishing a public education system. Mann praised the improvements that manufacturing was bringing to his state.

He argued that better-educated working men and women would bring greater prosperity for all.

In other states, such as Connecticut, companies responded to this broad appeal by building large halls for workers' lectures, concerts and political meetings. Some industries even built schools. Business began to use "scientific management" and industrial psychologists to formulate aptitude and performance ratings for workers. By 1910, 29 states provided some form of functional-context, industrial education. Ten states had opened technical high schools. Eighteen offered basic manual-skill training. Eleven states included skill-trade or industrial courses in public school requirements.

The effort to provide schooling and literacy in America supported an age of unprecedented social change and economic expansion. Literacy contributed to the establishment and growth of middle-class America. It created better occupations at higher pay. Literacy enhanced individuals' abilities and skills. It helped American culture flourish, and it ensured the United States a place as an emerging world power. Universal literacy became a cornerstone for modernization, democracy and the American consumer economy.[7]

By 1918, all 48 states had enacted compulsory school attendance laws that supported the expansion of literacy. But the task was far from complete. With America's entry into World War I in 1917, the first accurate national literacy tests were conducted for recruits by the U.S. Army. Twenty-five percent of all draftees were found to be illiterate. Ten million men registered for the draft. Approximately 700,000 were totally illiterate. It was not uncommon for federal officers to arrest illiterate "draft dodgers" who simply did not know about the draft or know that the country was even at war.

During the 1920s and 1930s, America's public schools continued to provide the greater population with training in functional, basic literacy skills. At this level they were highly successful. By the 1940 U.S. Census, completion of the fourth grade was considered evidence of literacy. Only 2.9 percent of all Americans failed to meet the 1940 standard. However, by the end of World War II in 1945, the military had rejected nearly 750,000 potential draftees because of educational deficiencies.

By 1950, over 10 million Americans had never attended school or had completed less than five years of education. During the Korean War, between 1950 and 1953, approximately 300,000 men were rejected for illiteracy. Of those who had enlisted, 10 to 15 percent had less than a fourth-grade education. During the 1950s, the Bureau of the Census reported that 6.8 percent of the entire U.S. work force had less than five years of schooling and were considered functionally illiterate. Of that group, 2 percent were totally unable to read or write.

Cook (1977) believes that by the 1970s, at least a ninth-grade education came closer to defining the functional reading needs of adults. Driver's license applications, banking forms and insurance claims require a tenth-grade level or higher. IRS tax forms have a readability level at or above twelfth grade. In its 1969 population survey, the U.S. Census Bureau reported that approximately 39 million people lacked a ninth-grade education. For the entire twentieth century, millions of Americans remained functionally illiterate by choice or public neglect. Their children grew up assimilating the same indifference. They are now an integral part of the work force of the 1990s.[8]

MEASURING THE WORK FORCE EDUCATION CRISIS

How extensive is adult "functional illiteracy" as America arrives at the twenty-first century? That depends on your measuring stick. A recent statement on literacy by the U.S. Department of Education established the adult literacy standard as "the ability to read, write, and compute . . . the ability to hold a decent job to support self and family, to lead a life of dignity and pride." But at what literacy level can an adult hold a "decent" job?[9]

At the lowest literacy standard, an employable adult can read simple texts, possibly parts of the daily newspaper with difficulty and street signs. This represents about the fourth- to sixth-grade level of "functional literacy." At this level, 16 to 27 million adults are considered functionally illiterate. (See Figure 2.1.)

A higher standard at the eighth-grade level requires the ability to read a driver's license manual, fill out a job application, read short digest articles or the newspaper and compute change when making a purchase. Forty-five million Americans do not have these educational abilities.

The highest literacy standard of high school (tenth to twelfth grade) includes the ability to read technical manuals, *Time* magazine and *Sports Illustrated*, read and compute an IRS tax return and write a simple letter. Between 44 to 82 million adults lack these simple skills. (See Figure 2.1.)[10]

Business communication and manufacturing modes are changing at an ever increasing pace. Computerization of the office and shop means that the great majority of future workers must learn to integrate and coordinate different reading, math and thinking abilities to perform most jobs. This requires a far higher level of functional literacy for the average worker in the 1990s than it did for workers in 1900, 1950 or even as late as 1970.

Trainers and developers from industry and adult-education specialists agree that a fourth-grade skill-level target for business is far too low. The reading and math materials that an adult needs to use in daily living are written at a level of difficulty far beyond a minimal fourth-grade ability.

Figure 2.1
Functional Illiteracy

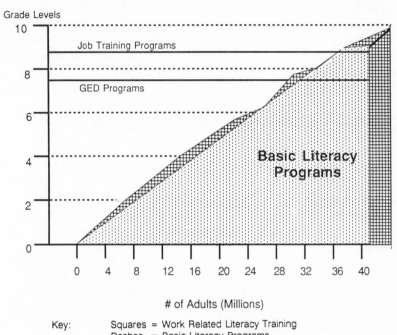

Key: Squares = Work Related Literacy Training
        Dashes = Basic Literacy Programs

For example, written material essential to many jobs for enlisted men in the U.S. Army exceed a twelfth-grade level of reading proficiency.

The twelfth-grade level is the most widely accepted standard now used (1991) by business and industry for functionally literate workers. Though some "grunt" labor jobs may still persist, by the year 2000 the vast majority of occupations will require twelfth-grade or even thirteenth-grade skills and aptitude. This means that 40 percent (82 million) of all U.S. workers today will require Work Force Education programs to keep America competitive in the world marketplace of the twenty-first century. To make matters worse, there is no relief in sight. As we have already seen, demographic figures suggest that the number and percentage of adults likely to seek literacy help will consistently increase well into the twenty-first century.

Who makes up this population of adult illiterates? Literacy abilities vary dramatically in contemporary America across racial and ethnic groups. Forty-one percent of illiterates are English-speaking whites. Blacks compose 22 percent, Spanish-speakers tie with 22 percent and 15 percent are other non-English-speakers. Less than half of adult functional illiterates have limited English abilities and are classified as English as a Second Language (ESL) learners. Most ESL learners are illiterate in their own native language as well. The larger proportion of adult functional illiterates were born in the United States. They attended school, some completing high school and others dropping out. However, it is increasingly evident that most of the members of this group have a basic learning block, or learning disability. These adults have had the same literacy difficulties since their earliest days in elementary school. What they personally experience is a failure to learn, not just a failure to read, calculate or write on the job. The largest number of these learning-disabled adults are clustered below the sixth-grade level (16 million to 27 million).[11]

In contrast, how do other adults perform at an advanced literacy stage (seventh to twelfth grade)? Today, nearly all young adults (ages 18–35) are considered to be literate by the U.S. Census standard of the last century. Eighty percent read at or above the level of the average eighth-grader. About 60 percent even read at or above the eleventh-grade level. Of those with a college degree, 80 percent read at an eleventh-grade level. However, numerous studies indicate a disturbing inability among young adults, working on complex tasks, to use information effectively above a literal concrete level. Only a small percentage, using their literacy skills, can carry out moderately complex tasks. Many have great difficulty synthesizing the main argument from a newspaper article, computing the cost of a meal in a restaurant or determining correct change from a stated amount. Only about 40 percent of all white students, 10 percent of black students and 20 percent of Hispanic students were found to be successful at these activities.[12] It is not surprising that an even more recent study by the Times Mirror Center reported that this same under-30 video generation "knows less, cares less and reads newspapers less" than any other generation in the past five decades. Only 30 percent of Americans under 35 reported reading a daily newspaper. This figure sharply contrasts to the 67 percent of young people who were reported to read a newspaper every day in a 1965 Gallup poll. The study also reported a 20 percent decline in knowledge of news stories and a 40 percent decline in the likelihood that these young adults could identify world newsmakers such as England's former Prime Minister Margaret Thatcher.[13]

An earlier 1988–89 Gallup survey commissioned by the National Geographic Society validates the growing ignorance of the average young American adult. One in seven could not find the United States on a blank world map. Twenty-five percent failed to find the Pacific Ocean. American students between the ages of 18 and 24 came in last among ten nations tested in geography. Fifty percent did not know that the Panama Canal reduces sailing time between San Francisco and New York. How can American business compete internationally if our entry-level workers and managers know so little about the world in which we live?[14]

A study by the American Council on Education in 1990 found that fewer and fewer of the 43 million American adults older than 18 who dropped out of school are seeking the high school "equivalency diploma" (GED). Since 1942, the GED has become a gateway to educational and economic opportunity for millions of adults. An individual must take an examination and surpass the performance of about 30 percent of graduating high school seniors to earn an equivalency diploma. Unfortunately, the study reported a 7 percent drop in the number of GED candidates between 1988 and 1989. Even more significant, the number of candidates who are typical entry-level workers, ages 18 to 24, declined by 26 percent. Only half of this huge drop can be attributed to a general population decline for this age group. The study concluded, "If young people are choosing to work rather than complete their schooling, the price may be high for both individuals and society—individuals lose opportunities for additional training, advanced education, better jobs and higher wages, while society loses the increased productivity of better-educated, more highly skilled workers."[15]

The local impact of this undereducated population can be observed in a 1991 report on Workforce Development from the Chicago Council on Urban Affairs. The council concluded that with a current school dropout rate of 50 percent, 35 to 50 percent of Chicago's 2.8 million residents, over the age of 16 and out of school, fall below the sixth-grade education level, or cannot read and write English above the sixth-grade level.[16] Although adults living in urban areas have recently been the target of such negative publicity, other studies clearly prove that adult illiteracy is even higher in the rural areas of America.[17]

As U.S. business and industry introduces increasingly complex computer technology into the plant and office, a staggering number of older and younger workers are becoming the new peasants of the information age. Our sophisticated technology cannot be supported by antiquated training and education programs. But we must also understand that by the year 2000, more than 70 percent of America's jobs will not require a college degree. In 1989, out of 117 million employees, 40 million (34%) held jobs requiring less than a high-school education. These service, manufacturing or construction jobs are being displaced by technology that requires a better-educated worker or, more likely, are being exported overseas. Those workers with truly few skills by the year 2000 will find that only one job out of ten will remain. Forty-two million Americans (36%) are skilled workers with jobs that require additional technical/professional education beyond high school but not a four-year college diploma. These employees are skilled-trade workers, secretaries, mechanics, technicians, EDP workers, police, fire fighters and other apprenticed trades. These jobs will in the future require more workplace-based education and training. Many employers already report significant shortages of workers to fill these jobs. The college-educated (35 million, 30%) are the managerial and professional workers. Even at this level, more in-house company education will be required of specific workers to improve personal communication skills and to compete in international markets.

Before the end of the 1990s, the U.S. Department of Labor estimates, 75 percent of job classifications will require some postsecondary training for entry-level positions. This is a 25 percent increase, which we are ill-prepared to handle. Unlike other countries, contemporary America does not focus on either vocational education or personal growth and development. Instead, the public schools stress behavior and attitudes appropriate to good citizenship and moral behavior. Lately even this agenda has broken down.[18]

Recently, parents and businesses have sought to reinstall ethics and moral behavior into the curriculum. A Rockford, Illinois, high school district has begun offering employers a guarantee that it will take back any graduates who prove unprepared for the workplace and will tutor them until they are ready. The school's goal is to graduate "a thinking employee, one who gets to work on time and rarely is absent, one who has a positive attitude about producing a quality product." To earn a "Certificate of Employability," a student must maintain a 4-point grade average on a 5-point scale and must average no more than six days a year of absenteeism excluding a serious illness. Teachers also rate students on their work-ethic attitudes. Similar programs are operating in Wisconsin, Missouri, Colorado and Maryland. This solution is workable for some students, but what about the majority who will never qualify?[19]

Another response by business to prepare a better work force is a throwback to the "company schools" of the past centuries. If you need better-educated workers, start your own school. In an unprecedented modern experiment in urban education, the Corporate/Community School was established in 1988 in North Lawndale, one of Chicago's most notorious slums. This is a tuition-free school financed by corporate giants such as United Airlines, Baxter International, Quaker Oats and 13 other corporations. They have raised $3 million to educate 300 children, with per-pupil costs about $4,000 a year (the same amount spent by the Chicago Board of Education). The students, age two through eighth grade, are local inner-city youngsters. The school exists to demonstrate what can be accomplished in an urban setting if teachers are given broad discretion on how to teach, parents are involved at school, parents are visited at home by school staff and the principal can terminate any staff member who has not measured up. The companies financially supporting the school see this as a long-term model for reeducation in urban America, a model they hope will be copied by others.[20]

Schools alone cannot do the job to motivate and fill in the literacy gap.

Personal motivation for learning comes from giving every employee and student a meaningful opportunity to apply Work Force Education skills at a job or in preparation for work. Functional illiteracy mainly threatens America both economically, as our international competitiveness wanes, and politically, as a large number of adults vote less and are less critical of government. An illiterate adult becomes an easy target for those seeking to manipulate U.S. public opinion.

We must resist the notion that the United States is experiencing an "unprecedented literacy tailspin." Americans are not less literate today than they were in 1900. In many ways, the overall population is more literate. However, we have forever thrown away our old "yardsticks" and today demand a much higher level of personal education and/or technical skills. A crisis exists because the needs of a proportionally larger group for increased literacy have outpaced the public school system's ability to educate or train.

It is our view that a solution must be found in the short term by mobilizing corporate America behind Work Force Education programs at the local company level. However, Mikulecky (1990) reported that employers provide only 10 percent of employees with formal training and another 15 percent with informal on-the-job training. This is a long way from giving all workers the functional-context education they need for the twenty-first-century workplace. A dramatic increase in company training programs must be teamed with a long and overdue revamping of U.S. schooling and an engagement of family social values in support of the American work ethic and Work Force Education goals.[21]

In the next chapter, we will examine what is currently being done across the United States to meet the Work Force Education challenge. Many programs already exist that have great potential for contributing to a successful Work Force Education effort within corporate training and development organizations.

NOTES

1. Marie Costa, *Adult Literacy/Illiteracy in the United States: A Handbook for Reference and Research* (Santa Barbara, Calif.: ABC-Clio, 1988), 46–47.

2. Harvey J. Graff, *The Legacies of Literacy* (Bloomington: Indiana University Press, 1987), 388–89.

3. Geraldine Joncich Clifford, "Buch and Lesen: Historical Perspectives on Literacy and Schooling," *Review of Educational Research* 54 (Winter 1984): 472–500.

4. Arthur Luehrmann, "Computer Literacy, What Should It Be," *Mathematics Teacher*, December 1981, 683–90.

5. Philippe Aries and Georges Duby, *A History of Private Life: Passions of the Renaissance* (Cambridge: Harvard University Press, Belknap Press, 1989), 111–15; Graff, *Legacies*, 163–65, 173–74, 179, 260–62, 343–44, 351, 375; Carl F. Kaestle, "Literacy and Diversity: Themes from a Social History of the American Reading Public," *History of Education Quarterly* 28 (Winter 1988): 523–49.

6. Clifford, "Literacy and Schooling," 475; Costa, *Adult Literacy*, 4–7; Carl F. Kaestle, "Introduction to Special Issue on the History of Literacy," *History of Education Quarterly* 30 (Winter 1990): 487–91.

7. Edward W. Stevens, Jr., "Technology, Literacy, and Early Industrial Expansion in the United States," *History of Education Quarterly* 30 (Winter 1990): 523–44; Nell P. Eurich, *Corporate Classrooms* (Princeton, N.J.: Carnegie Foundation, 1985), 30–36.

8. Wanda Cook, *Adult Literacy Education in the United States* (Newark, Del.: International Reading Association, 1977), 11, 58, 64, 72, 105.

9. Clifford, "Literacy and Schooling," 476–78.

10. J. S. Chall, E. Heron, and A. Hilferty, "Adult Literacy: New and Enduring Problems," *Phi Delta Kappan* 69, no. 3 (November 1987): 190–96; Costa, *Literacy*, 75.

11. Graff, *Legacies*, 397; Clifford, "Literacy and Schooling," 476; Robert Galvin, Speech to Region V ASTD Conference, 1 November 1988, Schaumburg, Ill.; Chall, Heron, and Hilferty, "Adult Literacy," 191–93; "Fresh Statistics," *Report on Literacy* 2, no. 17 (May 1990): 77; *Cases in Literacy: An Agenda for Discussion* (Newark, Del.: International Reading Association, 1989), 11.

12. Costa, *Literacy*, 64–65.

13. Robert J. Samuelson, "The College Charade," *Washington Post*, 13 June 1990, 6.

14. "The Tuned-Out Generation," *Time* 136 (9 July 1990): 64.

15. "Study: Fewer High School Dropouts Seeking GED," *Chicago Tribune*, 22 October 1990, Sec. 1, 12.

16. "Chicago Challenge: Workforce Development," Chicago Council on Urban Affairs, February 1991, 6.

17. Susan T. Ferrell and Aimee Howley, "Adult Literacy in Rural Areas," *Journal of Reading* 34, no. 5 (February 1991): 368–71; J. Behrstock, "Reaching the Rural Reader," *Journal of Reading*, vol. 24, iss. 8, 712–18.

18. *America's Choice: High Skills or Low Wages* (Rochester, N.Y.: National Center on Education and the Economy, 1990), 26–28.

19. Jack Houston, "School to Offer Its Graduates a Job Guarantee," *Chicago Tribune*, 2 July 1990, Sec. 2, 1; Sonia L. Nazario, "Bearing the Brunt," *Wall Street Journal*, Special Section, "The Knowledge Gap," 9 February 1990, 20; Kaestle, "Literacy and Diversity" 523–49.

20. Karen Thomas, "Corporate Chicago Plunges into the School Business," *Chicago Tribune*, 19 August 1988, Sec. 1, 1–2; Eileen Ogintz, "Education, Inc.," *Chicago Tribune*, 4 December 1988, Sec. 5, 1, 10.

21. Larry Mikulecky, "National Adult Literacy and Lifelong Learning Goals," *Phi Delta Kappan* 72, no. 4 (December 1990): 304–9; Anabell Powell Newman and Caroline Beverstock, *Adult Literacy* (Newark, Del.: International Reading Association, 1990), 49–50; Stephen Franklin, "For Unskilled, Best Hope Is to Find Their Abilities," *Chicago Tribune*, 6 January 1991, Sec. 20, 23–24.

3

A Variety of Answers

To enhance our understanding of the Work Force Education problem confronting American business, we need to investigate how adult workers acquire different kinds of skills and aptitudes. An important related issue is the assessment of the various delivery systems available for Work Force Education. Who are the appropriate clients? What are the results?

In this chapter we explore a variety of answers to Work Force Education devised over the last 30 years. We will sketch a representative group of programs, equipment, tests and materials, and their "target population."

How can we fairly evaluate these programs? Definitely not in terms of current political rhetoric and the "marketing hoopla" that frequently clouds the adult-literacy arena. Instead we will evaluate aspects of each type of program in the following manner: Who should be targeted for education? At what educational levels has research pointed toward success? Why is the program effective? When is it available for workers? Where can the program be held?

We will first examine the oldest sector in this debate over solutions, the nonprofit, volunteer and governmental programs. After this we will turn our attention to the later entries, computer-based training and interactive video. Specific reading/math programs, training materials and adult skills tests will be our third focus. Finally, we will tell the story of how a growing number of American corporations, both large and small, are currently operating their own in-house Work Force Education programs. (See Table 3.1.)

The overall national educational response to preparing a work force for the twenty-first century has clearly been inadequate in terms of both the

Table 3.1
Principal Categories of Adult Literacy Responses

   I. Federal Programs

  II. Volunteer/Nonprofit Programs

 III. Computer-Based Training (CBT)

  IV. Interactive Videodisc (IVD)

   V. Textbook Series/Periodicals/Tests

  VI. Corporate In-House Programs

---

number of adults served and the resources allocated. It is estimated that less than 5 percent of adults who need workplace literacy skills are being helped. In addition, the approximately $100 million per year of federal funding devoted to literacy programs for adults provides an average of $160 per student per year when divided among the states.[1]

Program quality remains an even more serious issue. Current review of these programs shows that a large portion of the students learn little or nothing at all. Successful adult-literacy programs report that it takes from 50 to 100 hours of practice for adults at low-level literacy to become competent in reading and comprehend a sentence as long as the typical newspaper headline. For such low-level literates to master reading and comprehend a newspaper, several hundred hours will be needed. Only 10 to 15 percent of adults currently in literacy programs achieve that level. Published reports on adult-literacy programs cite the problem of part-time, often inadequately trained and underpaid teachers and staff members.[2]

The U.S. Department of Education reported that the national average attendance and retention rates were 60 percent for state-administered adult-education programs. Drop-out rates are commonly as high as 50 percent, often during the first few critical weeks of the program.[3]

The proliferation of small community-based and corporate programs has given few effective mechanisms for HR managers to make well-informed choices. This fragmentation of Work Force Education also has reduced the sharing of information among community programs competing for funds or among corporations citing dubious "proprietary information." Many of the reports and conferences on this topic lack the rigorous evaluation procedures found in other areas of training and education. Too much time is being spent by individual companies in "reinventing the wheel." A Work Force Education "literacy gap" has continued to grow as HR managers search, largely in vain, for reliable, understandable, useful information.

THE FEDERAL RESPONSE

Government funding of Work Force Education had its contemporary beginnings during the War on Poverty in the 1960s. The Economic Opportunity Act of 1964 inaugurated the "Adult Basic Education" (ABE) concept. The Adult Education Act and programs in federal agencies financially supported adult-literacy education programs in many states, and still do. These programs range from community-based volunteer literacy education to local community college GED classes. Employment training is also federally funded nationally through the Job Corps. Federal ABE activities in 1985 exceeded $345 million. In 1991, 12 separate federal agencies administered 78 programs related to adult literacy. What follows is a review of selected programs that are the main focus of federal government efforts.[4]

In 1964 Job Corps training centers were first established as another War on Poverty program; 107 Job Corps Centers are now located in 42 states, the District of Columbia and Puerto Rico. These training centers were designed to prepare disadvantaged young men and women ages 16 to 21 for employment through vocational training. It should be noted that the Job Corps also offers a remedial reading program that is linked to its training activities and programs for the development of appropriate social skills and work habits. About 90 percent of enrollees reside at the centers during their training. The Job Corps program offers educational and vocational-skills training using competency-based, individualized instruction.

Adult basic education and a new program (1991) that is designed to focus on adult learning problems are part of the Job Corps educational curriculum. Seventy-seven Job Corps Centers are "contract centers" operated by major corporations and nonprofit organizations. Educational/vocational programs include areas of business and administrative support, construction, engineering and its related technologies, marketing and distribution, mechanics and repair, precision production, electrical appliance repair and other occupational categories.

Typical business or industrial sponsors will employ the younger disadvantaged worker in a job that has broad occupational application for both men and women. The sponsor makes a donation of equipment or funds to establish this training linkage. Start-up time varies, but one and one-half to two years may be necessary to negotiate and staff a new Job Corps program.

The combining of a Work Force Education program and vocational training at a specialized residential facility for young adults makes good business training sense. With a successful completion ratio of 66.5 percent in 1990, the Job Corps translates into meaningful jobs at the local level for large and small businesses whose manpower requirements will increasingly need younger entry-level workers. (For more information about Job Corps, contact 1-800-TRAIN-YOU.)[5]

In 1988, the Adult Education Act was revised to include a "National Workplace Literacy Program" through 1993. Using model partnerships among business, industry, labor organizations and educational institutions, the program provides assistance for demonstration projects that teach literacy skills needed in the workplace. These model projects are designed to train adult workers who have inadequate basic skills and are unable to perform their jobs. Their eligibility for career advancement is contingent on improvement of their basic skills. Information on selected model programs funded by the Department of Education is disseminated throughout the United States to encourage broad replication by business. Funding for 1988 was $9.5 million, in 1989 $11.9 million and in 1990 $19.7 million. Manufacturing, service industries and union partners have all received project funding.

The National Workplace Literacy Program was designed to encourage the investigation of innovative approaches in business and industry. However, it was never conceived as funding a government solution to this workplace manpower program. Funds are very limited and usually help finance only a one-year project. In 1990, over 300 proposals were submitted, and about 71 programs were funded. There are other "demonstration projects" in adult literacy at the Departments of Education and Labor. Contact your local regional office for more information. A current difficulty is the high dropout rate among participants because of ineffective Work Force Education programs. Many participants need very high-powered, work-related, basic educational skills training with immediate "payoffs." These low-skilled workers can become easily frustrated and drop out of the program.[6]

The new National Literacy Act (1991) will establish a National Institute for Literacy to conduct research and policy analysis, and distribute this information to literacy providers. The institute represents an interagency agreement between the Departments of Education, Labor and Health and Human Services to pool most literacy programs. It will be housed in separate offices, and operate as an independent agency.

The Job Training Manpower Partnership Act (JTPA) provides over $1.7 billion in specific job training for entry-level, "high-risk" workers (i.e., minority, low socioeconomic, unemployed). However, basic educational skills training is not funded separately but is part of a grant process requiring both the recruitment of "high-risk" workers and their placement at "real" entry-level jobs. For this reason local Private Industry Councils

(PICs) have been created across America to facilitate matching workers to jobs.[7]

VOLUNTEER/NONPROFIT PROGRAMS

Throughout the United States in both urban and rural areas, there exists a multitude of community-based literacy center offerings: Adult Basic Education (ABE), GED (General Equivalency Diploma) (i.e., a high school equivalency program), Literacy Volunteers of America or Laubach Literacy programs. Some offer assistance to dropouts; others help welfare recipients upgrade their skills so they can obtain employment and leave the welfare rolls. Other programs teach English to recently arrived immigrants and refugees. There are numerous classes and tutoring sessions taking place in public housing projects, jails and libraries and an increasing number at work locations.

Laubach Literacy Action (LLA) is among the oldest contemporary nonprofit adult-literacy groups. Established in 1955, it is based on the work of Dr. Frank Laubach, who developed the "Laubach Method" and materials as a carefully sequenced, phonetic method. Instruction begins by teaching the adult the alphabet, associated with individual pictures. The use of special symbols makes the spelling of words more phonetic. The Laubach Method uses specially prepared sequenced materials in the form of charts, workbooks and readers accompanied by a tutor manual.

Laubach Literacy Action provides training to volunteers in reading, English as a Second Language (ESL) and writing skills. In 1989, LLA deployed over 80,000 volunteer tutors to help 100,000 learners across America. LLA publishes its own materials through the New Readers Press and provides training through 750 local area programs.

Tens of thousands of adults have become successful readers using the Laubach Method. However, there are several limitations to this highly sequential phonetic reading program. Many adults have auditory dyslexia (i.e., an auditory perceptual handicap). They lack the ability to remember much of what they hear. Similar-sounding letters or words are not easily distinguished. It is very difficult for these adults to learn how to read if the system used is based on the sound-recognition system used in phonetic instruction.[8]

Literacy Volunteers of America (LVA) was founded in 1962 by Ruth Colvin, a Syracuse, New York, housewife. LVA has trained more than 50,000 volunteer tutors across America to provide basic instruction both on a one-to-one basis and in small groups. LVA uses a "whole word approach," rather than phonics, to teach reading. This method relies on learning vocabulary and the use of sentence structure and paragraphs to help adults learn reading skills. LVA publishes its own course materials and provides training programs for its volunteer tutors. The LVA program, like Laubach, is designed to serve adults with reading levels below the fifth grade.

Since LVA relies on volunteer tutors, its systematic approach to teaching reading has only a limited diagnostic testing component. Why did the adult worker fail to learn these basic skills originally as a student? Unfortunately, many potential learning problems, if not recognized, will frustrate the volunteer tutor following the LVA or Laubach systematic reading programs. Specifically, since LVA uses "a whole word method," if adults suffer from visual dyslexia (i.e., a visual perceptual handicap), they will confuse letters and words or lose their place on the page while reading. In other words, some adult students will become increasingly confused and helpless the harder they try to apply this "whole word" reading-skills method.[9]

The absence of a credible diagnostic procedure to diagnose and remedy dyslexia (i.e., a learning disability) is a major limitation of both the Laubach and the LVA adult-literacy curriculums. It is also difficult to objectively measure an adult's progress in either program, since neither normally uses nationally standardized pretests and posttests. Another limitation is the teaching of skills in isolation from an adult's job. Volunteer tutors follow a sequential series of lessons, vocabulary drills, books, etc. However, normally little is done in these programs to analyze specific job-content skills and to relate the general reading, math, writing or problem-solving application skills to everyday on-the-job skill requirements.[10]

Many other national organizations, associations and foundations are involved in literacy activities. The Barbara Bush Foundation offers seed money to fund local community literacy projects. Reading Is Fundamental (RIF) and Project Literacy are primarily information services heightening public awareness.[11] The foundation-supported Business Council for Effective Literacy (BCEL) in New York publishes a free newsletter on business-related literacy, the *BCEL Bulletin*. This publication contains "how to" guidelines for business literacy programs in addition to comments on corporate educational programs and research across the nation.[12] Another similar, although subscription-based, biweekly newsletter is the *Report on Literacy Programs*, published by Business Publishers of Silver Spring, Maryland. This publication on basic skills and workplace literacy provides reviews of legislation, books, "white paper reports," upcoming conferences and state-by-state activities on adult work-based education programs.[13]

To supplement this information on work force literacy resources and to direct adults to a local program, many states maintain "Literacy Hotlines." Project Literacy U.S. (PLUS) sponsors a toll-free national hotline for business literacy.[14] Libraries in some communities are also very active in working with local businesses. All types of libraries, large and small, urban and rural, receive grants from the U.S. Department of Education's Library Literacy Program (Title VI of the Library Services and Construction Act, LSCA). Approximately 230 grants totaling $5 million are awarded annually to libraries in almost every state. Thirty-two percent of all projects address Work Force Education to some degree. In Grand Junction, Colorado, a Fortune 500 company new to the community agreed to assist the Mesa County Public Library in developing a program for adults in the workplace. The tutoring program became a model Work Force Education project for other companies that have developed similar on-site programs to assist their employees.[15]

All of these nonprofit Work Force Education programs rely on volunteer tutors. Many feature one-to-one tutorials that can boost an adult learner's confidence and help conquer the fear of failure and helplessness that has been deeply ingrained after years of disappointment as an unsuccessful child or adolescent struggling to "cut it" in a school classroom. However, volunteers need to be trained and constantly retrained. They must work under the guidance and collaboration of paid professional educators and trainers. More full-time adult Work Force Education professionals are needed by most community-based nonprofit programs to improve instructional quality. Many programs cannot accept additional volunteers because of a national delivery system that is stretched to the breaking point with too many students, too few dollars, and numerous competing local nonprofit programs.

We must also keep in mind the evidence that volunteer tutoring will take considerably longer to achieve results when compared with the alternative of using a paid professional staff. Also, volunteer tutors can provide only several hours of tutoring each week. Company Work Force Education efforts must consider program cost factors in relation to how much time will be needed to achieve required worker-productivity gains or product-quality improvements.

Even after more than 30 years of concerted volunteer effort, less than one-half of 1 percent of all functionally illiterate adults in the United States are now receiving Work Force Education services. The existence of so many wide-ranging volunteer service organizations has sometimes resulted in greater confusion. Why? Volunteer programs are severely underfunded. Laubach's total annual budget is under $5 million; the budget of Literacy Volunteers of America is less than $3 million. Funding for local literacy programs, both public and private, now tends to be divided among numerous local or neighborhood-based literacy centers. There is little coordination among programs for student referrals or for volunteer recruitment and training. Technical assistance and staff development often remain fragmented at the local level.

The federal literacy programs and the nonprofit/volunteer sector have thus far borne the brunt of increased corporate demands for Work Force Education. These programs have reached their breaking point without additional corporate contributions or government funding. The outlook remains bleak for massive increased public funding. Moreover, the serious question arises whether large-scale volunteer efforts are, in the long term, the most expeditious or cost-effective mechanism for business to achieve a significantly higher twenty-first-century Work Force Education standard (twelfth-grade skills and work performance).

Human resource managers can make good selective use of local volunteer projects as one component of their on-site programs. Volunteer literacy training or GED classes will usually not meet all the different levels of reading/math skills needs and adult-learning problems found in the typical workplace. At their best, these volunteer programs can help mobilize groups of company employees as trained volunteer tutors to work with less-skilled workers in a company-sponsored cross-training program. This approach is particularly useful as a component of your overall Work Force Education effort or as an "icebreaker" to initiate your company training efforts.

COMPUTER-BASED TRAINING

A great deal of attention has been focused on computer-based training (CBT) applications for Work Force Education programs. The computer has long proven to be a reliable tool for self-paced instruction. However, it is not an end in itself. HR managers must become knowledgeable about the many CBT systems and software packages available today. CBT must provide for a broad range of applications in problem solving and information processing. You must learn how to evaluate CBT in terms of how well it can be integrated into the context of a total educational program.

Another related issue is the questionable appropriateness of adult basic skills software that has been adapted from children's materials. Computers have been widely used by children in school to learn concepts, let students practice or provide drill. But materials that are very beneficial for a ten-year-old fourth-grader may not be suitable for use by an adult learner. That is to say that the use of rabbits, cows and witches as reinforcers makes much of the available software inappropriate for adult education.

Although some CBT materials remain inappropriate for adults, the recent explosion of new software makes CBT highly desirable as part of your total Work Force Education effort. CBT helps adults learn efficiently. A concept or skill can be broken down and restructured in a step-by-step sequential manner. Computer-based instruction reduces peer pressure and embarrassment. It is very patient. The computer will wait for the adult to respond. Slower students may take longer on a task and may drill as long as necessary. Most software presents items in different combinations, letting a student perform the task with interesting variations. The computer can be an instrument fostering creativity and teaching vocational skills, time management or health and safety issues. For adults with low reading, math and writing skills, effective CBT can foster vocabulary development, comprehension and thinking/problem-solving skills.

However, it is important to keep CBT in proper perspective by asking the following questions: Who are the appropriate audiences for its use? What is the best software to get the job done? When should CBT be introduced during the instruction program? Why will CBT do a better job than other learning alternatives such as the use of worksheets, workbooks or text reading? Judicious use of CBT will keep its effectiveness rating high. Overuse and inappropriate software content will negate these advantages and actually slow the adult-learning process.

At a fundamental level, microcomputers are excellent program managers. They can grade tests, track individual progress and maintain complete student records. Computers facilitate the adult learner's entry and exit from a software package at any time. Absent students called away for a day, a week or a month return to the same display of their last class.

CBT can also be used for supplemental instruction. This gives program instructors time away from group teaching and accommodates individual tutoring for students who need special assistance.

At the top level of the CBT hierarchy, the computer becomes the primary instructor. The teacher facilitates the learning process through records management, software selection and tutoring.[16]

Interactive videodisc (IVD) systems have expanded the uses of CBT training. Since the technology was first introduced in the early 1980s, the software has been increasingly "debugged." Courseware and hardware are now being developed on a significant scale. These are powerful workstation systems, a ten-inch disc storing up to 54,000 images, or 256 megabytes of data. That is enough memory to store all the text and pictures of the *Encyclopedia Britannica*. Standardized software programs are emerging for literacy and other higher-learning applications in electronics, hydraulics and mainframe management.[17]

COMPUTER-BASED ADULT-LITERACY SYSTEMS

CBT adult-literacy packages are designed for use as a total instructional system. They each have different strengths and weaknesses that bear careful review by HR managers.

Programmed Logic for Automatic Teaching Operations (PLATO) is the acknowledged "granddaddy" of CBT. Since PLATO's birth in the 1970s, it has evolved into a local area network delivery system with instructional testing, management and reporting capability. Its software has changed substantially, offering mainly tutorial instruction, instead of only drill-and-practice lessons.

Computer Curriculum Corporation (CCC) offers a similar Work Force

Education program. Developed by Dr. Patrick Suppes (Stanford University, Math Institute), CCC is a part of many vocational/occupational training programs. CCC features instructional delivery at home via the telephone, as well as English as a Second Language (ESL) in six languages.

Both of these competency-based, sequential skill systems are designed for the adult reader whose reading level is between grades 6 and 12. PLATO curriculum includes reading, math, GED and English; CCC offers reading, ESL, writing, GED and language skills. The price for an eight-station PLATO/CCC system with workbooks, worksheets and supplemental materials begins at over $50,000.[18]

Billed as the "world's largest computer-based on-line prescription for basic skills," the Job Skills Education Program (JSEP) was developed for the U.S. Army starting in 1982 by Ford Aerospace Corporation and Florida State University. JSEP was designed to teach the basic skills needed for military jobs. It contains more than 300 lessons covering over 200 basic skills, including reading, writing, computational skills and study skills. Lessons are job-related, self-paced and individualized. A Student Management System (SMS) tracks each student's progress and career plans. Mastery tests follow each lesson. When passed, the student moves on to a new lesson. If the student fails, SMS begins a skill-development lesson. Tutorial intervention by a teacher occurs after a second failure. Learner strategies taught by JSEP lessons include time management, motivational skills, reading strategies, test taking and problem-solving skills.

JSEP curriculum comes in both a military and a civilian version. A PLATO mainframe delivers monochromatic or color versions. In 1990 the U.S. Army began post-by-post implementation of the JSEP program. JSEP was transferred for civilian use in 1988 through the Department of Education, with the assistance of Florida State University. During its "demonstration phase" at eight sites in 1991, 30 different "occupational prescriptions" were developed for industry. JSEP does not teach below the third-grade level, nor does it diagnose or treat dyslexia (learning disabilities). A research "JSEP Final Report" is available from the Department of Education.[19]

Other CBT programs, such as Educational Technologies or Basic Academic Skills for Employment (BASE), use motivational and instructional videotapes to teach phonics, reading, writing and comprehension. BASE presents a typical CBT approach to basic skills. A program pretest is given to measure job-related basic skill abilities. The software offers the program administrator and the student a detailed listing of what skills need to be mastered to achieve specific job proficiency. The computer offers lessons from the early "prescription" and tracks posttest and up-to-the-minute student progress.

All CBT systems for Work Force Education require a professionally trained director. Most vendors will offer your company's representative an in-depth train-the-trainer program. However, for best overall results, consider employing an educator with a background in adult education, reading, adult-learning problems or adult literacy. With the growing list of educational software, only this educational specialist can hope to decipher the most applicable CBT courses for your employee job training.[20]

INTERACTIVE VIDEODISC TECHNOLOGY (IVD)

IVD is a further development of CBT in which the adult learns reading and math skills through an encoding or writing process. Interactivity gives the student choices. They either watch what passes before them or leave the lesson and delve into material that offers further explanation or more in-depth information. Laser-disc technology offers the student random access that moves to any point on the disc. Many IVD programs have multiple audio channels that blend still pictures and text with full-motion video.[21]

IBM's Principles of the Alphabet Literacy System (PALS) was developed by a retired Florida educator, Dr. John Henry Martin. PALS is a spin-off of "Writing to Read," an early childhood reading and writing education program also marketed by IBM. In a similar vein, PALS teaches adult nonreaders to read by teaching them to write. Using a phonics program, adults discover by both sight (a touch-sensitive info-window station) and sound (headphones) that the sounds of speech can be written. They learn to spell phonetically most words they can say.

PALS uses IVD to enable the learner to listen to and view animated stories on a personal computer. Students watch a story unfold, hear dialogue spoken by various voices and answer questions or make choices about the story by touching the computer screen. The adult learns touch-typing as part of PALS and uses the keyboard to fill in blanks in the narrative or move to the next frame.

IBM markets the PALS system and its related software as a total systems solution for adult literacy, starting with the totally illiterate adult and progressing to a high school GED level. A complete 15-station PALS lab begins at $80,000.

Some field research has been published on PALS. One such report was done by an Ohio vocational school district (Ciancio, 1988), which compared standardized pre- and posttest reading scores for adults who had completed a 20-week PALS class program. Thirty-one percent of the students improved two or more grade levels, 31 percent between one and two grade levels and 23 percent less than one grade level; 15 percent showed no improvement. In discussing the PALS program with a program teacher coordinator, the authors discovered that other learning materials in addition to PALS were used with adults enrolled in the program. Many of the enrolled adults had significant visual or auditory dyslexia (learning disabilities) and had difficulty understanding the phonics materials they heard or the letter/word/numbers they saw presented by the videodisc system. If adults in the Ohio program continued to demonstrate these problems, they were given an alternative whole-word reading program and were completely removed from the PALS instructional system.

Another more recent study was completed in 1990 by Evaluation Research of Newton Highlands, Massachusetts Board of Library Commissioners. It confirmed the above findings. Moreover, the Massachusetts study challenged IBM's marketing claims that PALS is suitable for anyone reading at the fifth-grade level or below. "The program was found far too difficult for persons at the lowest end of this proficiency spectrum." Evaluation Research concluded that PALS, in its current form, is "one example of the 'quick fix' computer-assisted instructional programs . . . flooding the expanding adult literacy market."[22]

IVD is a valuable learning tool, since students retain much more of what they can hear, see and do. But we must also recognize that the illiterate adult at the low end of the literacy spectrum (grades 1–6) often possesses serious learning problems never previously solved or, in many cases, even diagnosed while attending school as a child. The adult illiterate does not simply lack reading skills or math skills per se. Before using any Work Force Education teaching approach, even a "high-tech" system, a Work Force Education program must first uncover potential learning blocks and then plan a sequence of appropriate training activities. Without such diagnosis, many adult students run a high risk of continuing to fail in the corporate classroom and ultimately on the job.

In contrast to IBM's PALS is the ongoing work of Eunice Askov, Director of the Institute for the Study of Adult Literacy, and her staff at Pennsylvania State University. They have long been in the forefront of functional-context education development using computer-based training for adults reading at a fourth- to eighth-grade level. The Institute for the Study of Adult Literacy has field-tested a variety of these CBT programs with adults at correctional institutions (Askov, Bixler, Maclay, 1986). A separate program, R.O.A.D. to Success, in conjunction with the Pennsylvania Department of Transportation, has the purpose of upgrading literacy skills while commercial drivers study for the Commercial Drivers Licence (Brown, 1990). These programs have been found to be highly effective in teaching adult beginning readers. Much of the courseware developed is interactive, branching and responding to the user's answers and needs.[23]

Many other IVD programs are now available with business training applications. The Wisconsin Foundation for Vocational Technical and Adult

Education (VTAE) has developed "Interactive Modumath" for adult learners who are enrolled in vocational-technical training programs and lack basic math skills. The videodiscs cover whole numbers, fractions, decimals, percentages, signed numbers, equations and word problems. VTAE has also pioneered producing interactive electronics training systems for the work site.

Project Star from Hartley Courseware offers a basic adult-reading instruction program that also is an IVD system. Language experience activities and application modules of vocabulary and comprehension activities are available for adult learners. Some provisions for potential adult-learning problems have been designed into the software. A Project Star software package sells for about $13,000.

Canada's Pathfinder Learning System also offers the integrated components found in other IVD systems, together with a coordinated library of non-CBT-based print and audiovisual education resources appropriate for use with different adult-interest levels of reading. In addition to a basic reading program (cost $87,000), modules are available in math, science, social studies and employment life skills at an individual module cost of $14,000.

Some CBT programs emphasize hand-eye, perceptual therapy. This software offers treatment for visual perceptual disorders that may interfere with the adult's ability to read. (See Chapter 4.) Vendors include Psychological Software Services, Indianapolis, Indiana; Cognitive Educational Series, Chula Vista, California; Computer Programs for Neuropsychological Testing and Rehabilitation, Fountain Valley, California; public domain programs: Logo Voice Print, Fire Organ, PR #2 and Special Needs #10.[24]

New CBT programs are being added to the market each year. Before you make any decisions about purchasing a major CBT system, it is recommended that your HR staff perform a needs analysis that clearly defines the specific business goals and objectives to be met by this technology. Some key considerations during the planning process include:

1. Who is the primary user population that will have access to this technology?

2. What are the main goals to be reached by the CBT system? Increase program attendance? Improve achievement? Enhance motivation? Are computers to be added to an ongoing program, or is a new training effort to be designed around them?

3. Will the CBT be used as the main curriculum? Or will CBT become integrated to reinforce the present program? If so, who will integrate CBT with existing training materials?

4. Will train-the-trainer become a major issue in using the new technology? Who will staff and operate the CBT program?

5. Where will the system be located? Will there be a need to tie sites together? Are the physical arrangements in the training area conducive to CBT? What are the safety, security and electrical needs of the system?

Evaluating CBT educational software is critical for a Work Force Education program's success. New software appears almost daily. One of the most extensive and critical checklists for evaluating educational content, technical features and support materials was written by the Adult Literacy and Technology Project, and funded by the Gannett Foundation (1987–90). (See Appendix 1 for details.) These selection criteria will change as the sophistication of software and hardware increases during the next decade. The following publications will assist in your review of current and new software programs:

Apple Journal of Courseware Review
20525 Mariani Avenue
Cupertine, California 95014

Computing Teacher
1787 Agate Street
University of Oregon
Eugene, Oregon 97403

Electronic Learning
Scholastic, Inc.
730 Broadway
New York, New York 10003

Micro SIFT Reviews
300 S.W. Sixth Avenue
Portland, Oregon 97204

The Reading Teacher
International Reading Association
800 Barksdale Road
Newark, Delaware 19711

Software Reports: Guide to Evaluated Educational Software
10996 Torreyana Road
San Diego, California 92121

Teaching and Computers
Scholastic, Inc.
730 Broadway
New York, New York 10003

Writing Notebook
Box 1268
Eugene, Oregon 97440-1268[25]

Another resource for consideration by HR professionals is the index matrix prepared by Eunice Askov and the Institute for the Study of Adult Literacy at Pennsylvania State University. This index lists software that can be customized for a specific student population's use in building up workplace vocabulary and reading skills. (The index matrix appears in Appendix 2 and has been reprinted with the permission of its authors.)[26]

Contemporary expert opinion on the use of computer technology as an instructional tool may be characterized as "the promise of the technology remains but a promise." The courses developed to date do not yet fully utilize the capacity of state-of-the-art hardware and software. Unfortunately, too many of the currently available CBT programs are little more than "electronic page turning." Product development lags because vendors argue that the business market has not yet developed sufficiently for most companies to even consider purchasing their technology. In addition, a lack of consensus on how to evaluate the adult learner's performance has prohibited meaningful systematic evaluation of CBT as a Work Force Education training/instructional tool.

CBT can be interactive, keep records and offer scheduling flexibility. However, many programs are numbingly dull, reduced to repetitive drill activities. IVD offers sophisticated audio/graphics, yet very few IVD software packages are properly designed for the Work Force Education market. Those that do exist are not adaptable to job-specific content and make little provision for dyslexia (i.e., learning disabilities); nor do they always possess an adult-learner context. The courseware as of yet does not deliver the full potential of the hardware in teaching educational skills side by side with occupational and life skills.

Current examples of published CBT and IVD evaluations are limited and sketchy. There are many reasons to believe that the use of these instructional tools with the right audience will save instructional time. However, we will not know with certainty until CBT and other instructional methods of Work Force Education are carefully tested and compared with one another, using well-established evaluation criteria with a large number of adult students and with results published in recognized professional journals.

As we approach the year 2000, many entry-level jobs (machine operators, food preparers, bank tellers, cashiers, supply clerks and numerous other occupations) will require daily work at a computer terminal. There is little doubt that employers will turn to CBT and IVD to teach job simulations interactively on an individualized basis. Ultimately, Work Force

Education programs will be combined with job-simulation training. Corporations with a strong sense of strategic planning will invest now to develop their own custom job courseware. Vendors will ultimately develop off-the-shelf software products answering these job content and educational skill needs.[27]

BOOKS AND PERIODICALS

High-interest/easy-reading materials for adults whose skills vary between grades 1 and 12 have an important central place in a Work Force Education program. This genre consists largely of book series on similar topics and themes. In some instances, books portray central characters or settings. A series is similarly packaged and is usually advertised and purchased as a set.

Hardcover books, paperbacks, workbooks and periodical materials are currently available from major and small publishers in reading, math, ESL, GED, life skills, employability, career development and other workplace-related topics. Many of these materials are supposedly designed for an adult audience. However, more high-quality, low-reading-level books are needed for adults who lack certain academic skills and related job skills or adults who have major learning problems (i.e. learning disabilities).

Various questions need to be addressed before selecting Work Force Education print materials. The following suggested guidelines were adapted from the American Library Association:

1. Does the appearance of the material make it suitable for an adult?
2. Does the book contain pictures or drawings of adults or children?
3. How well do these graphics relate to the text?
4. Can the book's narrative stand on its own without these graphics?
5. How is the type size presented?
6. Would an adult feel comfortable with this type size?
7. Do the book's shape, size and overall design make it appear as an adult book or set it apart?
8. Does the subject of the book have appeal for adult readers?
9. Will the book stimulate adults to want to read further?
10. Can the book bridge the adult into more difficult subject materials?
11. If the publisher has indicated a reading grade level, is it correct?
12. Does the book's glossary or index make it more useful?
13. Overall, how readable is the book?

The following publishers have book series that are designed for the adult reader or at least offer high-interest/low-ability levels. Reading and math publishers include Academic Therapy; Addison-Wesley; Alemany Press; Barron's BLS; Book-Lab; Cambridge (PHR); Contemporary Books; Crestwood House; Delta; Dormac; EDT; Educational Activities; Fearon; Globe Book; Hammond; Janus; KET; Longman; MECC; Media Materials; Modern Curriculum Press; New Readers Press; NTC Publishing; Phoenix Learning Resources; Prentice-Hall Regents; Raintree Publishers; Quercus; Scholastic; Scott, Foresman; Steck-Vaughn; Sunburst and Sundance Publishers.

At present, periodicals that meet the high/low criteria are more limited in availability. Publishers include Field Publications, Scholastic and, from Canada, *Voices: New Writers for New Readers*, available through Delta Systems Company, 570 Rock Road Drive, Unit H, Dundee, Illinois 60118-9922.

Specific information on all of the above publishers (except *Voices*) is available in the *1990 ABLE Curriculum Guide*, Royce and Royce, 1938 Crooked Oak Drive, Lancaster, Pennsylvania 17601, (800) 992-2283 (a project supported by the U.S. Department of Education and the Pennsylvania Department of Education). Another valuable companion guide is *Easy Reading: Book Series and Periodicals for Less Able Readers*, International Reading Association, 1989.

Ellen V. LiBretto's *High/Low Handbook*, R. R. Bowker, is now in its third edition, listing books, materials and software for the problem reader. The handbook mainly considers materials for children and adolescents. However, its extensive list of computer software and high/low book series makes it an invaluable tool for planning or updating a corporate Work Force Education program.

THE TESTING MAZE

There are many standardized achievement tests designed to measure scholastic aptitude. Unfortunately, in the field of Work Force Education, many programs do not use a widely recognized standardized pre/post-test to assess the adult's rate of progress in the program. When tests are used to evaluate student progress, usually the Tests of Adult Basic Education (TABE) or the Adult Basic Learning Exam (ABLE) are employed.

To help bring some perspective to this issue, the Educational Resources Information Center (ERIC) has published *Measures for Adult Literacy Programs* (1990). This is an extremely useful reference book for HR managers, since it provides thorough, easy-to-read, candid evaluations of 63 Work Force Education tests. These tests include basic reading, math, writing, ESL, self-esteem, work-ethic and critical thinking. ERIC is a neutral information source acting as a massive nonprofit clearinghouse that offers sophisticated computer software and print databases on a wide diversity of published educational materials.

The most comprehensive published guide for potential adult tests is the *Mental Measurement Yearbook*. This publication has been available for many decades and provides detailed authoritative reviews of all published tests now available for children, adolescents and adults. It is constantly being updated, is massive in scope and is written for an educational audience.

One note of caution before you use these guides for test selection: If you have not been professionally trained in test measurement, read at least one standard reference text on the topic to assist you with interpreting the contents of these standardized tests. The most commonly used college texts include *Essentials of Psychological Testing* (L. Cronbach), *Psychological Testing* (A. Anastasi) and *Standards of Educational and Psychological Testing* (American Psychological Association). Another alternative is hiring an educational consultant in Work Force Education to facilitate test selection. As we will discuss at greater length in a subsequent chapter, there are no valid educational reasons to avoid using recognized pre/posttest measurement of your Work Force Education program. A wide variety of tests is now commercially available, fairly treating a diversity of ethnic backgrounds, abilities and cultures.

CURRENT CORPORATE PROGRAMS

Corporate classrooms are busy today all across America. As noted earlier, U.S. corporations in 1989 spent over $30 billion on training and education and over $130 billion when adding on-the-job training (American Society for Training and Development estimates). The Carnegie Foundation estimates that nearly 8 million employees attend these corporate classrooms. These revenues and attendance numbers approximate all of America's institutions of higher learning.

The American Society for Training and Development also estimated that only $500 million of the these training dollars are being spent on basic skills. However, this figure is deceptive. As we have already noted, the Work Force Education crisis is much broader than basic skills or literacy education for entry-level or blue-collar workers. A critical report by the Center for Public Resources on "Basic Skills in the U.S. Work Force" (1983) broadly surveyed basic academic skills. The survey found that of the 184 corporate responders, 75 percent had some type of Work Force Education programs.[28] The following list examples are selected from several different types of companies and in no way indicate the complete coverage of training programs in any one company:

American Institute of Banking—New York City
　—Reading and Study Skills Development
　—Reading and Writing English Skills for the Foreign-Educated
　—Conversational English for the Foreign-Educated
　—Speech

Chrysler Corporation
—Reading Skills
—Introduction to Writing
—Writing Skills
—Speech Skills
—Accelerated Reading

Consolidated Edison
—Effective Reading
—Effective Listening

IBM: Software Engineering Institute
—Self-Study courses in Algebra, Math Preparation and Review, Logical Expression

Manufacturers Hanover
—Effective Communications—Listening
—Basic Arithmetic

NCR
—Basic English Grammar
—Effective Business Writing
—Effective Technical Writing

Polaroid
—High School Chemistry and Physics
—Algebra and Trigonometry
—Metric System
—Literacy Training Tutorials
—Reading Labs

Standard Oil of California
—Better Letter Writing
—Put It in Writing
—Technical Writing
—Practical English and the Command of Words
—Effective Communicating

The Carnegie Foundation's special report *Corporate Classrooms: The Learning Business* concluded: "The repetition in course titles shows how pervasive and similar the problems are. . . . And such courses are not limited to entry-level employees. Some of the same titles will be found in courses designed for management and other personnel categories at differing levels." It is our strong belief that many more companies are conducting such training, but due to the stigma attached to the public conception of "literacy training" or "basic skills" training, they are often reluctant to publicly report such information.[29]

Fortunately, as the decade of the 1980s advanced, more companies, both large and small, began to share information on the effectiveness of their Work Force Education programs. In the mid-1950s, Polaroid began offering job-related Work Force Education courses in math and science. By the mid-1980s, one-third of Polaroid's 5,000 hourly Boston-area plant workers participated in these courses. In 1970 the company launched an expanded course offering including ESL, basic reading, basic math and writing skills. The students included production employees, senior engineers, assembly operators and machine operators. Tutorial groups of one or two students met with a teacher-tutor for 30 instruction hours over 10 weeks. Employees and their supervisors negotiated time off for these courses. Local teachers were hired as independent contractors to act as tutors. The job-related curriculum was designed to account for adult learning problems that might frustrate successful instruction in any subject area. Pre- and posttests designed for the program assessed program effectiveness. However, all courses were voluntary and results confidential. A manufacturing manager told the authors that improving employee motivation was considered to be a critical factor. Even without formal written assessment reports, workers can certify in a practical skills area and thereby earn more pay. Some employees were reported by their managers to be "just like a new person."

Polaroid's Work Force Education program was not just a nice benefit for management to give employees. As one manager said, "It's survival!" This does not mean that this program is a solution for all the competitive problems found at Polaroid, one of the few American manufacturers left in the international camera industry. However, it is obvious that Polaroid acknowledges the value of its "human capital," which may give the company a significant strategic advantage.[30]

Motorola, located in suburban Chicago, has followed another path. In 1986 it contracted with Harper Community College to send teachers to its Schaumburg and Arlington Heights plant locations. Courses included remedial and basic skill courses similar to those offered at Polaroid, as well as advanced algebra. The two-hour classes of 15 to 25 students included one hour on company time, the second on the employee's own time. Motorola invested $5 million for over 1,500 employees to attend these classes. Future higher wages motivated these workers to attend. Motorola's own corporate motivation was enhanced competitiveness for the international telecommunications marketplace. The company needed people who were more highly skilled to work in a "sixth sigma quality," error-free, computerized production environment. Susan Hooker, a senior manager in training and development at Motorola University, stated, "There is a powerful improvement in the workplace and in the product you're building if you attend to the needs of your work force." There are also expectations at Motorola that the present program will be expanded until it can effectively train the company's entire work force. Other additional Work Force Education alternatives are now being considered for expansion of the entire program.[31]

GM, Ford and Chrysler have teamed with the United Auto Workers (UAW) in establishing a wide variety of Work Force Education initiatives.

These range from basic skills to blueprint reading, robotics, master programming controllers with applied electronics and many other academic and technology courses. Program methods range from traditional classroom instruction to PLATO-CBT and interactive videodisc. To build a "world class car," the big three automakers and the UAW have learned a hard lesson from their German and Japanese competitors. To make a superior technological product, you must invest in a work force that is knowledgeable and capable of using up-to-date, cutting-edge manufacturing innovations, or any manufacturer will rapidly lose market share.[32]

A different approach is being taken by Inland Steel's Best University in East Chicago, Indiana. Using cross-training tutorials (peer tutoring), one employee tutors another. Volunteer tutors are drawn from throughout the company, then trained and paired with other employees. The key motivator is gaining certification for higher-paying jobs.

A company-wide effort at empowering workers on-the-line revealed that many lacked the needed verbal, written and comprehension skills to complete reports, read manuals or lead meetings. Advanced production technology has been placed in Inland's plants, but many workers lacked the math skills or application problem-solving abilities to properly utilize the equipment. Inland Steel needed to "put money in people not just machines," according to Dale Rediger, President of Inland Bar and Structural, a division of Inland Steel Corporation. Thus, Best University was founded in 1989. Laubach peer tutoring at Inland is supplemented by using PALS and other CBT software products. Inland will expand Best University's programs to enroll more workers in cooperation with the local steelworkers' union.[33]

Smaller companies are also beginning to offer these programs. At Heinemann's Bakeries of Chicago, 60 of 190 production employees signed up for a classroom ESL program taught by Daley College. Heinemann's is a member of the Chicago Consortium for Worker Education, a coalition of 15 unions. The consortium was partially funded by a $69,000 grant from the Illinois Secretary of State's literacy program. This consortium was created to serve unionized workers struggling to cope with advanced technology.

Keith Ervin, the education director of the Midwest region of the International Ladies Garment Workers Union and chairman of the consortium, believes, "This is one of the few areas where the union and the employers have a vested interest that is the same." The next generation of skilled bakers will come from the foreign-born workers now in this program. They need to pass a written English test indicating they can understand written recipes and communicate with the shop floor. This qualifies an employee to become a trainee in a three-year-long baker apprenticeship program.

In addition to the motivation of job advancement and helping management resolve a long-term manpower problem, the program is designed to help integrate foreign-born workers into the wider society. "This will help for everything from work to home," says Monica, a Heinemann employee and Polish immigrant who moved to the United States ten years ago.[34]

The Central Labor Council-Consortium for Worker Education Workplace Literacy Program is the result of the collaborative efforts of eight New York City trade unions and the City University of New York. The program uses state-certified teachers and provides both basic education (English as a Second Language, Adult Basic Education, and General Educational Development) and opportunities for degree-bearing programs (B.A. and M.A.). Four programs illustrate the variety of approaches being taken to address workplace literacy issues:

1. The ACTWU Worker Education Program addresses the needs of workers in the apparel industry, most of whom are Spanish-speaking immigrants with very weak formal education. The program provides workshops on immigration procedures as part of the curriculum, individual counseling, classes in Spanish literacy and ESL and GED classes. The program places students in various ESL levels based on results of a pretest. Evaluative measures use pictures, questions and stories to measure speaking, reading and writing ability.

2. The Skills Upgrading for Dislocated Sewing Machine Operators is run by the Garment Industry Development Corporation. Students are largely non-English-speaking immigrants. All have lost their jobs and are seeking new skills for reemployment. The program centers on short-term literacy and technical skills needed for reemployment; the long-range goal is workplace literacy. Students participate in four cycles, each of which is five weeks long, with students attending for 35 hours a week. Students work on sewing-machine skills with a technical teacher in the morning and attend ESL and health-and-safety classes with literacy and health-and-safety instructors in the afternoons. Evaluation focuses on vocabulary development in both written work and conversation, improvement in oral and written expression (particularly use of tenses, pronouns, word placement and simple sentences), development of detailed oral responses and increase in reading fluency.

3. The Teamsters Local 237 Workplace Literacy Program for Supervisors of Caretakers serves students who are mostly male, both native- and foreign-born. The major goal of the program is to prepare students for civil service examinations. Thus, reading, writing and math skills needed for specific jobs are addressed. Students attend classes three hours a night, two nights a week, for six to eight weeks. Evaluation is centered on students' completion of specific instructional outcomes (e.g., vocabulary mastery, essay writing, statement of an argument, etc.).

4. The consortium-wide Computers and Literacy Program is designed to enhance the literacy of ESL students by using the computer as a writing tool. Students attend class every Sunday for fifteen weeks, three hours per Sunday. The weekly classes focus on Basic Education of ESL, together with computer lab practice.

A key feature of the consortium programs is the experimentation with assessment measures. Programs use a wide variety of assessments, including in-house tests to measure mastery of content for civil service exams, certification or citizenship exams; student notebooks and essays; performance ratings of technical skills; job placement rates; and student self-reports.

All of these programs are representative of the great diversity of Work Force Education efforts across America. Other similar programs are now being offered by Prudential Insurance, Reynolds Tobacco, the Bank of Boston, Bank of New England, Massachusetts General Hospital, Allstate Insurance Company, CNA, Pratt & Whitney Group of United Technologies, Planters Peanuts, the Travelers Insurance of Hartford, UNISYS, Hewlett Packard, Domino's Pizza of Ann Arbor, Advanced Thermal Products, Clorox, Courtyard by Marriott and IBM. These Work Force Education efforts span the United States and represent the service, industrial and manufacturing economic sectors. In a subsequent chapter we will present in-depth case studies analyzing specific Work Force Education program applications.

What conclusions can we reach from this variety of answers for Work Force Education now available to HR managers? Can we somehow rank the overall effectiveness of each type of program? Leading researchers (Kulik, Kulik, Bangert-Drowns, 1990) have already rated the different educational methods used by these training programs, in descending order of effectiveness:

1. Mastery Learning, that is, a form of small-group tutorials (to be discussed in the next four chapters)
2. Cross-Training (peer tutoring)
3. Computer-Based Training (when appropriate)
4. Programmed Learning Materials (when these can be successfully used by independent learners)
5. Traditional classroom instruction.[35]

All of the Work Force Education programs we have just reviewed fall into one or more of these categories. However, large numbers of adults are still failing these classes. They easily become frustrated, since learning often does not happen rapidly. Many workers drop out of programs. Some quit their jobs; others remain employed, but at a lower-productivity job. In the next chapter we will find out the factors causing these learning failures. Who are these people? Why wasn't this need met by the local schools? How has current cutting-edge research pointed a possible way out of this worker-productivity training dilemma? When and where can HR departments plan employee training that will successfully address both corporate productivity/competitive needs and employee motivation for a better job?

NOTES

1. Forrest P. Chrisman, "Toward a Literate America: The Leadership Challenge," in *Leadership for Literacy*, ed. Forrest P. Chrisman (San Francisco: Jossey-Bass Publishers, 1990), 14–17.

2. G. M. Diekhoff, "An Appraisal of Adult Literacy Programs: Reading Between the Lines," *Journal of Reading* 3 (Fall 1988): 624–30; T. Sticht, "Adult Literacy Education," in *Review of Research in Education*, ed. E. Rothkoph (Washington, D.C.: American Education Research Association, 1988); J. S. Chall, E. Heron, and H. Hilferty, "Adult Literacy: New and Enduring Problems," *Phi Delta Kappan* 63, no. 3 (November 1987): 190–96.

3. J. McGrail, *Adult Illiterates and Adult Literacy Programs: A Summary of Descriptive Data* (San Francisco: Far West Lab for Educational Research and Development; Andover, Mass.: Network of Innovative Schools, 1984), ERIC doc. no. ED 254 756.

4. Carman St. John Hunter, *Adult Illiteracy in the United States* (New York: McGraw Hill Book Company, 1979), 63–71; Ernest Z. Rothkoph, *Research in Education* (Washington, D.C.: American Educational Research Association, 1988), 61; *Federal Register*, Part VIII (Washington, D.C.: Department of Education, August 18, 1989), 34408; *Federal Register*, Part II, (Washington, D.C.: Department of Education, April 17, 1990), 14382; Wanda Cook, *Adult Literacy Education in the United States* (Newark, Del.: International Reading Association, 1977), 84–85.

5. *Training Opportunities in Job Corps* (Washington, D.C.: U.S. Department of Labor, 1990); Sara Levitan and Frank Galbo, *A Second Chance* (Kalamazoo, Mich.: W.E. Upjohn Institute for Employment Research, 1988), 123–58.

6. "FY 1991 Conference Agreement on Appropriations," *Report on Literacy Programs*, 1 November 1990, 172.

7. Interview, Peggy Luce, Director Job Development, Chicago Association of Commerce and Industry, 20 March 1991.

8. Marie Costa, *Adult Literacy/Illiteracy in the United States: A Handbook for Reference and Research* (Santa Barbara, Calif.: ABC-Clio, 1988), 103–4. For more information, contact: Laubach Literacy Action (LLA) New Readers Press, 1320 Jamesville Avenue, P.O. Box 131, Syracuse, NY 13210, (315) 422-9121.

9. For more information on LVA, contact: Literacy Volunteers of America, Inc. (LVA), 404 Oak Street, Syracuse, NY 13203, (312) 445-8000.

10. Hunter, *Adult Illiteracy*, 60–63; Cook, *Adult Literacy Education*, 75; Anabell Powell Newman and Caroline Beverstock, *Adult Literacy* (Newark, Del.: International Reading Association, 1990), 95; Judy Cheatham and V. K. Lawson, *Small Group Tutoring* (Syracuse, N.Y.: Literacy Volunteers of America, 1990), 2–40.

11. For a fairly comprehensive directory of literacy organizations, see Costa, *Literacy*, 91–109.

12. To receive a free copy of the *BCEL Bulletin*, write to: Business Council for Effective Literacy, Inc. (BCEL), 1221 Avenue of the Americas, New York, NY 10020, (212) 512-2415.

13. To inquire about receiving *Report on Literacy Programs*, contact: Business Publishers, Inc., 951 Pershing Drive, Silver Spring, MD 20910-4464, (301) 587-6300.

14. Call Project Literacy U.S. (PLUS) Toll-Free National Hotline at: (800) 232-2946. Call Illinois Literacy Hotline at: (800) 321-9511.

15. *Library Literacy Program 1988*, U.S. Department of Education, Office of Educational Research and Improvement (Washington, D.C.: U.S. Government Printing Office, 1989), 5:23.

16. Ellen V. LiBretto, *High/Low Handbook* (New York: R. R. Bowker Co., 1985), 57-59; Terilyn C. Turner, "An Overview of Computers in Adult/Literacy Programs," *Lifelong Learning* 8, no. 11 (1988): 9-12.

17. Paul Kringle and Dick Schaaf, "Interactive Training Beginning to Produce," in *Interactive Technologies* (a supplement to *Training*), September 1989, 5-6.

18. Turner, "Overview of Computers," 10-11.

19. Lois S. Wilson, "Workplace Literacy: Using the Job Skills Education Program," presentation at Workplace Literacy and Education Solutions, by Institute for International Research, Peat Marwick Executive Conference Center, Chicago, 19 March 1991.

20. Lois S. Wilson, "An On-Line Prescription for Basic Skills," *Training and Development Journal*, April 1990, 36-41.

21. Doran Howitt, "Experimental Software Boosted," *Info World*, 29 October 1984, 29-30.

22. Jean Ciancio, "Literacy: The Basic Skill," *Vocational Educational Journal*, March 1988, 41-42; Interview, May 8, 1989, Great Oaks Vocational School District; "PALS: A Closer Look," *Business Council For Effective Literacy Newsletter*, 25 October 1990, 4.

23. Eunice N. Askov, Brett Bixler, and Connie Maclay, *Evaluation of Computer Courseware for Adult Beginning Reading Instruction in a Correctional Setting* (University Park: Pennsylvania State University, 1986), 1-6; Eunice N. Askov, "Functional Context Education," *Research on Literacy* 1 (1 February 1991): 1; Emory J. Brown, *Evaluation of the R.O.A.D. to Success Program* (University Park: Pennsylvania State University, 1990), 1-34.

24. Dominick M. Maino, "The Process Approach, Microcomputers and Therapy," *Computers and Vision Therapy Programs* 1, no. 6 (March 1988): 227-34.

25. LiBretto, *Handbook*, 57-80, 82, 86-89, 105-6.

26. Eunice N. Askov and Cindy Jo Clark, "Using Computers in Adult Literacy Instruction," *Journal of Reading* 34, no. 6 (March 1991): 434-49.

27. Turner, "Overview of Computers," 12; Hanna A. Fingert, "Changing Literacy Instruction: Moving beyond the Status Quo," in *Leadership for Literacy*, ed. Forrest P. Chrisman (San Francisco: Jossey-Bass Publishers, 1990), 31; Arnold H. Packer and Wendy L. Campbell, "Using Computer Technology for Adult Literacy Instruction: Realizing the Potential," in *Literacy*, ed. Chrisman, 122-43.

28. James F. Henry, Susan Raymond, "Basic Skills in the U.S. Work Force: The Contrasting Perceptions of Business, Labor and Public Education" (New York: The Center For Public Resources, 1983).

29. Nell P. Eurich, *Corporate Classrooms: The Learning Business* (Princeton, N.J.: Carnegie Foundation, 1985), ix-x, 60-63.

30. Morton Ritts, "What If Johnny Still Can't Read," *Canadian Business*, May 1986, 54-58; Interviews, Polaroid Corporation Managers, 17 April 1990, and 9 May 1990.

31. Gretchen Reynolds, "Training Tomorrow's Work Force," *Chicago*, January 1990, 113-32; Irwin Ross, "Corporations Take Aim at Literacy," *Fortune*, 29 September 1986, 48-54.

32. "Automated Learning and Information Systems," *UAW-GM PLATO* (Con-

trol Data Corporation, 1989); *Skills 2000* (UAW-GM Human Resource Center, 1989).

33. Interview, Doris Scott Baker, Best University, Inland Steel, East Chicago, Ind., 7 July 1990.

34. Merrill Goozner, "On Training, Union, Bakery Speak Same Language," *Chicago Tribune*, 10 December 1989, Sec. 7, 6–7.

35. Chen-Lin C. Kulik, James A. Kulik, and Robert L. Bangert-Drowns, "Effectiveness of Mastery Learning Programs: A Meta Analysis," *Review of Educational Research* 60, no. 2 (Summer 1990): 265–99; S. D. Collins, M. Balmuth, and P. Jean, "So We Can Use Our Own Names, and Write the Laws by Which We Live: Educating the New U.S. Labor Force," *Harvard Educational Review* 54, no. 4 (1989): 454–69.

4

Adult Learning in a Work Force Education Environment

Work Force Education is the "poor man" of human resource development and the "bastard" of the American educational system. Born in adversity and mired in political controversy, it has remained isolated from the mainstream of corporate training and development until now. Work Force Education programs are deprived of adequate training budgets. They lack the specialized personnel for program development that ensures successful training of employees.

A FAILED INFRASTRUCTURE

In 1984–85, California's state-funded adult basic skills programs reported a 50 percent dropout rate after 100 hours of instruction. The same demographic trends held true on the East Coast for the 40,000 adults who quit literacy programs in New York City. In the Midwest, only six out of ten pass the Illinois GED high-school equivalency exam. A study by Women for Economic Security, a Chicago-based research organization, looked at the dropout problems in the region's adult-education basic-skill programs. The study found inadequate teaching, often by unqualified instructors who had never taught adults. Even if the teacher was not a volunteer, questions were raised about the wisdom of history teachers instructing adults, often with learning disabilities, in reading, math, writing or English as a Second Language. Little or no individual attention was given to GED students. Motivational problems abounded. Adults enrolled expecting a tie-in between on-the-job skills and the educational program. However, they found little or no relevance to what they learned and soon dropped out of the program.

Throughout America, in 200 Work Force Education programs, 49 percent of the students, on average, received less than 25 hours of instruction before terminating their enrollment. Even the one-on-one tutoring programs offered by the National Affiliation for Literacy Advances reported that most adults completed less than 50 hours of tutoring.

Why do so many Work Force Education students drop out of these programs? It is well known that some adults have less learning "potential" than other workers. Many of these adults probably carry over a lifetime of undiagnosed serious learning problems that defeat many local programs.

The underlying fallacy of current corporate Work Force Education is the assumption that the employee already knows "how to learn" new skills and "how to apply" that knowledge on the job. To the contrary, many adults can't, won't and never will learn or apply knowledge, unless they are first taught the "how to."[1]

A general lack of funding for research on Work Force Education has prevented the development of a cadre of related training and development professionals. This has contributed to a failure in understanding that children and adults learn basic skills in very different ways. Too many adult-literacy programs are derived from experience with children. The results can be disastrous, based on erroneous testing or the use of curriculum inappropriate for the adult's life context.

There have been numerous studies on the misuse or abuse of standardized pre- and posttesting that yielded inflated program results. Darling (1982) reported on basic skill programs that ignored time limitations for standardized tests. The accepted practice by the teachers was to "allow students as much time as they desire" to complete the test. This completely nullified the test results. Sticht (1987) reviewed 32 different studies on basic-skill programs involving U.S. Army, Navy and Air Force programs, national nonprofit-based adult reading programs of over 20,000 students, the Job Corps literacy program and CBT for adult literacy. He found gains of six months to three years after 2 to 141 hours of instruction.

But the credibility of these scores is undermined by an unbelievable lack of understanding regarding standardized testing procedures. This contributed to such common practices as offering "warm-up" tests (i.e., using a test as a teaching tool and then using it again for postprogram evaluation) and giving the same pre- and posttest rather than differing forms and administering different subtests at the beginning and end of the program. These erroneous test-taking procedures undermine the positive claims made in many adult-literacy programs, where bogus evidence is offered that a few hours of instruction produce one, two, even three or more "years" of reading improvement. A lack of understanding regarding the use of pre/post standardized test results and how adults go about the learning process has led to many literacy training programs making promises that are unrealistic. A community college president reported that his students gained one year in their reading skills after 20 hours of CBT. He claimed that after 60 hours of instruction, these adults would make a three-year achievement gain. This impossible extrapolation demonstrates why there is a widespread need for a better understanding of how adults learn.

Research by Park (1983) and Boraks and Schumacher (1981) on adult reading strategies indicates that Work Force Education students process written information differently than children. Once again, many standardized readings and math tests designed for use with children cannot be used as the sole indicator of program results when applied to an adult audience.

HOW ADULTS LEARN

Much of the crisis environment that surrounds Work Force Education newspaper headlines has resulted in a "quick-fix" programmatic mindset. Adults are suddenly expected to magically gain "years" of educational knowledge in weeks or months. Yet many of these individuals made little, if any, educational progress during 12 years of formal schooling. How can adults suddenly learn at such a comparatively rapid rate?

For example, a typical child during grades 3–12 adds 3,000 new words per year to a reading vocabulary, or some 30,000 new words over a ten-year period (Graves, 1986). A fifth-grade student reads an estimated 1,000,000 words a year both in and out of school and encounters up to 16,000 to 24,000 unknown words while reading (Nagy, Anderson and Herman 1987). Even with all this extended practice, children do not acquire an adult reading speed (130 to 220 words per minute) until sometime between the sixth and the eighth grades (Sticht, 1974). How can you consider funding a corporate Work Force Education program if it takes all this time for adults to learn and apply new reading abilities?

Our personal field research indicates that literacy is not an entirely generic set of time-acquired, discrete skills. Individual adults have learned reading, writing, math skills and application abilities during diverse formal and informal lifetime learning experiences. A decade of research with military personnel (Sticht et al., 1975, 1977) found that individuals with special background knowledge relevant to the job's reading tasks (e.g., a person with an aptitude for aircraft mechanics) performed better on a specific reading task test than someone with no specialized background knowledge. How can this be explained?

There is an important social nature to the workplace. Adults work in social groups and draw on the individual skills of other adults in their work group. One worker may ask for information from another rather than reading the information. Interpersonal interaction, common sense, abstract reasoning and problem-solving abilities are used by adults in a collaborative manner in which they share literacy tasks at work. Until recently, typical mass-production job-related reading requirements were very repetitive and limited in content and context. Adults used what educational skills they possessed to help them comprehend a relatively small number of word or number symbols appearing on the job. The introduction of computers, robotics, new quality controls and specialized orders/manufacturing has in a sense overwhelmed socially learned, on-the-job literacy.[2]

These coping skills, which have well served many adults over a lifetime, mask potential learning problems and the need for more information and skills. Outside of their natural work group, nonreading adults can feel the stigma that society associates with illiteracy and may act to conceal it. These feelings of personal shame reinforce adults' test-taking fears. Many employees are intimidated by standardized testing, which may remind them of previous unpleasant school experiences. Typically, Work Force Education program pretests do not provide the individually tailored information needed to plan necessary individualized instruction through a specific diagnosis of the adult's learning disabilities.

A study of typical company in-house or off-site programs (Baar-Hessler, 1984), showed how many American businesses are repeating the same school failure already experienced by low-skilled adults. Typical class sizes range from 10 to 35 students. Because of these large classes, little individualized instruction occurs and the inability to read or apply skills to the job remains the "employee's problem." Little thought is given to modifying the company's Work Force Education program or changing the teaching procedure itself to better address the individual employee's failure to learn.

There is a reasonable alternative to duplicating the "schooling" approach that failed many of these adults as children. Your company's Work Force Education instructional activities need to be based on diagnosed learning strengths and weaknesses. Diagnosis means asking specific questions about learning abilities while teaching. The instructor, over a period of classes, gathers anecdotal information and test data on student skills. A picture will emerge of the adult's learning disabilities and of how to adapt the instructional content and methods for precision teaching.[3]

UNDERSTANDING ADULT DYSLEXIA/LEARNING DISABILITIES

What proportion of the adult-basic skill population suffers from dyslexia or learning disabilities (L.D.)? Current estimates are as high as 80 percent. Even though many adult workers in this group are non-English-speaking foreigners, the larger proportion are U.S.-born. Many have completed high school or have dropped out. In our field-based research program, we also found many instances of L.D. adults who had even completed college and were now managers. These individuals experienced the same basic-skill and application problems as in their first days in elementary school. Numerous follow-up studies (Chall, 1987) of L.D. children provide evidence that many learning disabilities are not outgrown unless treated and may manifest themselves in new ways during adulthood. Many of these adults spurn educational assistance. Fairweather (1991) found on average that less than 50 percent of young adults with L.D. problems participated in postsecondary education or training programs when compared with nondisabled young adults.[4]

In interviews conducted by researchers and also by the authors with Work Force Education program staff members, great concern was expressed for the many L.D. adults who had not reached functional literacy even after several years of company-sponsored instruction. Company trainers repeatedly said that these adults needed diagnosis of their specific learning disabilities and individualized instruction in small groups or on a one-to-one basis.

What is a "learning disability"? The authors' field research with adults has identified over 300 potential skills used in learning reading and math concepts. This "total learning profile" includes important learning abilities needed by everyone to process information, reach understanding and apply skills. These skills include not only reading and math content areas but also vision, speech and hearing and the social-emotional aspects of learning and achievement. These 300 skills in our "total learning profile" are in constant daily use. We draw on some of them as we read this book, attend a training class, write a letter or carry on a group discussion. Our learning abilities are gradually sharpened as we grow physically, mature psychologically and develop mentally through school attendance and other self-improvement activities.

L.D. adults lack some of these learning abilities. Their intelligence quotient (IQ) is not the issue, for most possess average to above-average intelligence aptitude (i.e., to learn and adapt to problem-solving situations). However, L.D. adult learners have an inherent difficulty in processing information. They have an imperfect ability to listen, think, speak, read, write, spell or do mathematical calculations. Why? The major areas of concern we have uncovered with these adults center on perceptual problems. An adult may have perfect vision and hearing abilities (acuity). However, he/she may have impaired abilities for the brain to receive, understand and correctly process visual or auditory information (perception).

Visual perception is the ability to organize and recognize visual images as specific shapes. Making sense of letters, words or numbers requires visual memory, visual tracking from left to right on a page and visual discrimination between different similar symbols (e.g., b-d, m-n, 6-9).

Auditory perception is the ability to organize and recognize different sounds as letters or words. These sound patterns require our personal development of an auditory memory, auditory discrimination (e.g., dad-bad, bit-hit, through-though) and auditory comprehension (the ability to follow oral directions).

Many adults in Work Force Education programs lack these and other related thinking-processing skills. They are unable to learn phonics because they cannot discriminate between similar sounds. Others cannot concentrate on a computer screen because they cannot read words or symbols without making many mechanical errors that substantially reduce their comprehension.

From your own personal experience of foreign travel, or an experience of a business associate, recall your feeling of helplessness on first arriving in a non-English-speaking country. Even if you had taken some foreign language instruction, you may not have been prepared to comprehend the rapid rate of a foreign tongue when giving directions or making announcements in a train station or airport. Did you board the right train on your first outing? How well can you remember directions given in French, Italian or German? This is not an issue of your intelligence or desire to learn, but a lack of practice by that part of the brain that controls auditory perception (in a foreign language). As you are probably aware, true verbal language fluency takes the average executive years to acquire. This example is similar to the difficulties faced by many of your employees with auditory perception difficulties as they struggle to improve their educational skills.

Perhaps you can recall your first efforts at communication with a waiter in a foreign restaurant? Maybe you could pick out the meaning of a word or two on the menu, but the rest was confusion. Hopefully what you ordered at that meal was digestible! Adults with a visual perception problem face the same confusion in translating letters, words and numbers into comprehensible messages.

If an adult has difficulty recognizing sound patterns (auditory perception), will a phonetic-based instruction program successfully teach reading or math? If adult workers skip or insert words, lose their place on the page or confuse letters and numbers (visual perception), they will need special training before experiencing success as a reader. Most traditional literacy programs, whether based on texts, CBT or interactive videodiscs, will fail these adults. The successful diagnosis of potential learning disabilities will substantially increase the success rate of low-skilled or underskilled workers and managers.

DISCOVERING THE KEYS TO ADULT LEARNING

There is no one best HRD programmatic answer to the Work Force Education puzzle. As an HR manager, you have probably helped build your company's multilayered management-training program. Your company develops the inexperienced supervisor into a middle manager, and some become senior executives. As managers move up in your organization, they are offered more difficult business and personal development programs. The company seldom offers the same training program to all levels of the organization, recognizing the different levels of employee readiness and experience.

Work Force Education demands the same approach to adult learning. A variety of answers, not just one training program, recognizes the different levels of employee readiness to learn and of personal on-the-job application experience.

Current trends in educational psychology have brought a new surge in the development of programs designed to train all levels of workers to think more efficiently. These programs teach problem-solving strategies in the classroom while focusing on developing appropriate thinking skills. This national trend has been accompanied by a growing understanding that intelligence is not an unchangeable, fixed entity. What in the past has been viewed as innate aptitude/behavior or cognitive (thinking) ability appears to us now largely as a matter of offering an appropriate learning opportunity to acquire the skills essential for success in the office or workshop. Research shows that adult learners do best when they see a clear relationship between what is being taught and the attainment of their own goals. In our work, the greatest success was achieved by those for whom the completion of a basic or advanced educational program was directly related to a personal work goal. This included learning a foreign language for overseas marketing and advanced writing for key business reports, as well as ESL, basic reading, math or blueprint reading for employment retention or job advancement. Adult learners must clearly recognize the need for skill training. You must also give them an incentive to improve their skills.

However, cognitive (thinking and problem-solving ability) training cannot be the same for all students. To succeed, it must adapt to the learning characteristics of the adult. In some ways, this is contrary to your experience as an HR/training manager. Company training programs generally are behavior based, seeking to instill the appropriate company solution or responses for management, supervisory or technical applications. You know that the behavior-based, Skinnerian approach to training works. However, you now face a different challenge, not only to induce rote learning but also to foster abstract thinking skills throughout your company. We know that some people learn more readily than others. The Work Force Education challenge is to understand why these individual differences occur and devise programs that help less successful adult learners improve their higher cognitive-learning abilities.[5]

SOCIAL LEARNING

One such model originally derived by the behaviorist learning camp is the social learning model. As an HR manager, you are probably familiar with Skinner's behavioral model of learning. The basic idea is that you reinforce desired behavior and "shape" a person's performance. The Skinnerian model has been the basis for much organizational training.

Bandura (1978, 1989) and other social learning experts believe that in addition to using external reinforcement and punishment procedures to shape behavior, we learn by observing and modeling. If a model is rewarded, the learner is more likely to model the behavior than if the model is punished. Adults are more likely to emulate a rewarded fellow worker's behavior than that of a "punished" worker. For example, we can attend a violent film and learn how to be violent, but if the violence depicted in the film is punished rather than rewarded, hopefully most of us will not engage in the violent behavior.

The social learning model is very important to corporate trainers, since much of what is learned in the company classroom is learned in a social context. Most learning is internalized. We imitate the behaviors of those around us (trainers, peers, managers). While learning to model the models, we are making no overt responses that can be selectively rewarded or punished. From a social learning standpoint, what is taking place is the internalizing of the thinking and problem-solving process (cognition). In addition, this thinking process includes three interrelated components: the learner's behavior, individual differences (intelligence, personality) and the learner's environment (the physical learning site).[6]

THE REMODELING EXPERIENCE

The behaviorists believe that successful training consists in learning a large number of habits. The greater the number of accumulated habits, the greater the problem-solving ability of the learner. In contrast to a cognitive perspective, it is not the mere accumulation of experience but rather the "remodeling of experience" that is of primary importance in learning. One of the best indicators of what a person will learn at the start of a new training class is what the adult student already knows. It is evident that adults build on their past experiences. For this reason, pretesting—a precise diagnosis of the adult's learning profile, both strengths and weaknesses—is an essential initial component for Work Force Education. With this process, the trainer uses the diagnosed existing learning strengths to cope with learning skill weaknesses, thereby accelerating the entire new learning process.

MOTIVATION AND THE WORK ETHIC

In addition to understanding adult learning, we need to also consider a motivational element for Work Force Education. Most HR managers previously assumed that employees' "work ethic" automatically triggered their motivation, channeled work behavior and supported individual goals. For many employees, we can no longer rely on this formula.

What causes motivation on the job, and how can it best be built into Work Force Education programs? One explanation is that motivation consists of some sort of internalized physiological-drive mechanism. Perhaps a much more useful view is that motivation results from a thinking process called "cognitive conflict" (Silvan, 1986). For example, the way to motivate employees is to give them a problem-solving situation that generates a great deal of cognitive conflict (disequilibrium). Once the adult learner arrives at a solution to the problem, cognitive conflict is reduced, and the learner is ready to go on to the next task. We must make training as realistic as possible by basing at least part of the Work Force Education curriculum on job-related problems, simulations, role-plays or case studies. This cognitive conflict in turn motivates and maximizes an adult learner's performance. Motivation is the key stimulus that transforms Work Force Education into improved on-the-job performance. The increasing use of "work-teams" and "worker empowerment" reinforces a problem-solving training approach to improved motivation. Substituting the negative stigma of "illiteracy" with the positive attributes of studying the solutions to real work problems improves employee motivation, stimulates interest in quality/precision issues and increases personal involvement with job tasks.[7]

PERCEPTION AND REASONING ABILITIES

As a person ages into adulthood, the mind pigeonholes a tremendous amount of information into the brain's long-term and short-term, or working, memory. No matter how well we may motivate, the brain unceasingly filters this information acquired through vision, hearing and sensory (physical-motor) activities into its separate control areas (templates). The brain's encoding (receiving information) results in learned perceptions (skills up to concepts). Through these perceptual templates, the adult learner filters and stores all information. However, if the past encoding and decoding of the brain has been faulty, the visual/auditory perceptual templates set up roadblocks (disabilities) that interfere with the learning process. So each adult's existing internal perceptual-cognitive abilities influence the manner in which information is initially encoded in short-term memory and stored for later use in long-term memory.

The capacity and duration of an adult's memory may be substantial, but it is limited by many factors including individual attention, organizational abilities, practice (formal/informal educational activities) and the presence of perceptual disabilities (learning disabilities).[8]

HOW COGNITION WORKS

Cognitive psychologists have expanded our view of how an individual's abstract-reasoning abilities (thinking-cognition) grow over time. What develops? An adult usually develops a greater attention span than a child. The average person can concentrate on no more than seven different ideas (plus or minus two ideas) at any one time (Miller, 1956). As a person ages, the number of these chunks of information that can be mentally manipulated at one time remains constant. However, as the chunks become more complex letter and number symbols (i.e., vocabulary expansion, fractions, decimals, ratios, equations), the individual concepts become larger and require more sophisticated reasoning ability.

Children and adults perceive things differently because they are able to comprehend different details of a problem at lesser or greater depth based on their developed perceptual-thinking abilities. However, if an adult has not acquired these abilities through a combination of school and work activities, then reading, math, writing and problem solving will remain underdeveloped. Unschooled or underschooled adults have limited problem-solving abilities across tasks in the workplace. Years of formal successful schooling seem to be necessary before the emergence of spontaneous memorization and thinking skills (Olson, 1977). As an example, it is generally accepted that if a student studies for an exam only the night before, as opposed to spacing out the study over time, the depth of learning will not be as great. This is one of the primary reasons why short-term, quick-fix literacy programs fail for a large number of poorly educated employees.

If this explanation of learning is true, does it make corporate Work Force Education programs unrealistic and too costly, since we must consider enrolling an adult for years of training? The answer is a resounding NO! You cannot modify employee differences in temperament and maturity. But most of the elements in the cognitive approach to instruction can be taught and learned by adults. Cognitive information processing can be taught when adult learners are actively participating in the learning task: discussion, practice, analyzation, problem solving, sharing personal thoughts, understanding and knowledge. The authors designed training programs, in applied work settings, that include instructional procedures to modify cognitive components (attention, visual/auditory perception, memory, language, math, reading and writing skills) and that accelerate learning without sacrificing retention. Our goal was to help the individual adult move away from merely "knowing what" to "knowing how" and finally "knowing that." In the next three chapters, we will review these working cognitive Work Force Education models that have been successfully used by hourly workers and managers.[9]

RECIPROCAL TRAINING

Another successful cognitive learning method is the small-group instructional model found in reciprocal training. This learning strategy improves adult comprehension and accelerates new skill acquisition and information applications across changing job tasks (Glaser, 1990).

In the first step of reciprocal training, the instructor teaches self-regulatory strategies that employees can predict, analyze, summarize and apply to their work. The second step allows practice of these skills in small groups with different members taking turns directing the learning/application process.

Even though initially the trainer assumes the role of expert, reciprocal training focuses on the adult's interest in the social aspect of teaching and small-group learning. The assumption is that better training takes place in a cooperative environment and is a social group-type of experience. The reciprocal teaching process enables adult learners to realize their potential (Brown & Campione, 1986). The employee moves from external learning to internalizing the information and successfully applying it in diverse work projects (Vygotsky, 1978; Kosulin, 1986).

Motorola uses this approach to initiate production employees into Computer Integrated Manufacturing (CIM). The trainees are paired up at computer workstations, and the instructor leads them step-by-step through the different types of equipment and computer controls. Trainees learn operation of the robot arm and simulated programming and gradually become conversant in modern automated factory terminology. By the end of the training, assembly-line workers understand how a computer will program a robot for creative job tasks. Workers then begin to ask specific questions about applying robotics to their own jobs on the line. This relatively low-cost reciprocal training effort builds on factory workers' knowledge of everyday technology, uses social learning in small groups, and extends a basic foundation of knowledge to the lab's robotic technology. The training equipment has the realistic features of industrial equipment but is smaller, far less expensive and easier to operate (Cheng, 1990). These workers are walking away from their computer training program with a cognitive learning strategy that will enhance productivity and quality for the manufacturing of many future, diversified products.[10]

A TRAINING REVOLUTION

All of the training strategies we have reviewed have at their core improving the adult's thinking, judgmental and decision-making abilities. For Work Force Education success, the employee needs not just better skills but also the thinking and problem-solving abilities demanded in the high-tech office or factory. As a tool-and-die maker puts it, "Actually a machine tool shop is one big think tank." We view this learning as "central information processing" by the brain. Work Force Education must encompass a successful diagnosis of the adult's learning profile and reorganization of perceptions (vision, hearing, achievement, motivational "work ethic" issues). Of course, learning is limited by the individual differences among learners (e.g., knowledge, language, personality, learning disabilities), which may severely limit higher-level thinking, learning and problem-solving behavior.[11]

A recent study by the Public Agenda Foundation, a New York–based research and educational organization, concluded that most company training has not kept pace with advances in the workplace. Some progressive U.S. companies have addressed the need to include these higher-level thinking-business skills in their Work Force Education agenda. On their shop floors, self-directed work teams or incentive programs, such as "pay for knowledge," give workers more money to learn the skills for another position. The program enables employees to move from one assembly line to another as needs arise, enhancing productivity and quality. However, these programs remain the exception in America.[12]

The authors have applied cognitive learning principles that improved productivity in a diversity of company on-site Work Force Education programs. This mode of training reliably raised the level of employee personal commitment and lessened resistance to change.

COGNITION AND LITERACY

By this point you may be thinking, "These are nice theories, but how does all this relate to literacy training?"

Most trainers/educators have long agreed that relating content to an adult's life and interests increases motivation and improves thinking skills (cognition). However, the reality of typical literacy programs is that employees spend most of their time with boring reading, writing and math materials. Contemporary programs argue that basic skills can be taught in the abstract and that relevant content is nice but not necessary.

In our view, resourceful programs must integrate basic-skills instruction with general and specific job skills.[13]

What employees read, write and calculate in the office or workshop is highly diversified. Letters, proposals, forms, memos, manuals, minutes of meetings, brochures, charts, graphs, computer screens, computer printouts and computer control-boards all require specialized information-processing skills. The average worker is required to read work-related materials at levels of difficulty from the sixth- to the twelfth-grade level or even higher.

The basic purposes for reading at work fall into several categories. "Reading to do" (80%) involves information to accomplish a specific task. Most often, this information is not retained after the job is done. "Reading to learn" (25%) requires learning information and retaining it for later use. "Reading to assess" (16%) features considering a material's usefulness for a specific task, purpose or group of people. Other broader uses of reading/math/writing skills include gaining background information, analyzing problems, responding to problems and solving problems. All of these activities require higher-level thinking skills, which can be facilitated through Work Force Education.[14]

Three instructional reading models predominate in contemporary adult education.

Model I: Top-Down or Meaning-Emphasis

The assumption here is that the real purpose of reading for adults is to gain meaning from the text. Very little phonics instruction is given, since it stresses analysis of words. The meaning-emphasis model argues that adult learners are more able to use contextual clues to decode unfamiliar words. Adult reading tasks provide more context clues and thus generally differ from those encountered by children.

Model II: Bottom-Up or Code-Emphasis (Phonetic)

This reading instruction model teaches the phonetic analysis of words. It enables readers to decode words and gain meaning from a text at any level of reading. Many traditional adult-literacy programs are based on this concept.

Model III: Interactive

This combines the above two strategies but places more emphasis on reading for meaning. Reading is a cognitive process that gains meaning from the text. Phonetic analysis is one of several tools that may or may not be useful in learning unknown words.[15]

The meaning-emphasis model is highly cognitive in nature. It demands the application of abstract reasoning skills and the retention in long-term memory of information that is used by the short-term memory in reading for meaning.

The phonetic reading process, at the other extreme, relies on the memorization of rules (sound patterns) to unlock word meaning. By adopting these rules, the adult learns a successful set of behaviors that build the learning of word meaning into text comprehension.

The combined interactive model seems to work best for most adult learners. On the one hand, it acknowledges the aspects of higher-level reasoning that adults possess and that children lack. It simultaneously recognizes that certain adult perceptual templates (vision/auditory perception) may be strong enough that the use of phonetic instruction will speed up the accumulation of basic reading skills. However, interactive instruction does not penalize the adult who has learning disabilities (weak perceptual skills) and cannot decode sound patterns. It offers a balanced teaching approach that enhances adult reading to almost any level.

WORK FORCE EDUCATION PROGRAM RECOMMENDATIONS

In light of this information on learning and reading, we offer these successful teaching practices for Work Force Education programs:

1. Diagnose the adult's learning disabilities. This includes not only giving a pretest in reading, math, problem solving, grammar, writing or other pertinent skills but also making careful observations for potential learning difficulties and/or disabilities. Additional diagnostic tests can be used, if needed, to determine the direction of remedial teaching.

2. Teaching materials must be relevant to adult needs. The curriculum for the manager, clerk, or shopworker must be organized by job tasks. It must be built on the employee's knowledge of job content. Other useful everyday informational materials need to be included based on personal employee interests and need.

3. When appropriate, the teaching program should give the employees an opportunity to work together and learn from each other.

4. Adult trainees must receive constant feedback on their progress.

5. Effective Work Force Education programs use an array of evaluation methods to improve content, instruction methods and overall employee success back in the workplace. Standardized tests alone will not do the job and may give false impressions of skill needs and program results.

6. Individual adult goals and objectives must be clearly defined for enrollment in the program.

7. Successful Work Force Education programs will link the goals of the company with the goals of participating employees.[16]

THE FAILURE OF PAST LITERACY PROGRAMS

If we know so much, why have current literacy programs failed so many adults? There is a shocking lack of adult-literacy-focused "applied research" devoted to upgrading the state of the art based on any of the instructional approaches we have reviewed in this chapter. Few wholly "new" systems for adult learning are being tried in the American workplace.

At most, only a dozen first-rate researchers have focused their attention on this field. Until the late 1980s, very little government, foundation, university or corporate funds were offered to find new solutions. Without more funding, neither pure nor applied research will be forthcoming in the 1990s.

Recent scholarly contributions are meager and scattered. Few empirically based studies of applied field research are available, since many corporations shield results for so-called proprietary reasons. Too many contemporary "research" articles give repetitious information or relate "horror stories" about literacy training. Others offer glowing program descriptions without giving solid evidence on results or without detailing the "how-to" of the curriculum. In most articles, there is little solid research on individualized instruction or learning in the context of work.

As Taylor (1989) has said about the literacy field, "The essence of scholarship does not lie in creating theories that fit our research." Work Force Education needs to create explanations that tell us something about what we are studying. Too often, adults are penalized by programs that fail them as employees and cannot adapt to their learning profile as students. Of course, as children, these low-skilled adults followed the same defeatist path in school. Contemporary company HRD literacy programs have now become the educator of last resort. But you do not need to repeat the school's fundamental teaching mistakes.[17]

It is our belief that a better Work Force Education program can be built on a mastery learning model combining testing and case-study reports. Mastery learning fits the employee's need for applied learning. It can measure the long-term effect of employee participation in Work Force Education programs.

Mastery learning is built around a sequence of individualized learning goals tracked class-by-class through written instructional objectives related to those goals. This tracking of prescriptive learning for adults in the workplace uncovers important factors that strengthen and accelerate employee training. Mastery learning uncovers the processes used by adults to acquire problem-solving abilities using verbal and mathematical job-related skills. As a training competency approach, it can also be used across a wide variety of managerial, support, skilled and semi-skilled jobs.

Other literacy researchers (Sticht, 1988) support the notion that Work

Force Education can best be taught by this integration of educational skills with job knowledge development. In the next three chapters, we will discuss how such Work Force Education programs have operated. We will investigate how to accelerate employee learning. The instructional techniques for the diagnosis of difficult adult learning problems and effective teaching strategies will be illustrated across job types. We will review various management teaching strategies at different worksite environments. Details will be given on how to create relevant program evaluation/performance standards that are measurable and easily interpreted. Case studies from company programs for shopworkers, support staff, supervisors, managers and professionals will provide on-the-job illustrations of how you will be able to plan your own HR Work Force Education applications.[18]

NOTES

1. Thomas G. Sticht, "Adult Literacy Education," in *Review of Research in Education*, ed. Ernst Z. Rothkopf (Washington, D.C.: American Educational Research Association, 1988), 59–96; Carol Jouzaitis, "Adult Education Failing to Spell Success in GED," *Chicago Tribune*, 25 November 1990, Sec. 1, 1, 10.

2. S. Darling, *Submission to the Joint Dissemination Review Panel* (Washington, D.C.: U.S. Department of Education, 1982), 6; T. G. Sticht, *Functional Context Education: Workshop Resource Notebook* (San Diego, Calif.: Applied Behavioral and Cognitive Sciences, 1987); R. J. Park, "Language and Reading Comprehension: A Case Study of Low Reading Adults," *Adult Literacy and Basic Education* 7 (1983): 153–63; N. Boraks and S. Schumacher, *Ethnographic Research on Word Recognition Strategies of Adult Beginning Readers* (Richmond: School of Education, Virginia Commonwealth University, 1981); M. F. Graves, "Vocabulary Learning and Instruction," in *Research in Education*, ed. Rothkopf (1986), 49–89; W. E. Nagy, R. C. Anderson, and P. A. Herman, "Learning Word Meanings from Context during Normal Reading," *American Educational Research Journal* 24 (1987): 237–70; T. G. Sticht et al., *Reading: A Developmental Model* (Alexandria, Va.: Human Resources Research Organization, 1974), 82–95; T. G. Sticht, *A Program of Army Functional Job Reading Training* (Alexandria, Va: Human Resources Research Organization, 1975); T. G. Sticht et al., *The Role of Reading in the Navy* (San Diego, Calif.: Navy Personnel Research and Development Center, 1977); T. G. Sticht et al., *Integrated Job Skills and Reading Skills Training* (San Diego, Calif.: Navy Personnel Research and Development Center, 1977).

3. Jonita M. Ross, *Learning and Coping Strategies Used by Learning Disabled Students Participating in Adult Basic Education and Literacy Programs* (University Park: Pennsylvania State University, 1987), 1–58; Nancy D. Padak, Jane L. Davidson, and Gary M. Padak, "Exploring Reading with Adult Beginning Readers," *Journal of Reading* 34, no. 1 (September 1990): 26–29; Madeline Baar-Kessler, "An Analysis of the Concept of 'Literacy' and Investigation of the Role of the Fortune 500 Companies in Literacy Training" (Master's Thesis, Rutgers, State University of

New Jersey, 1984), 58; Anne McGill-Franzen, "Failure to Learn to Read: Formulating a Policy Problem," *Reading Research Quarterly* 22, no. 4 (Fall 1987): 475–90.

4. Ross, *Learning and Coping*, 1–3; J. S. Chall, E. Heron, and A. Hilferty, "Adult Literacy: New and Enduring Problems," *Phi Delta Kappan* 69, no. 3 (November 1987): 190–96; James S. Fairweather and Debra M. Shaver, "Making the Transition to Postsecondary Education and Training," *Exceptional Children* 57, no. 3 (December/January 1991): 264–69.

5. Miriam Alfassi, "An Investigation of the Role of Individual Differences in Cognitive Growth Explored within the Context of a Reciprocal Teaching Instructional Environment" (Ph.D. Dissertation, Loyola University, Chicago, 1990), 2, 3; Susan Foster, "Upgrading the Skills of Literacy Professionals," in *Leadership for Literacy*, ed. Forrest P. Chrisman (San Francisco: Jossey-Bass Publishers, 1990), 80.

6. A. Bandura, "Human Agency in Social Cognitive Theory," *American Psychologist* 44, no. 9 (1989): 1175–84; A. Bandura, "The Self System in Reciprocal Determinism," *American Psychologist* 33, no. 4 (1978): 344–58.

7. E. Silvan, "Motivation in Social Constructivist Theory," *Educational Psychologist* 21, no. 3 (1986): 209–33.

8. R. Glaser, *Advances in Instructional Psychology* (Hillsdale, N.J.: Erlbaum, 1978), vol. 1, vol. 2 (1982), vol. 3 (1986); D. Ausubel, *Educational Psychology: A Cognitive View* (New York: Holt, Rinehart and Winston, 1968).

9. G. A. Miller, "The Magical Number Seven Plus or Minus Two: Some Limits on Our Capacity for Processing Information," *Psychological Review* 63 (1956): 81–97; D. Olson, "The Language of Instruction: On the Literate Bias of Schooling," in *Schooling and the Acquisition of Knowledge*, ed. R. C. Anderson and R. J. Spiro (Hillsdale, N.J.: Erlbaum, 1977).

10. R. Glaser, "The Reemergence of Learning Theory within Instructional Research," *American Psychologist* 45, no. 1 (1990): 29–39; A. L. Brown and J. C. Campione, "Psychological Theory and the Study of Learning Disabilities," *American Psychologist* 41, no. 10 (1986): 1059–68; L. S. Vygotsky, *Mind in Society* (Cambridge, Mass.: Harvard University Press, 1978); A. Kosulin, "The Concept of Activity in Soviet Psychology: Vygotsky, His Disciples and Critics," *American Psychologist* 41, no. 3 (1986): 264–74; Alex F. Cheng, "Hands-On Learning at Motorola," *Training and Development Journal* 44, no. 10 (1990): 34–35.

11. Marya Smith, "First Person: Tool and Die Maker, 'A Machine Tool Shop Is One Big Think Tank,' " *Chicago Tribune Magazine*, 9 December 1990, Sec. 10, 36.

12. Connie Lauerman, "Take This Job . . . America's Changing Attitudes toward Work," *Chicago Tribune Magazine*, 25 November 1990, Sec. 10, 16–22.

13. Hanna A. Fingert, "Changing Literacy Instruction: Moving Beyond the Status Quo" in *Leadership for Literacy*, ed. Charisman 28–32.

14. Larry Mikulecky, Jeanne Ehlinger, and Avis L. Meenan, *Training for Job Literacy Demands: What Research Applies to Practice* (University Park: Pennsylvania State University, 1987): 3–4.

15. William R. Kitz, "Adult Literacy: A Review of the Past and a Proposal for the Future," *Pro-Ed* 9, no. 4, (1988): 44–50.

16. Valerie Meyer, "Lingering Feelings of Failure: An Adult Student Who Didn't Learn to Read," *Journal of Reading*, December 1987, 218–21; Patricia Dunn-

Rankin and Drake Beil, "A Primer for Workplace Literacy Programs," *Training and Development Journal* 44 (August 1990): 45–47.

17. Fay F. Bowren, "Adult Reading Needs Adult Research Models," *Journal of Reading*, December 1987, 208–12; Judith A. Alamprese, "Strengthening the Knowledge Base," in *Leadership for Literacy*, ed. Chisman, 98–102; Forrest P. Chisman, "Toward a Literate America," in *Leadership for Literacy*, ed. Chisman, 17; Sticht, "Adult Literacy Education," 77, 83; Denny Taylor, "Toward a Unified Theory of Literacy Learning and Instructional Practices," *Phi Delta Kappan* 71, no. 3 (November 1989: 184–93.

18. Sticht, "Adult Literacy Education," 74–75; Alamprese, "Strengthening the Knowledge Base," 104–13; Stanley Deno et al., "Educating Students with Mild Disabilities in General Education Classrooms; Minnesota Alternative," *Exceptional Children* 57, no. 2 (October/November 1990): 150–61.

5

Individualized Instructional Programs (IIP) for Work Force Education

As technology has advanced in the office and factory, the need has grown for human resources to develop vastly improved training systems that link applied learning theory to business goals. In this chapter we will study the specific idea of breaking down job tasks into their identifiable educational/training learning components. We will examine advanced teaching strategies that give trainers the resources to work with employees who are problematic trainees.

It has already been stated that improving adult learning for Work Force Education is determined mainly by enhancing cognition (thinking and problem-solving abilities) but that learning may be constrained by individual differences (language, knowledge, attitudes, personality and learning disabilities).

We already know that (Vélis, 1990) the acquisition of functional reading, math, writing and problem-solving abilities is a cumulative process that takes the average person many years to attain. (Twelve years of formal schooling is typical for almost everyone.) The higher the standard of initial schooling, the greater will be adults' interest in acquiring more training, education and personal knowledge during the rest of their lives. Unfortunately, the converse is also equally true. Weak, ineffective initial schooling patterns, for whatever reason, make it much harder to reeducate a functionally illiterate adult using a standard schooling format (i.e., typical large-group classroom instruction). From the findings of our field-based research program, we have crafted detailed, empirically derived task analyses of instructional skills associated with many occupations. This training is designed to enhance reasoning and problem-solving abilities embedded within the context of an academic, job-related skill curriculum. Identification of individual differences in information-processing abilities was utilized to design remedial instructional programs that compensated for particular learning problems. This specific diagnosis was used to pinpoint learning difficulties at all educational levels and helped the employee make the gradual transition to job-appropriate educational fluency.

When called on to design a specific Work Force Education program, we have developed instructional procedures that develop up to 300 cognitive learning skills in relation to occupational and individual worker aptitudes. It is our belief that the mastery learning program of instruction has many potential ramifications for Work Force Education programs, since we have found that many job-related learning and thinking skills can be taught.[1]

MASTERY LEARNING

John B. Carroll (1963) proposed that the degree of learning is a function of the ratio of two quantities: (1) the amount of time a learner spends on the learning task, and (2) the amount of time a learner needs to learn the task. (See Table 5.1.)[2]

This model has served as a behaviorally based theoretical anchor for much of Benjamin Bloom's (1968) work related to mastery learning instruction. Carroll's formulation implied that by allowing sufficient time to learn a task (i.e., permitting the numerator of the ratio to be larger) and by improving instructional conditions (i.e., decreasing the denominator), most students should be able to reach a criterion of mastery. Mastery learning is an educational procedure in which a learning hierarchy is developed and learners are required to master each unit of the hierarchy before beginning a subsequent unit. Mastery usually is determined by end-of-unit tests that learners must pass. Bloom (1971, 1976) has argued that mastery learning research (Block, 1971, 1974; Block & Burns, 1976), supports his claim that mastery learning strategies can raise the achieve-

Table 5.1
Carroll's Model of Mastery Learning

Degree of learning =   Amount of time spent on task

Amount of time needed to learn to
learn the task

---

ment levels of approximately 80 percent of students to levels achieved by the upper 20 percent under nonmastery conditions. It should be noted that these findings apply to many academic content areas (e.g., reading, writing and math) and to different types of thinking and problem-solving situations. From these reviews, it seems that most investigators recognize that the tutoring and mastery learning research findings confirm the achievement claims but that the time claims require further investigation. Most tutoring and mastery learning theorists acknowledge that during the initial learning sequences, extra time must be provided to less able learners. However, this extra time is viewed as a temporary "crutch" that becomes less and less necessary with practice (Bloom, 1976).[3]

A number of critics of mastery learning instruction (Anderson & Burns, 1987; Buss, 1976; Greeno, 1978; Guskey, 1987; Mueller, 1976; Resnick, 1977; Slavin, 1987a, 1987b) have argued that in regular nonmastery school situations, in which time is held constant for all learners, individual differences among students are reflected primarily in differences in achievement outcomes.[4] To bring less-able learners up to the desired mastery level, schools must provide additional time for both learners and teachers. Since individual differences among learners are assumed to be relatively stable, critics claim that these time costs remain relatively constant throughout mastery learning instruction (i.e., time is traded for the increased achievement of less-able students, and time inequality is traded for achievement equality).

From the results of numerous investigations, almost always with students attending elementary or secondary schools, we know that mastery learning programs, when compared with traditional approaches to instruction, produce positive gains in academic achievement and student attitudes (Block & Burns, 1976). However, as Berliner (1989) pointed out, we also know that in practice, many of these programs receive negative reviews. To explain these poor results, Berliner has hypothesized that we need to examine teachers' beliefs and thoughts about their roles within the context of mastery learning instruction. "The teachers' conception about what is 'proper' student behavior is challenged in mastery approaches (e.g., ability is a time variable not a genetic quality of the individual), and their capacity to manage heterogeneity—30 individuals proceeding at their own pace—is also strained." In other words, it is very difficult to individualize instruction for a classroom of 30 students.[5]

There is considerable evidence indicating that the effectiveness of the mastery approach depends on the length of the experiment and the type of outcome measure used. Slavin (1987a) found that experiments lasting four weeks or longer yielded more positive findings than those experiments lasting less than four weeks. Finally, there may be a "Robin Hood effect" associated with the use of mastery learning approaches to instruction. Mastery learning may help slower-learning students at the expense of faster-learning students. The important educational resources of teacher time and attention may be used to benefit the slower learners at the expense of faster ones.[6]

PERSONALIZED SYSTEMS OF INSTRUCTION (PSI)

Although mastery learning and PSI approaches were derived from different theoretical perspectives, they are similar in many ways. Bloom's (1971) learning-for-mastery strategy evolved from Carroll's (1963) theory of school learning and has had its major impact, thus far, on elementary and secondary school educators, not corporate trainers. In contrast, the personalized system of instruction (PSI) strategy developed by Keller (1968) evolved from Skinnerian behavioral theory and has had its major impact on the thinking of university and college educators and in some training applications.[7]

The basic components of PSI include self-pacing, the use of proctors, the mastery requirement, immediate feedback, and frequent testing over relatively small units. Regular teaching procedures do not encourage enough responses or provide enough opportunities for reinforcement. Keller (1968) proposed that subject matter be divided into brief instructional units, enabling students to study at their own rate and to progress to the next unit when mastery (an 80 to 90% correct score) is achieved. Those students who do not master an instructional unit the first time are provided with additional time and tutoring until mastery is achieved.[8]

Kulik, Kulik, and Cohen's (1979) meta-analyses of PSI indicated that when compared with traditional instruction, PSI produces superior student achievement, considerably less achievement variation, and higher student evaluations of college courses. In addition, PSI procedures were found to be unrelated to increased study time or course withdrawals. Considerable disagreement exists over the respective contributions of each of the components to the effectiveness of PSI. For example, Calhoun (1973) found that all of the components make important contributions. However, Block and Burns (1976) reported that the mastery requirement produced the strongest effects. Finally, the "Robin Hood effect" cited above as a potential problem with mastery learning instruction does not manifest itself with PSI because students work independently (Calhoun, 1973). That is, since students work independently with PSI, a teacher's time and attention are not used to benefit slower learners at the expense of their faster peers.[9]

In sum, PSI gets generally favorable marks when compared with traditional instructional methodologies, appears to be easily adapted to a wide variety of instructional situations and has few, if any, empirically demonstrated negative side effects.

TUTORING

Gordon and Gordon (1990) reported that large-group-based schooling has dominated the twentieth century but that individual and small-group tutoring approaches to instruction still hold an important role. Peer-tutors, after-school remedial programs, homebound instruction, and the "home-schooling movement" are modern expressions of tutoring. Between the years 1500 and 1900, tutors demonstrated that a child's education was a highly personalized process, supported by the family and guided through the assistance of literate teachers. At their best, tutors remained the best equipped to assess individual differences among their students and to engineer stimulating learning environments. In the nineteenth and particularly the twentieth centuries, tutoring became an actual part of "schooling." Some of the most important philosophers of the West developed educational theories based on their practical experience as tutors. Their tutorial philosophy led to the development of many of our modern educational principles such as continuous assessment, remediation, encouragement and support. It is important to note that these principles are the same as those assumed to be of importance to advocates of mastery learning and PSI instruction.[10]

A review of the literature indicates that tutoring usually produces positive results. Annis (1983) reported that tutoring procedures appear to produce good effects on both tutees and tutors. Summarizing research on tutoring, Gage and Berliner (1988) indicated that these positive effects have been consistently found on measures of achievement and on affective measures of self-esteem and intrinsic interest in the subject matter being taught. A meta-analysis of the studies of the effects of tutoring (Cohen, Kulik, & Kulik, 1982) indicated an initially high rate of success in a relatively short time (usually measured in weeks) common to achievement gains from tutoring. In most studies, these initial gains appeared to diminish over time after four weeks of tutoring.[11] In addition, numerous cross-age, peer-tutoring studies conducted with learners across the life span have yielded positive findings (Lippitt, 1969; P. Lippitt & R. Lippitt, 1970; R. Lippitt & M. Lippitt, 1968). In sum, tutoring appears to be a very powerful technique for enhancing student learning across a wide sample of different types of students and content areas.[12]

INDIVIDUALIZED INSTRUCTIONAL PROGRAMS (IIP) AS AN ENHANCED COGNITIVE SCIENCE MODEL OF MASTERY LEARNING, PSI AND TUTORING

It is the authors' view that it is now time to embellish the behaviorally based mastery learning model originally proposed by Carroll (1963) to include a number of cognitive variables. The Individualized Instructional

Table 5.2
The IIP as an Enhanced Model of Mastery Learning

Degree of learning = Time spent (willing or allowed)

Time needed (aptitude, i.e.,

individual differences) +

(quality of instruction x

ability to understand

instructions)

Where: Student <u>aptitude</u> would consist of the

biological differences of attention,

temperament and maturational stages of

development and the psychological differences

of existing knowledge and language templates,

cognitive styles, attitudes, expectancies, mood

and learning disabilities.

<u>Quality of instruction</u> would be viewed as the

ability of the teacher to organize instruction,

to give it meaning, and to set up problem-

solving situations that enhance critical

thinking.

<u>Ability to understand instructions</u> would

consist of the same components as quality of

instruction.

Programs (IIP) model is presented in Table 5.2 as an enhanced cognitive science model of mastery learning, PSI and tutoring.

From a cognitive scientist's perspective, individual differences in student aptitude would consist of differences in attention, temperament, maturational stages of development, existing knowledge and language templates, cognitive styles, attitudes, mood, expectancies and learning disabilities. Quality of instruction would relate to the ability of the tutor to organize instruction and to set up situations that would enhance meaning and contribute to the development of critical thinking and problem-solving skills.

It is recognized that we are unable to modify biological differences in temperament and maturational stages. But most of the other components listed in the embellished cognitive science model can be learned. We can enhance knowledge and language templates. It is generally accepted that how efficiently we learn depends to a great extent on what we already know. From a cognitive science perspective, a major constraint on atypical adult learners is that their knowledge base and ability to code and store information may be very limited. There is a literate bias in training, which is viewed as enhancing our thinking and problem-solving behaviors. The assumption is that this literate bias allows the expert learner (artist, writer, reader) to interpret environmental events (a painting, a proposal, a story) differently than the novice learner. It is further assumed that students with an internally controlled, field-independent cognitive style interpret their environment in a way that differs from the externally controlled, field-dependent learner. For example, internally controlled students would attribute their successes to effort, persistence, and hard work, whereas externally controlled students would be more likely to attribute their success to luck. Negative attitudes, low expectancies and bad moods constrain cognitive performance. Again, the point to be made here is that knowledge and language templates, cognitive styles, attitudes, expectancies, mood and potential learning disabilities can be modified by the IIP tutor.

One might get the impression that the authors are advocating a diagnostic-prescriptive framework for improving the achievement of learners. However, this is not the case. It is recognized that the current thinking (Arter & Jenkins, 1977; Kavale & Forness, 1987) in remedial curriculum and instruction departs from the diagnostic-prescriptive model, at least for the mildly and moderately handicapped learner, in that it focuses narrowly on deficits, does not recognize and build on strengths and does not consider the complexity, connectedness and holistic nature of learning.[13]

Much of what we present here is derived from the field of cognitive information processing, a field replete with overlapping ideas and concepts expressed in multiple terms. There are those practitioners who would claim that the field is too complex and the instructional procedures derived from it too cumbersome to use. Although most of us may agree that trainers should utilize cognitive information-processing principles in the curriculum and instructional designs they create for all learners, we may not think that this complex theory of learning and instruction can be directly applied to pragmatic instructional situations. Should trainers be expected to monitor and shape the cognitive information-processing capabilities of adult learners? Can trainers modify an adult student's attention, cognitive styles, expectancies and memory? The research indicates that they can (Frisby, 1990; Glaser, 1984; Gordon, Ponticell, Morgan, 1989; Glaser, 1990).[14]

It has been argued that individual differences in cognition (knowledge and problem solving) and perception can both constrain and facilitate learning. Our view is that individual differences, especially the cognitive bases of differences of the problem adult learner and instructional task, appear to have a valid place in training and development if the training program uses concepts found in mastery learning, PSI and tutoring instruction. It is the authors' belief that the information-processing and neo-Piagetian cognitive science approaches have potential for use in diagnosing poorly educated adults and, most important, may suggest appropriate educational prescriptive interventions for each. The information-processing and neo-Piagetian development theories of instruction would appear to be particularly valuable in diagnosing reasons for current learning difficulties and in suggesting the mastery learning, PSI and tutoring instructional procedures (prescriptions) for overcoming these difficulties. From these theories we have devised an advanced IIP tutorial model that facilitates the adult Work Force Education program.[15]

THE IIP TUTORIAL TRAINING MODEL

We have designed a tutorial delivery system that helps the trainee learn more efficiently, master subject material and improve long-term retention. This tutorial system also best encompasses a teaching of reading that combines reading for meaning and phonetic analysis. Adults are motivated by the immediate application of these new skills. Our tutorial program integrates the learning of job content material and instruction in reading, composition/grammar, applied math concepts and a foreign language or English as a Second Language. Tutoring is already widely used in the corporate training environment. One example is the Johns Hopkins University Directed Listening-Language Approach (DL-LEA) (Gold & Johnson, 1982) as a tutorial method of teaching adults to read. The DL-LEA method integrates the learning of any subject matter and a tutorial reading program. Since 1989, Boston University's Corporate Education Center has trained thousands of employees using Accelerated Learning Techniques (ALT). This program uses methods to decrease the amount of time required to cover a given subject area. Skills are taught in intense, shortened time frames. Accelerated learning is possible if training programs are designed by content/learning/training experts who determine how to break a job down into tasks, functions, skills and related competencies.

Another superior component inherent in an organized tutorial system is a personal needs assessment that determines training capabilities. Tutoring will more efficiently answer the primary question of what must be learned by the individual employee. This is a difficult and painstaking task that is far more important than CBT high-tech bells and whistles or than physically attractive corporate training environments. What tutoring facilitates is a collection of employee information that can be used to modify the Work Force Education program. It also establishes a criteria for individual employee success. A tutorial-training evaluation process will provide for a continual modification of the Work Force Education program based on individual employee learning needs and occupational skill/application requirements.[16]

THE IIP

A tutorial-based Work Force Education program has been developed by the authors and used in many corporate field settings with hourly workers, office support staff and business managers. It is based on a cognitive, mastery learning model that offers a variety of curriculum scripts (45) designed to diagnose specific adult learning problems while tutoring for mastery of related job skills. It is designed around a sequence of individualized learning goals tracked by written instructional objectives related to those goals.

The Individualized Instructional Programs (IIP) are specifically designed to bring about rapid, verifiable skill training. Each IIP, with its associated written methods and reporting materials, is designed to help the trainer follow a thoughtful, sequentially arranged, systematic presentation with a group of up to five adult students or on a one-to-one basis. The IIP program emphasizes administrative quality control, student learning awareness and constant feedback to company management during the training.

The IIP curriculum was written in an attempt to avoid duplicating many of the pitfalls of traditional large-group classroom instruction. Many illiterate adults dropped out of school to become entry-level employees because of personal underachievement and frustration in the classroom. The IIP small-group (1:5) or individual (1:1) training format takes into account individual differences among the participants. It is easily adapted to many different adult learning problems.

A typical IIP (small-group) training module consists of 40 hours of instruction. Classes meet for two hours and are held twice a week for ten weeks. (1:1 instruction is done during one-hour classes held twice a week for ten weeks, totaling 20 hours.) This tutoring module structure recognizes the importance of extending learning over time rather than offering short-term massed practice. We need this time to assess how an adult learner approaches the learning task; to discover what specific sequential subject-matter skills are missing; to reorganize the adult's achievement/study habits; and to assess and improve employee motivation, which supports learning related to the workplace. The hallmark of the IIP program is precision individualized diagnosis and applied training that allow employees to learn at their own pace.

To facilitate better individualized tutoring across types of educational/job-related skills, we designed specifically crafted curriculum scripts to teach competencies at the introductory, maintenance and mastery levels. We have systematically designed into these IIP curriculums up to 300 learning descriptors that are used to document academic skill achievement, selected job-related competencies and personal motivational outcomes. The 300 learning descriptors are assessed throughout the 40 class hours through tutor observations, diagnostic/developmental testing, criterion-referenced tests and normed achievement testing.

IIP STRUCTURE

How does a trainer decide if an employee has learned a particular skill concept or work procedure and is ready to move on? The IIP curriculum script is a loosely ordered but well-defined set of skills and applied work concepts that the adult is expected to learn. What drives the instructional process is the skills the employee brings to the learning task. The IIP facilitates the gathering of this information individually from student performance cues (300 skills) and student learning strengths to attack learning difficulties or skill misconceptions.

The content areas used to teach these new skills are taken directly from the daily work assignment or future jobs in the office or factory. Thus the IIP curriculum script is the major determinant of the content for the tutoring class, not a trainer's rigid, preconceived lesson plan. Curriculum scripts used in our research program include basic reading and math, learning disability areas, grammar training, managerial/executive writing skills, English as a Second Language, 15 foreign languages (including French, Spanish, German, Italian, Portuguese, Japanese, Russian and Chinese) and office practice (typing, shorthand, computer literacy, computer software). (See Tables 5.3 and 5.4.)

The IIP's formal/informal test-tutor-test format helps establish meaningful employee learning goals and objectives. The specific attainment of job-related skill goals is reported, in great detail, back to the adult student throughout the training classes. The use of realistic job-training goals and objectives motivates adults to persist to any desired level of lit-

Table 5.3
IIP Comprehensive Reading Checklist

| Directions: | Please check appropriate box as an indicator of skills levels and developmental progression. This is FOR YOUR USE WITH <u>EVERY</u> CLASS.   After the last class for this unit, you must indicate the Final Instructional Skill level. |

Ex: 3^1 (first 3 mos. of grade) 3^{mid} (4 to 6 mos.) 3^2 (7 to 9 mos. of grade)

	FINAL INSTRUCTIONAL SKILL	INTRODUCING SKILL	EMPHASIZING SKILL	MASTERING SKILL
A. Sight Vocabulary				
B. Acquired Vocabulary				
1. Context Clues:				
a. pictures				
b. listening				
c. verbal				
d. word meaning				
C. Visual Discrimination & Analysis				
1. Developing left to right sequence				
2. Recognizing letters, capitals and lower case				
3. Likeness and differences in word forms				
D. Total Phonetic Skills (See attached Phonetic Skills Checklist)				
1. Single Consonants				
a. initial				
b. final				
c. medial				

eracy or advanced educational fluency. The IIP gives adults a concrete picture of their progress and establishes a positive self-motivational training process.

The IIP curriculum script provides an overall inclusive structure that is used to track the daily performance of a particular tutoring class. A primary component of each class is the tutor's ability to use task analysis to track the sequence of successive steps the adult must take to attain a particular learning goal. For each of the written learning objectives that the tutor records, task analysis describes exactly what skills the adult must

Table 5.4
IIP ESL (English as a Second Language)

Beginning Level

Speaking

		FINAL INSTRUCTIONAL SKILL	INTRODUCING SKILL	EMPHASIZING SKILL	MASTERING SKILL
A.	Structures				
1.	This/that				
2.	Verb to be - is/am/are				
3.	Singular/plural noun forms (regular and irregular)				
4.	Possessive adjectives (my, your, etc.)				
5.	Personal pronouns in subject and object forms. Example I/me, she/her, etc.				
6.	Contrast of statement and question forms with verb to be Example: The book is white/Is the book white?				
7.	Imperative forms Example: Go to the store/Don't sit there.				
8.	Present continuous Example: I am walking/You are walking, etc.				
9.	There is/are Example: There is an elevator in the building.				
10.	The habitual present tense Example: I go to class every Monday.				
11.	The future tense with will Example: I will go				

learn to achieve mastery. Task analysis has been used by HRD for many years to break down job-training requirements. The IIP has taken it a step further by including both requisite educational skill requirements and employee learning aptitudes. Thus the IIP not only serves as a diagnostic tool uncovering employee learning difficulties but also recognizes the importance of laying out for the trainer specific subject-matter content. Our attempt to better organize and structure skill content related to on-the-job performance has improved the rate of sustainable adult learning and retention over time.

When applied, these individualized tutorial programs (40 hours) have shown a distinctive pattern for employee learning. Initially, the learner makes negligible gains because of previously unresolved and interrelated learning problems. Then there is gradual progress while basic skills are being diagnosed, reorganized and taught. A significant breakthrough usually occurs at about the fifteenth hour of instruction as the student responds to the IIP restructuring of abilities and learning materials. Performance differences over time (fewer than 10 hours of tutoring, 10 to 20 hours, 20 to 30 or more hours) have been repeatedly documented by the authors. Maximum grade-level improvement occurs around the thirtieth hour of tutoring. The majority of individuals enrolled in an IIP Work Force Education module of 20 to 40 hours attains six months to a year of skill improvement. (See Appendix 3 for IIP statistical research data and Appendix 4 for an explanation of grade-level equivalency improvement as a result of training.) At the end of an IIP training module, employees needing additional training are easily regrouped with others who have been diagnosed as needing similar assistance. (See Figure 5.1.)

THE IIP AND L.D. FACTORS

Individualized diagnosis of learning disabilities (L.D.) is embedded into IIP small-group tutorial classes. The anecdotal account of actual classwork is recorded on both a short "class outcome report" and the appropriate IIP checklist. A trained tutor closely observes and records a student's learning skills from class to class. An accurate diagnosis of specific learning disabilities can be made by observing, for a particular learner, behaviors in vision, auditory-speech and achievement.

Visual memory/tracking/discrimination, auditory discrimination/attention/memory and achievement/work-ethic attitudes are some of the learner characteristics that may be related to a learning problem. Each of these categories is defined, and specific observable aspects of learning are rated by the tutor. (See Table 5.5.) If visual tracking (i.e., the ability of the student's eyes to follow written material from left to right without moving his/her head) is a problem, the student possibly ignores punctuation; loses his/her place in a sentence, in a paragraph or on a page; distracts easily; tires easily. The tutor observes and documents these notable characteristics and rates the student on the visual tracking errors during the course of the tutoring classes. If the number of errors is high, diagnostic tests are used to pinpoint the visual perceptual skill problems. Remedial work is then done by the tutor to improve visual tracking skills using employee work-related materials.

Figure 5.1
Comparison of Instruction Modes to Academic Gains

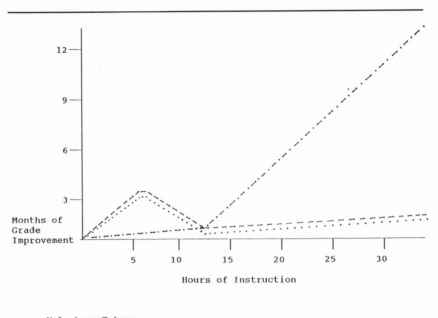

- - - Volunteer Tutors
-.-.- Individualized Instructional Programs (IIP)
..... Classroom Training

We have found that the IIP L.D. curriculum scripts are very accurate at pinpointing specific learning disabilities using this test-tutor-test approach rather than administering lengthy, comprehensive L.D. diagnostic tests. The curriculum script is in itself a diagnostic test that allows maximum class time to be used for job-skill tutoring and minimum time for necessary testing. The IIP helps minimize the risk that important L.D. skill areas will be inadvertently overlooked by the tutor. Finally, it should be noted that diagnosis is an ongoing IIP process in all the classes and is not bunched up in pretesting, as is found in many traditional adult classroom programs of study.

IIP METHODS

The IIP curriculum scripts are updated as the tutor teaches each class. The tutor fills out the checklists after the first class to indicate skills observed at a "mastery level" (i.e., the specific grade level that has been established for this group as a final target by the end of the ten-week module of classes). Specific skill weaknesses, observed from students'

Table 5.5
Vision and Motor Skills

Directions:	Circle the number that best describes the student's performance of each individual skill. For each given category, if you have observed and tested few programs, mark the skill <u>Adequate</u>, if some weaknesses were apparent, mark the skill <u>Fair</u>, if many strong problems were diagnosed, mark the skill <u>Inadequate</u>. Comment sections are provided for further amplification. <u>THIS IS FOR YOUR USE WITH EVERY CLASS.</u>

Number Key: 1 - Excellent
                2 - Very Good
                3 - Good
                4 - Fair
                5 - Poor

<u>Visual Memory:</u>

The ability of the student to retain and recall information assimilated through visual means.

Time durations to be considered by teacher:

	1	2	3	4	5
One minute to another:	1	2	3	4	5
Early to later part of same class:	1	2	3	4	5
From class to class:	1	2	3	4	5
From beg. to mid UNIT:	1	2	3	4	5
From beg. to end of UNIT:	1	2	3	4	5
Follows written directions:	1	2	3	4	5
Circle:	Adequate		Fair		Inadequate

classwork, are supplemented by diagnostic tests. As the tutor introduces, maintains or achieves student mastery over designated job-related skills, students are tracked class-by-class on the appropriate IIP checklists. Over 40 different subject-area curriculum scripts have been developed and tested within the context of our ongoing field-based research project. Subject-area experts were formed into curriculum committees, which systematically prepared and reviewed each subject-specific curriculum script. This field research has extended over 23 years (1968–91), with approximately 7,000 participating students. This is still an ongoing process. Every effort has been made to lay out and update the potential skills needed by a student for a wide variety of work-related academic skills. This has saved tutors a great deal of class time. Tutors are now better able to concentrate their time on the diagnosis and analysis of individual employee skill problems and to select the best tutoring methods to maximize the adult student's learning.

Many adult students have motivational problems related to formal learning and a lack of a personal work ethic. They may possess a high aptitude but perform poorly on the job because of undiagnosed learning problems in their school years. Employee educational skills may be uneven (e.g., math computation skills may be high while reading comprehension skills may be low).

To motivate the adult learner, we begin the IIP tutorial process by working at an "independent skill level" (i.e., with skill-related materials that give the positive reinforcement of immediate personal success). An adult's recognition of his/her own ability to achieve is a sound method that begins the enhancement of personal motivation and builds a positive self-image as a student. This level of tutoring is related to an employee who has reading problems and who uses actual workplace vocabulary materials that demonstrate an understanding of job safety rules. The tutor moves rapidly in the classes to the adult's "capacity level" of learning. Here the student can still perform the skill functions but must rely on the tutor as a resource for additional coaching. At this stage the tutor is continuing to rebuild the adult's self-confidence in the classroom and gain his/her personal trust as a mentor. The "instructional level" of tutoring can then be introduced by the tutor without running the risk of traumatizing the adult learner. This stage presents new material that can be introduced-reinforced-mastered using the IIP's tutor-test-tutor learning system. At all costs, the IIP process avoids tutoring at the "frustration level," which duplicates many adults' previous large-classroom learning failures. In these past educational experiences, their poor academic skills were overwhelmed by instruction they did not understand, and never learned, leading to a perpetuation of the school dropout syndrome.

At every step of these instructional activities, the adult learner has a need to know, "How am I doing?" Immediate feedback to the adult student is critical for improved motivation. The greatest risk at the initial stages of a Work Force Education program is that the employee will come to think that the learning task is impossible. The IIP tutorial process is ideal in breaking down long-term learning goals into digestible small information chunks that adults can recognize, understand and master at their own pace.

However, this ideal is not always possible, since mastering significant skill problems is often related to poor study-skill behaviors. Far too many adults have few, if any, specific learned, study-skill strategies. They easily become overwhelmed and distracted when presented with complex independent homework/classroom exercises. In many instances, study skills were never formally taught in school. In other cases, the student simply ignored or misunderstood the material. Of course, a lifetime of using poor study skills is not changed in one tutoring class. Assigning a large amount of homework at the beginning of a Work Force Education program invites student failure and demotivates many adult learners. Formal study skill habits must be gradually taught by the tutor. They can be included as part of realistic employee/work-related skill exercises rather than presented independently, out of context. The tutor teaches more complex study-skill concepts as the adult progresses from the previously mentioned independent capacity and instructional skill levels. Homework assignments now take on an added work realism that encourages better study habits.

With these improved skills, homework/independent-work activities show the adult his/her own small but recognizable steps in learning. This new learning self-awareness builds self-motivation. As a result, adult learners enrolled in IIP Work Force Education come to see learning new ideas as a personal challenge that is attainable, not as a punishment to be feared or avoided.

Testing is another difficult hurdle for some adults who experienced repeated test failures over many years of formal education. Adults sense that skill tests will only once again prove how much they do not know. Instead of administering a long skill pretest, the IIP gives shorter subtests in several class sessions. The IIP format of comprehensive, observable curriculum scripts eliminates the need for many diagnostic tests. Instead, the tutor makes consistently recorded skill observations of each individual student's daily classwork. Testing becomes largely unobtrusive, since it is part of another regular class learning exercise.[17]

ADDITIONAL TUTORIAL TASKS

Barrows (1988), in his research on the tutorial process, uncovered several additional tutorial concepts related to the IIP process. A tutor's primary task is to ensure that no part of the skill-learning process is passed over or neglected until it has been fully understood by the adult.

Each phase of the learning process must be taken in its proper sequence. For example, some adults are poor readers because of specific learning disabilities. Until these L.D. problems are diagnosed and remedied, the adult will not significantly improve his/her reading ability. That is, offering only reading instruction becomes a self-defeating process.

Educational diagnosis means early recognition of not only learning disabilities but also reasoning difficulties, failure to understand concepts or weak application skills. The tutor must be certain that the student has reached the level of understanding appropriate to on-the-job applications. A tutor must push the student to realize what the adult already knows and to achieve better problem-solving and thinking skills. Constantly asking the appropriate who, what, when, where, or why questions will help the adult ultimately develop alternative solutions to an on-the-job problem. Learning will not be geared to new skill acquisition but ultimately to success at work.

The IIP small-group learning format helps adult students recognize and freely admit what they do not know. This is essential to stimulate new learning. All of us have probably felt the embarrassment associated with admitting our personal ignorance in a classroom environment. Small-group tutorials help everyone relax. Adults want to learn and will aid each other in areas of personal strength. The social context of this group learning process, as previously discussed, is a powerful incentive that helps adults make open, unembarrassed statements of what they do not know or understand.[18]

The IIP methods offer a special curriculum, written for trainers to successfully individualize instruction for almost any adult student. Most significant, the IIP Work Force Education program is flexible enough to accommodate a wide variety of learning problems based on careful observation and continuous reevaluation class-by-class. Skill training is built on assessing what the student already knows, then matching the tutoring/learning techniques considered to be most appropriate for that adult learner.

IIP INSTRUCTION ALTERNATIVES

The IIP was initially developed for 1:1 tutorials. Adults requested private instruction at home on work-related, applied skill training. This assured total privacy, since employees did not always want their employers to know they lacked educational skills. These programs proved highly successful in developing both the diagnostic strategies and accelerated learning methods inherent to the IIP process. This field research formed the basis for the IIP tutorial program's professional recognition and accreditation by the North Central Association of Colleges and Schools (1982) as a "special function" educational service. It was the first instance in the history of American education that any tutorial program had achieved professional, public recognition.[19]

These highly individualized 1:1 programs have also been used in-house by corporations to train numerous managers and professionals for all levels of writing, 15 foreign languages, English as a Second Language (ESL), public speaking, speech elocution, blueprint reading, speed-reading, basic reading and basic math and for overcoming learning disabilities. Administrative assistants and secretaries have used the 1:1 IIP for grammar training, shorthand, typing and computer skills.

The 1:1 format has the advantage of shortening training time. A typical module consisted of 20 classes of one-hour duration. Two classes were held each week, over a ten-week period. Precision individualization accelerated learning and improved retention at a ratio of 1:5 when compared with conventional classroom instruction (i.e., the educational/ training curriculum tutored in a 20-hour, 1:1, IIP module requires at least 100 hours of classroom teaching to achieve comparable results). Our short-term/long-term analysis of results indicates an 80 percent information-retention ratio six months after the students finished their IIP tutorials. This meets and exceeds standard classroom information retention standards.

Our many corporate training applications indicate that 1:1, IIP management/staff training yields a very high cost-benefit ratio. Increased employee job productivity far exceeds program cost. Corporate competitiveness issues are dramatically increasing the demand for training programs, such as the IIP, that will rapidly accelerate adult learning and improve long-term retention.

In other instances, where the number of employees to be trained was large, the IIP was conducted at a ratio of 1:5. As previously mentioned, these small-group tutorial classes consisted of 20 two-hour classes. Two classes were held each week over a ten-week period. Adult learning occurred at a ratio of 1:3 when compared with classroom teaching. The educational/training curriculum tutored in a 40-hour, 1:5, IIP module required at least 120 hours of conventional classroom attendance for an adult to achieve the same results. Small-group IIP long-term retention rates were found to be similar to the 1:1 tutorial program. Training content for the IIP small-group programs included all of the areas taught on a 1:1 basis.

From two to five adults tutored in this manner have consistently shown the above rates of learning. However, our research with the IIP tutorial model indicates that accurate diagnosis and significant individualized instruction significantly declines beyond a five-student class size.[20]

Another format for IIP Work Force Education programs is the use of cross-training (i.e., peer tutoring). In this instructional program, one employee tutors another employee. Peer tutoring has been used successfully for decades in contemporary American education. Ellson (1976), Harrison and Guymon (1980), Bloom (1989), as well as other researchers, have long advocated peer tutors as a powerful supplement to standard classroom teaching. Gordon (1990) has chronicled how peer tutors were successful in tens of thousands of one-room American schoolhouses for over a hundred years. Meanwhile, in the cities, peer tutors helped in nineteenth-century "Monitorial" schools to tutor small groups of students.[21]

This mode of cross-training is now frequently used in American industry for technical skill training. Two examples of cross-training applications in contemporary Work Force Education programs include the use of managerial volunteers to teach shopworkers basic skills (Best University, Inland Steel). Manager volunteers have also tutored local unemployed community residents at their worksite on company time (IBM, Chicago).

The IIP can be adapted for use by company peer tutors to reinforce the classes taught by subject-specialized tutors. For the cross-training to have maximum effect, peers must tutor peers. A literate shopworker will be more effective in tutoring a less literate peer than a supervisor or a management tutor volunteer. Why? Peers speak the "same language." Research has shown that students are able to explain what they do not understand to a peer far better than to a manager. Adult students' inhibitions are reduced with other adults drawn from their own work group. Peer tutor explanations become more relevant, since the information can be given in the work context of both tutor and tutee. Fear of displaying ignorance subsides, since the student knows the tutor is a peer, not a supervisor.

There are several key considerations that will enhance a cross-training program. Peer tutors must receive formal pretraining in tutoring techniques that motivate adult learners. A special subject-related curriculum must be laid out step-by-step so that the tutor can easily follow it. Tutors need to record daily results in a simple written reporting log. Peer tutors should also receive basic methods instruction in reading, math, learning disabilities or the appropriate skill areas to be tutored at the company. They will also need periodic retraining while participating in the cross-training program. Finally, peer tutors need the backup of subject-trained specialists who can intervene when the volunteer tutor hits a major learning roadblock that stops an individual adult's skill-building progress. Besides helping a fellow worker succeed, peer tutor volunteers must be offered other incentives by the company Work Force Education program. Peer tutors will probably never possess the technical expertise of a degreed teacher. However, HR professionals should not be intimidated by the acronyms of education. Intelligent adult volunteer tutors can teach basic skills and observe or remediate L.D. problems. Their rate of progress with the tutee will be slower than that of a teacher. However, furnished with an organized curriculum script, peer tutors will make a valuable addition to your company's Work Force Education program.

An IIP train-the-trainer program will be particularly useful if large numbers of employees are in need of an in-house program. Can current corporate trainers be prepared to tutor small groups in basic reading, math, learning disabilities or writing skills? We believe this approach will be successful if they are trained to use a mastery learning program using a curriculum-scripted format. Similar to peer tutors, trainers must learn the use of effective tutorial and skill-content methods in any train-the-trainer program. Content specialists need to backup these trainers' ongoing work, offer retraining sessions and provide direct intervention with more difficult adult learner problems. Company trainers will prove even more effective than volunteers as tutors, since many already have had positive experiences motivating adult learners. During the 1990s, the use of properly written train-the-trainer programs, combined with cross-training and tutoring by subject-area specialists, will emerge as "jump-start" solutions to America's Work Force Education dilemma. These are cost-effective remedies that will reach large numbers of adult workers at all levels. These tutorial formats will enable corporate HR departments to train the "untrainable" through specific diagnosis and enhanced remedial education. Countless adults will be prepared for work through corporate classroom training, adults who otherwise cannot be hired, may quit their jobs, or may act as an ongoing drag on company productivity. For managers, this specialized tutorial format offers HR a flexible tool for key executive training and individual career development.

Our research has clearly demonstrated that our use of the IIP tutorial system as an enhanced mastery learning model yields significant results in the diagnosis and training of adult workers with significant learning problems. Moreover, the field programs we have supported have demonstrated the adaptability of cognitive research to practical, job-training applications for managers, support staff and shopworkers. The results of these programs have shown a clear, sustained improvement in both the rate at which adults learn and their long-term ability to retain new information. In the next two chapters, we will review case studies that show the many applications of these mastery learning programs for adult employees and how these programs might be developed as part of your organization's training and development.

NOTES

1. Jean-Pierre Vélis, *Through a Glass, Darkly: Functional Illiteracy in Industrialized Countries* (Paris: UNESCO, 1990), 68–69; Wanda Cook, *Adult Literacy Education in the United States* (Newark, Del.: International Reading Association, 1977), 108.

2. J. B. Carroll, "A Model of School Learning," *Teachers College Record* 64 (1963): 723–33.

3. B. S. Bloom, "Master Learning," in *Mastery Learning: Theory and Practice*, ed. J. H. Block (New York: Holt, Rinehart and Winston, 1971), 47–63; B. S. Bloom, *Human Characteristics and School Learning* (New York: McGraw-Hill, 1976). On mastery learning research, see Block, *Mastery Learning*; J. H. Block, "Mastery Learning in the Classroom: An Overview of Recent Research," in *Schools, Society,*

and Mastery Learning, ed. J. H. Block (New York: Holt, Rinehart and Winston, 1974); and J. H. Block and R. B. Burns, "Mastery Learning," in *Review of Research in Education*, ed. L. S. Schulman, vol. 4 (Itasca, Ill.: Peacock Publishers, 1976).

4. L. W. Anderson and R. B. Burns, "Values, Evidence, and Mastery Learning," *Review of Educational Research* 57, no. 2 (1987): 215–24; A. R. Buss, "The Myth of Vanishing Individual Differences in Bloom's Mastery Learning," *Instructional Psychology* 3 (1976): 4–14; J. G. Greeno, "Review of Bloom's Human Characteristics and School Learning," *Journal of Educational Measurement*, 1978, 67–76; T. R. Guskey, "Rethinking Mastery Learning Reconsidered," *Review of Educational Research* 57, no. 2 (1987): 225–30; D. J. Mueller, "Mastery Learning: Partly Boon, Partly Boondoggle," *Teachers College Record* 78 (1976): 41–52; L. T. Resnick, "Assuming That Everyone Can Learn Everything, Will Some Learn Less?" *School Review* 85 (1977): 445–52; R. E. Slavin, "Mastery Learning Reconsidered," *Review of Educational Research* 57, no. 2 (1987a): 175–214; R. E. Slavin, "Taking the Mystery out of Mastery: A Response to Guskey, Anderson, and Burns," *Review of Educational Research* 57, no. 2 (1987b): 213–35.

5. Block and Burns, "Mastery Learning"; D. C. Berliner, "The Place of Process-Product Research in Developing an Agenda for Research on Teacher Thinking," *Educational Psychologist* 24, no. 4 (1989): 325–44.

6. Slavin, "Mastery Learning Reconsidered"; Slavin, "Taking the Mystery out of Mastery."

7. Bloom, "Master Learning"; Carroll, "School Learning"; F. S. Keller, "Good-Bye Teacher!" *Journal of Applied Behavioral Analysis* 1 (1968): 79–84.

8. Keller, "Good-Bye Teacher!"

9. J. A. Kulik, C. C. Kulik, and P. A. Cohen, "A Meta-Analysis of Outcome Studies of Keller's Personalized System of Instruction," *American Psychologist* 34 (1979): 307–18; J. F. Calhoun, "Elemental Analysis of the Keller Method of Instruction" (Paper presented at the Annual Meeting of the American Psychological Association, Montreal, 1973); Block and Burns, "Mastery Learning."

10. E. E. Gordon and E. H. Gordon, *Centuries of Tutoring: A History of Alternative Education in America and Western Europe* (Latham, Md.: University Press, 1990).

11. L. F. Annis, "The Processes and Effects of Peer Tutoring," *Human Learning* 2, (1983): 39–47; N. L. Gage and D. C. Berliner, *Educational Psychology* (Boston: Houghton Mifflin, 1988); P. A. Cohen, J. A. Kulik, and C. C. Kulik, "Educational Outcomes of Tutoring: A Meta-Analysis of Findings," *American Educational Research Journal* 19, no. 2 (1982): 237–48.

12. P. Lippitt, "Children Can Teach Other Children," *Instructor* 789 (1969): 41, 99; P. Lippitt and R. Lippitt, "The Peer Culture as a Learning Environment," *Childhood Education* 47 (1970): 135–38; R. Lippitt and M. Lippitt, "Cross-Age Helpers," *National Education Association Journal* 57 (1968): 24–26.

13. J. A. Arter and J. R. Jenkins, "Examining the Benefits and Prevalence of Modality Considerations in Special Education," *Journal of Special Education* 11, no. 3 (1977): 281–98; K. A. Kavale and S. R. Forness, "Substance over Style: Assessing the Efficacy of Modality Testing and Teaching," *Exceptional Children* 54, no. 3 (1987): 228–39.

14. C. L. Frisby, "Toward a Broader Role for School Psychology in the Thinking Skill Movement," *School Psychology Review* 19, no. 1 (1990): 96–114; R. Glaser, "The Reemergence of Learning Theory within Instructional Research," *American*

Psychologist 45, no. 1 (1990): 29–39; R. Glaser, "Education and Thinking: The Role of Knowledge," *American Psychologist* 39 (1984): 93–104; Edward E. Gordon, Judith Ponticell, and Ronald R. Morgan, "Back to Basics," *Training and Development Journal* 43, no. 8 (1989): 73–78.

15. J. Brophy, "Research Linking Teacher Behavior to Student Achievement: Potential Implications for Instruction of Chapter 1 Students," *Educational Psychologist* 23, no. 3 (1988): 235–86; A. L. Brown, "Knowing When, Where, and How to Remember: A Problem of Metacognition," in *Advances in Instructional Psychology*, ed. R. Glaser, 3 vols. (Hillsdale, N. J.: Erlbaum, 1978–86); R. Case, "A Developmentally Based Approach to the Problem of Instructional Design," in *Thinking and Learning Skills*, ed. S. F. Chipman, J. W. Segal, and R. Glaser, vol. 2 (Hillsdale, N.J.: Erlbaum, 1985); R. J. Herrnstein, "Doing What Comes Naturally: A Reply to Professor Skinner," *American Psychologist* 32, no. 12 (1977): 1013–16; R. J. Herrnstein, "The Evolution of Behaviorism," *American Psychologist* 32, no. 8 (1977): 593–603; J. Levin and N. Pressley, *Cognitive Strategy Research: Educational Applications* (New York: Springer-Verlag, 1983); W. J. McKeachie, "Psychology in America's Bicentennial Year," *American Psychologist* 31, no. 12 (1976): 819–33; N. Pressley and J. Levin, *Cognitive Strategy Research: Psychological Foundations* (New York: Springer-Verlag, 1983); B. F. Skinner, "Herrnstein and the Evolution of Behaviorism," *American Psychologist* 32, no. 12 (1977): 1006–12.

16. Mark L. Blazey and Karen S. Davison, "Keeping Up with the Factory of the Future," *Training* 27 (February 1990): 51–55; Philip J. Harkins, "The Changing Role of Corporate Training and Development," *Corporate Development in the '90s, Supplement to Training Magazine*, 1991, 26–29; Patricia Cohen Gold and John A. Johnson, "Prediction of Achievement in Reading, Self-Esteem, and Verbal Language by Adult Illiterates in a Psychoeducational Tutorial Program," *Journal of Clinical Psychology* 38, no. 2 (July 1982): 513–22; Irwin L. Goldstein and Patricia Gilliam, "Training System Issues in the Year 2000," *American Psychologist* 45, no. 2 (February 1990): 134–43.

17. Edward E. Gordon, Judith Ponticell, and Ronald R. Morgan, "Back to Basics," *Training and Development Journal* 43, no. 8 (August 1989): 73–76; Ralph T. Putnam, "Structuring and Adjusting Content for Students: A Study of Live and Simulated Tutoring of Addition," *American Educational Research Journal* 24, no. 1 (Spring 1987): 13–48; Edward E. Gordon, Judith Ponticell, and Ronald R. Morgan, "A Report on Results of the IIP Literacy Training Program: Implications for the Literacy Issue in American Business" (Paper presented at the Annual Meeting of the Midwest Education Research Association, Chicago, 19 October 1990); Edward E. Gordon, *Individualized Instruction Program (IIP) Curriculum, Administration and Methods Manual* (Oak Lawn, Ill.: Imperial Tutoring and Educational Services, 1991).

18. Howard S. Barrows, *The Tutorial Process* (Springfield, Ill.: Southern Illinois University School of Medicine, 1988), 6–11, 18–20, 23.

19. Edward E. Gordon, "Home Tutoring Programs Gain Respectability," *Phi Delta Kappan* 64, no. 6 (February 1983): 398–99. Imperial Corporate Training and Development, 10341 Lawler, Oak Lawn, Illinois, 60453-4714, (312) 881-3700, (708) 636-8852, was accredited in 1982 by the North Central Association of Colleges and Schools as a "special function" school of individualized tutoring. The program offers tutoring to children, adolescents and adults.

20. Gordon, "Home Tutoring"; Edward E. Gordon, "The Implications of Inte-

grating Business Skills with Appropriate Content Areas," *Training Today*, October 1988, 8–9; Susan Becker, "What You Should Know about Tutoring Centers," *Instructor* 6, no. 95 (February 1986): 88–90.

21. Douglas G. Ellson, "Tutoring," *The Psychology of Teaching Methods* (Chicago: University of Chicago Press, 1976), 130–41; Grant Von Harrison and Ronald E. Guymon, *Structural Tutoring* (Englewood Cliffs, N.J.: Educational Technology Publications, 1980); Benjamin S. Bloom, "The Search for Methods of Group Instruction as Effective as One-To-One Tutoring," *Educational Leadership* 41 (May 1984); Edward E. Gordon and Elaine H. Gordon, *Centuries of Tutoring: A History of Alternative Education in America and Western Europe* (Lanham, Md.: University Press of America, 1990), 196–200, 276–78, 309–12, 314–16; Gordon, "Integrating Business Skills."

6

Case Studies I: Hourly Workers

Beginning in 1968, the authors provided training to adult workers who lacked a wide variety of educational skills. These employees worked for manufacturers, retailers, petrochemical companies, law firms, craft unions, health care providers, the hospitality industry and other businesses.

Adults were tutored using Individualized Instructional Programs (IIP) with a specific Work Force Education application for the job they presently performed, job retraining, a job promotion or a new job for a new employee. The IIP training was conducted both in small groups (1:5) and on a 1:1 basis (as previously described in Chapter 5). Training classes were usually conducted at the employee's work site or office, but in some instances adults were tutored at home after work hours.

Many of these employees spent their entire working lives hiding poor educational skills. Literacy may be a problem, but "fluency," or a lack of "functional literacy," is a far more typical problem (see Chapter 2 for a detailed discussion of this issue). The majority of older hourly workers in the factory or office were hired in an era when reading, writing or math demands were far simpler. Personal computers (PCs), software and related office/factory automation demand far higher employee educational levels.[1]

Discovering who needs this Work Force Education program intervention can be a tricky task for any business. In many workplaces, it is tough getting employees to admit they need training.

"You can teach a class for three days and not know someone is not getting it," said Alice Barnes, the president of the Denver chapter of the American Society for Training and Development. "Someone can sit there and fake it . . . take their homework home and let their wives or husbands do it for them."[2]

Some of the work behaviors that may point to a Work Force Education training solution include:

- Employees use excuses to avoid reading or writing, such as mislaying their glasses
- Repeated absenteeism after high-tech equipment is placed at their work station
- Illegible, scrambled work orders or other carelessly prepared paperwork
- Machinery maintenance that is specifically neglected or improper, if requiring reading from technical manuals
- An employee refuses a promotion to a better job that requires higher educational performance

As we noted earlier, many of these adults do not seek training for fear of discovery and public humiliation. "I want to read and write so I can stop being the show of other people," lamented a functionally illiterate woman. Workers will go to great lengths to conceal educational problems before agreeing to accept help.

The following selected sample of case studies represents a cross section of both factory and office hourly workers who received Work Force Education programs from the authors. Though our work with individual employees remains strictly confidential, an overview of our programs will give HR managers a basic understanding of diverse job-training applications in a Work Force Education setting.[3]

CLOROX

The Chicago suburban plant of Clorox employs approximately 100 hourly workers and managers. Clorox distributes its household products through such plants strategically located across the United States. Each location assembles a finished product from the raw materials delivered at each site. Local manufacturing and product testing have become much more sophisticated during the past decade. In response to Workforce 2000, and declining demographics, Clorox is attempting to upgrade its workers' skills for the future introduction of high-tech manufacturing/assembly equipment. The majority of future jobs will require ninth- to twelfth-grade educational skills to comprehend training manuals and introduce additional productivity enhancements.

As is true for employees of the majority of U.S. manufacturers, Clorox's present work force includes individuals who never attained ninth- to twelfth-grade educational skill levels. These adults are at present good workers. Many have been with the company for 10, 15 or even 20 years. Management realizes that it is far better to retrain these loyal employees than to seek new hires in an even tighter, uncertain job market. Some of these adults have already failed GED classes. Others have never voluntarily admitted any educational problems to their employer.

A voluntary Work Force Education program was begun by Clorox with several worker-orientation sessions announcing the availability of the classes and their content and answering specific employee questions. The company paid for the entire program. The employees attended classes after or before their work shift. A two-hour class was held on-site twice each week, for a period of ten weeks, totaling 40 hours of training. The IIP curriculum was used with each employee (see Chapter 5 for a detailed review of IIP training).

Before the first classes, the program's trainers conducted a detailed analysis of employee job content, the work site and potential program goals and objectives. The readability levels of the technical manuals that Clorox would soon be using on the production line were determined.

Ten men and women composed the first two Work Force Education classes, with five employees per class. Initial testing showed that individual educational skills in reading and math ranged between the fourth grade and prereading levels. Some of these adults had significant learning disabilities that had prevented their prior success in school. We found, almost without exception, that once their learning disability problems were diagnosed, the students were capable of rapid skill growth and information retention. Overall, worker achievement averaged 12 months of skill growth over the ten-week training period. However, performance varied, with one adult advancing by only six months and another by two years. These variations of individual learning rates were traced to the presence or absence of personal motivational, aptitude or, in some cases, learning disabilities. One employee related how happy he now was reading the daily newspaper. For over 15 years, he had come to work everyday with a rolled up newspaper in his back pocket. This employee wanted to be like everyone else, so at break time and lunch he would "read" his newspaper, even though he understood very few words. Now that he was actually able to read his newspaper, his personal motivation for learning and his belief in himself were at an all-time high.

After the initial program, workers were regrouped and began follow-up training for another ten-week period. Our immediate goal remained: the elimination of significant learning problems. The program's long-term goal was to ultimately raise skill levels to the seventh-grade level, enabling the adults to attend local GED classroom instruction at a community college, on-site or near their home.

A second long-term goal was to reach all local Clorox employees with

Work Force Education needs. This would assure that the plant would be ready to use the high-tech equipment arriving within the next several years. It has been our experience that a program's first successful volunteers offer their peers much needed encouragement to participate. In many instances, these first "testimonials" for the Work Force Education program prove to other workers that the program is practical, is useful and makes a daily job simpler, safer and perhaps even enjoyable.

Supervisors were surveyed at the end of each ten-week class period. We needed them to determine if the employee's job performance had improved during the training process. Of equal importance was raising their awareness that Work Force Education was making a noticeable difference in employee daily work patterns. Supervisory support of the program was also essential to encourage active worker participation. They reported that among employees who participated in the Work Force Education program, production errors dropped, employees became more interested in advancing to more complex jobs, job problem-solving/troubleshooting skills increased and personal job motivation improved.

There are now men and women at Clorox in Chicago who have just begun experiencing the pleasure of success at learning on the job and at home. Their worries over how they will cope in an increasingly complex, high-tech manufacturing environment have begun to fade. Instead, these employees are more optimistic about themselves, their products and their future at Clorox. The local HR manager felt that "ten tons had been removed from my back" with the initiation of the Work Force Education program. The demographics of the work force, and a lack of information on how to address this issue, had given him few alternatives. He can now partner with his workers to successfully face the high-tech factory of the twenty-first century, arriving soon at his local plant.

RESIDENCE INN AND COURTYARD BY MARRIOTT/ADVANCED THERMAL PRODUCTS

The Chicago Association of Commerce and Industry (CACI), a non-profit business-economic enhancement organization, partnered with the authors to provide Work Force Education company models for small and medium-sized companies. CACI pilots groups of workers and companies available through its "On-the-Job-Training" programs. It funds this program through the Job Training Partnership Act (JTPA), which helps organizations hire and train economically disadvantaged adult workers.

With the Marriott organization, we trained workers in CACI's "Future Tech Program" for basic reading and math applied to the housekeeping function. Another group of maids was enrolled in an ESL program. The small-group tutorial classes met on-site over a ten-week period.

One of the results of the training was that the daily newspaper became "user friendly" to the students. During the tutoring classes, they read help-wanted ads, learning about their job requirements and specifically about hotel positions that would become available to them as they acquired more knowledge and problem-solving skills. CACI placed them with a hotel because it provided good, upward career ladders. However, without this Work Force Education program, they would not have known about higher-level jobs or how to get them.

The basic-skill trainer characterized some of their work with the following comments:

They [the students] talked about recipes and reinforcing measuring skills. The use of the newspaper to increase knowledge of current events and job responsibilities helped reinforce good basic living-job skills. General information of all sorts that is sometimes taken for granted by many of us was eagerly learned by these adults. Sometimes thought of as trivial information, this was found to be beneficial to these adults. They had never been exposed to, or taught such knowledge.

The fact that their employer offered training that would improve their quality of living had a major motivational impact for these employees. In too many instances, the unemployed minority worker is viewed by companies as a "high-risk" employee. There are few business-education programs providing anchors for these adults in the daily conditions of effectively functioning in a modern urban society. The authors believe that Work Force Education programs have considerable potential for providing these life-style/work "anchors" that build a more stable, dedicated national work force.

The ESL students had very different experiences. Their ability in their native language was at best approaching the third-grade skill level. Their language training focused on housekeeping vocabulary, and vocabulary commonly used with hotel guests. The ESL trainer typified their work with these comments:

The ESL training provided them with a good inner feeling that each of them is capable of learning! They were surprised with their own learning ability and realized that with more exposure and practice, they could each begin to speak English. . . . This exposure to the English language, and to a learning environment, gave them an incentive to learn to communicate better.

Imparting this employee "incentive" translates into transferring the "work ethic" to the present American generation. We believe this to be an achievable goal for Work Force Education programs.

CACI has learned through these past program experiences that the training must be scheduled at least partially during working hours. Students had been volunteering an hour at the end of the workday. Many ended up with poor class attendance, which reduced individual skill gains. Also the company has to designate a permanent training class-room so everyone knows where to report and acclimates to the setting. It is not recommended that the training space be moved around to what-ever space is available that day.

CACI and the participating companies recognized the value of a 1:1 or small tutorial group setting. The IIP offered them a prescriptive learning method that tailored the program content to the individual student's best learning abilities. Even though these tutorial classes are more expensive in relation to traditional classroom teaching, the learning outcomes were far greater, with the corollary of a positive training experience that en-hanced employee motivation. Given these positive results, CACI is con-tinuing these Work Force Education programs, placing great confidence in the future enhancement of worker performance.

GM/UAW – CARPENTER – WAREHOUSE FOREMAN

Until the early 1980s, adults' basic skill needs were a "closet issue" for many workers and the majority of American businesses. For these adults, the shame associated with their poor educational record drove them to hide their literacy needs from employers, friends, children and even spouses. Even though some of these adults enrolled in local com-munity GED and basic skill classes, many others continued to rationalize their educational weaknesses, at least until their daily livelihood at work came into jeopardy.

The authors had the unique opportunity to provide private, confiden-tial tutorials to these adults beginning in 1968 and continuing to the present. In what follows, several examples are presented from the many individual hourly workers who approached us for assistance.

Tom was an assembly-line worker at a General Motors plant located in the Chicago metropolitan area. For all of his adult life, he had struggled to cope with significantly weak reading and math skills. On his own, Tom contacted the authors and arranged for private 1:1 tutorials at his home. Through an employee tuition-assistance program, GM/UAW funded Tom's Work Force Education program in introductory and ele-mentary reading skills. This highly individualized instruction allowed him not only to increase his job productivity but also to improve the quality of his family life. Tom had significant learning disabilities that were undiagnosed while attending school. Many of these learning diffi-culties were addressed through use of the IIP, and his overall educational skill levels improved so that Tom successfully enrolled in a local GED class at the completion of our tutoring. Our Work Force Education pro-gram eventually allowed Tom to be promoted to a better job at GM.

Jim was a union carpenter who had graduated from a local parochial high school. Jim was twenty-two years old and had average intelligence. When he contacted the authors, we were surprised to discover that his basic educational skill levels were only at the first-grade level. Needless to say, both visual and auditory learning disabilities (see Chapter 4 for definitions and discussion) were major contributing factors. Jim had a very poor school record but somehow had actually graduated and entered the skilled trades. However, he was highly motivated to learn the necessary reading/math skills to improve his work performance (measuring skills, reading directions and blue-prints, etc.). His wife, a secretary, was very supportive in his personal educational quest and helped him with drill work and other homework assignments throughout the tutoring.

His 1:1 tutoring program occurred at home after work or on weekends. For more than one year, Jim persisted with this program. During that time, he received 100 hours of tutoring intervention directed at his learning problems, with the content being directly focused on work needs and personal life interests.

Three different reading/learning disability tutor-trainers taught him over this period. We have found from our research on both 1:1 and 1:5 tutorial programs that the intensive individualized nature of our work facilitates the formation of strong personal relationships between the tutor and the student. Our recommended practice has been to periodically change tutors to preserve objectivity in reporting results. This procedure prevents adult students from losing their "learning edge" (motivation).

At the beginning of such a program, it was necessary for the tutors to prepare many of the introductory reading materials to be used by Jim. This is difficult, since an adult at this level needs reading materials at a high level of interest and subject content but possesses a very basic personal vocabulary. Job/life interests are essential to draw on for educational materials. While Jim received educational diagnostic testing, he needed to see himself as learning and moving ahead toward his final goal. Like many other lower-skilled adults, Jim was afraid of testing. He had always performed poorly in tests in school, so why should our test be any different? This test-phobic behavior necessitated our breaking up the diagnostic testing over many class sessions. By observing Jim's learning strengths, how he best went about acquiring new information, we minimized our diagnostic work to only essential educational areas that needed improvement.

This test-tutor-test approach was followed even after we had a clear picture of Jim's educational strengths and weaknesses. The development and retention of his new abilities and their application to a variety of tasks were thereby confirmed during the tutorial class sessions. It is important to note that we did not base the results of our work only on a final posttest. We are happy to report that during Jim's Work Force Education program, he attained ninth-grade educational skills and problem-solving application abilities.

Peter was a middle-aged warehouse employee who had been promoted to foreman. Even though he had ably performed his prior work for 20 years at this warehouse, his new job now required higher reading and math skills. Neither his employer nor his children realized his weak educational background. Peter came to us because he needed rapid, confidential instruction that supported his new position.

The specially crafted Work Force Education program for Peter was provided at our administrative office in the evening to provide total confidentiality. Peter's wife accompanied him to every 1:1 tutorial session. The structure and content of his program were similar to that of the previous adult workers. However, he persisted in our program only long enough to handle the day-to-day reading, math and invoice writing demanded on the job (sixth grade level). Since he was older, and resistant to change, learning came more slowly, and learning disabilities were hard to overcome. Fortunately, these factors are not insurmountable (at Clorox many students were also middle-aged), but it does mean that more time and effort may be needed to successfully remediate skills and ensure their long-term application/retention.

We wish to caution the reader from thinking that the 1:1 or 1:5 IIP or a similar curriculum program is a "magic bullet" that always hits on target. Many adults have come to the authors for "GED instruction," only to discover that they needed a basic skills program. Many of these individuals were unemployed. They did not persist in our program and unfortunately dropped out at a very early stage. We have had our greatest successes with employed adults who intertwined their job-life needs with our tutorial system of training. Our finding indicates that adults need to feel a sense of realistic accomplishment in these Work Force Education programs of study. At higher skill levels (ninth to twelfth grade), adults may become more patient while learning harder, complex learning tasks. However, as we will see later, even management personnel tend to demand a sense of immediate accomplishment, particularly at the beginning of their personal training programs.

SECRETARIAL "OFFICE PRACTICE TRAINING"

Office clerical positions employ millions of workers. Their skills are usually at a high-school level. Some may have attended a postsecondary business school. As previously discussed, many of these workers have very poor academic skills, even though they have graduated from high school (see Chapter 1). Thousands of companies have seen an alarming rise in personnel screening costs for office support jobs. Many companies now offer classroom instruction programs in spelling, grammar, punctuation, letter writing, shorthand, typing and PC/software literacy for receptionists, clerks, typists, secretaries and even administrative assistants. This trend will probably not subside but will accelerate throughout the 1990s.

Beginning in 1984, the authors were contacted by corporations looking for a successful solution to this workplace dilemma. Many companies had already tried in-house training classes, public seminars or local educational programs. However, after completion of these programs, office workers were still making the same content errors. Corporations took an unprecedented step (for 1984) by asking us to "tutor" their secretaries on a 1:1 or 1:5 basis at their office during the workday. These companies have included Angus Chemical Company, Blue Cross/Blue Shield, Evans, Inc., Evangelical Health Systems, FMC, Morton International, and Pre-Mark International.

IIP tutorial programs in basic, and sometimes intermediate, written communication skills were provided to these secretaries, with programs lasting from 6 to 12 months in order to cycle all the office workers through the classes. Some needed only review work; other staff needed extensive new skills and practice. Prior employee work was analyzed by our business English tutors for errors. Company "model letters," documents or reports were incorporated into the IIP tutorial content.

Work Force Education programs for office practice covered an array of business skills, including grammar, spelling, punctuation, proper business letter forms, writing, speed typing, shorthand, PC use and PC software. Business communication training for executive secretaries helped employees learn how to correctly edit the writing errors of top-level managers. The secretaries became proficient in such areas as correct use of pronouns and modifiers, punctuation, parts of speech and sentence structure.

These "office practice" areas are part of the literacy-fluency gap that permeates the U.S. work environment. Many companies must now hire marginally educated entry-level clerical workers. As they are incorporated into the support service, a company may find promotable individuals based on their daily performance record. However, many cannot be advanced because of their weak educational preparation. Even major law firms have contacted the authors for secretarial training programs that focus on specialized legal vocabulary, legal correspondence and legal documents.

Many secretaries are now called on to assume managerial responsibilities. A newly promoted headquarters secretary found that her responsibilities included inner-office memo communications. Her training included learning advanced vocabulary and the proper use of colons and semicolons. At the end of the 1:1 writing program, she was able to compose appropriately worded, clear and concise memos.

In another instance, a corporate vice president dictated letters without following the basic rules of business writing. His secretary already possessed excellent grammar and punctuation skills. The IIP sessions were individualized for training in managerial and executive writing skills for editing purposes. Sessions emphasized establishing the proper tone of a letter, smooth topic transitions, getting to the point, filling in details and a proper summary close.

Health care and insurance organizations have used our IIP programs to improve accuracy and speed in patient data entry. Data entry clerks have received PC training that taught them both PC usage and software capabilities. At a major insurance company, grammar and speech skills were improved by the technique of taping conversations and learning correction through listening.

A leading Chicago law firm requested the authors' assistance in sharpening the shorthand skills of two executive secretaries. Although both individuals had a good knowledge of Gregg shorthand, they found it necessary to increase their speed and accuracy to meet the demands of more advanced assignments. An IIP tutorial increased their shorthand speed from 60 wpm to 100 wpm. Not only was their accuracy greatly improved, but they were also able to read other secretaries' shorthand notes. This has proven to be a labor-saving skill, since letters do not need redictation if another secretary is absent.

FOX COLLEGE "BUSINESS PRACTICE LAB"

Many U.S. proprietary secretarial schools have suffered from a decline in educational standards and very high student loan default rates. Previous generations of women were well educated after attending these schools. Most parents now encourage their daughters to attend a college or a university and not "just become a secretary." It is important to emphasize that the "brain drain" away from business colleges is by no means universal. However, far more lower-skilled high school graduates now fill the business school classrooms then in past decades. What has been the response of these schools to the basic skill needs of our current high school generation? In a word—nothing! There are rare exceptions. However, many functionally illiterate business school graduates fail to find or hold jobs in industry because of significantly deficient basic educational skills. This should not be surprising, since we earlier noted that only 40 percent of all nonminority U.S. public high school graduates attain the twelfth-grade level of skill usage by graduation, with a 10 percent attainment rate for minority students. A few progressive U.S. business schools are now attempting to cope with this educational challenge.

For over 50 years, Fox College has operated as a private secretarial school in the Chicago metropolitan area. They have long been considered one of the finest business colleges in Illinois and the United States. Their graduates are eagerly sought by Fortune 500 companies as executive secretaries and administrative assistants. In an effort to ensure the high quality of graduates, the president of Fox College reportedly "wipes out" 30 percent of a new class's poorest performing students over the first 30 to 60 days of their enrollment.

During the past 15 years, Fox College has referred to the authors individual students who lack basic reading, math or writing skills, are poorly motivated or possess weak study habits. Many of these young adults have enrolled in IIP tutorials that helped them gain admission and successfully graduate from Fox College.

Over this same period (1976–91), the dramatic downturn in educational skills accelerated among high school graduates. To accommodate a current underskilled generation, Fox College began working with the authors to test all incoming students. We established a "business practice lab" for those students testing below the tenth-grade skill level (25 percent) in reading comprehension, vocabulary, grammar, spelling, punctuation, capitalization or computation skills. The small-group IIP tutorials incorporated business content materials into classes held on-site, several days each week. Our goals were to reduce both the voluntary dropout rate and the number of students forced to leave the school because of repeated test failures, poor study habits and weak self-motivation for school and the world of work.

This application of a Work Force Education program in a vocational educational setting uncovered previously undiagnosed learning disabilities and a wide array of basic skill deficiencies. Student motivation remained very high, since most individuals were anticipating future success as an executive secretary. They now saw how to overcome learning problems that had plagued them year after year in school. The IIP sessions acted as both an introduction and a reinforcement for their business classes. These young adults were never stigmatized with the feeling that these were "literacy classes" for the slower student. In fact most of the participating adults scored at average to above average on intelligence tests administered by the college.

There is every reason to believe that over the next decade our Business Practice Lab at Fox College will tutor an ever larger proportion of their entering young adult and returning older adult population. (The current level is about 20 percent.) Automation in the office will demand greater and faster use of support-staff educational skills. Problem-solving abilities, application of knowledge to abstract issues and a stronger ability to learn new technologies on the job will require secretaries to develop stronger, higher-level thinking skills for the twenty-first century office.

SUMMARY RECOMMENDATIONS

The economic infrastructure of the United States is now collapsing, in part from the prolonged effects of a greatly cheapened, out-of-step public educational system. American schools increasingly prepare fewer and fewer young adults for productive twenty-first-century jobs. Exacerbating the public school's failure, most U.S. companies exclude hourly workers from their formal training programs.

The selected sample of case studies presented in this chapter confronts both these powerful regressive social and economic issues. We have demonstrated how advanced educational programs in a Work Force Education environment successfully accomplished a variety of job needs and radically enhanced employees' education levels. These are convergent, mutually supportive issues that reinforce the traditional American work ethic. Based on our applied field research, it is our view that employees will learn to value productivity, quality, punctuality and job problem solving if employers invest in their human resources through serious Work Force Education programs.

NOTES

1. Jean-Pierre Vélis, *Through a Glass, Darkly: Functional Illiteracy in Industrialized Countries* (Paris: UNESCO, 1990).

2. David Lewis, "Employees Find Ways to Hide Their Illiteracy," *Rocky Mountain News*, 11 January 1991, 1.

3. All case studies used in this chapter are confidential and are on file at the business office of Imperial Corporate Training and Development, 10341 Lawler, Oak Lawn, Illinois, 60453-4714, (312) 881-3700, (708) 636-8852. Please direct phone or mail inquiries regarding this data to Dr. Edward E. Gordon, President.

7

Case Studies II:
Management Employees

Do managers need Work Force Education programs? One national survey of business places the functional illiteracy rate of managers at 20 percent.

Supervisors and managers are victims of a high-tech skill-upgrade squeeze at work. They were educated as accountants, managers, marketeers, financial analysts, engineers or in other professional collegiate programs. A highly skilled secretary was once always available to correct writing, grammar or spelling errors. Those days are coming to an end. Now you must compose your own letters, memos, reports or proposals on a PC. Even if secretarial help is available, you cannot always rely on the current generation of secretaries for rewriting or corrections. In a heightened competitive environment, engineers and accountants are finding that they must learn how to take highly technical information and write a clear, concise summary that a client understands and buys.

The current generation of foreign-born professionals working in the United States has many difficult communication problems. Even though their English comprehension may be excellent, many have difficulty being understood at a meeting or in one-on-one conversations. Writing or speaking "American" business English can be a disaster for this group. English as a Second Language (ESL) programs have proven even more of a necessity for foreign executives on a "tour of duty" with a U.S.-based company.

More American businesses are looking to overseas markets for expansion. Increasingly, it has become necessary for managers to possess some degree of fluency in a foreign language and local business customs to achieve successful business penetration. This is a major corporate roadblock. Before the 1980s, typical U.S. executives had not given serious consideration to foreign language literacy as part of their higher educational business preparation. Most managers are often unprepared for foreign assignments. A recent survey of 320 high-level U.S. executives now working in the Pacific Rim and Western Europe indicated that 82 percent received no training on foreign business practices. Only 15 percent were given any language training. The Columbia University Graduate School of Business indicates that by the year 2000, a significant shortage will exist of U.S. managers equipped to run global businesses.[1]

At present, many business schools at universities across America are offering specialization for international business. One of the authors was discussing the above literacy issues with a current business undergraduate who informed him that she was conversant in four languages: Spanish, French, Italian and Greek. Even though this is an encouraging development, it will take at least a decade before there are adequate numbers of university-trained entry-level international business executives. Until then, American business must marshal its own internal training resources to master the foreign competitive challenge.

A collage of other literacy issues has also caught management unprepared. In many cases, executives or professionals are now assuming extra duties for which they were not trained or educated. Additionally, for many executives, the downside of the PC revolution means more paperwork, not less, to be read and understood.

How many managers or first-line supervisors lack appropriate basic skills or have learning disability problems? This is a very sensitive personnel issue that very few businesses will even discuss, let alone admit. Since beginning the public dialogue on managerial basic skills, the authors have often been approached by corporate trainers who relate how they inadvertently uncovered this problem. They told us how new managers, middle managers and even senior executives, while enrolled in typical company management-training classes, could not read or write at an appropriate educational level. The learning disability problems that were described earlier (see Chapters 4 and 5) can affect managers as well as hourly workers. How have these individuals with educational problems graduated from college and even risen to executive levels? The answers lie in the fact that they can learn, but possibly at a slower rate. Educationally underskilled managers have survived and prospered by finding ways around their inadequacies. This is becoming an HR issue now because layers of middle managers have been reduced by corporate downsizing. Senior executives must read and write more than ever before. An older generation of highly literate secretaries is retiring to be replaced too often by less skilled staff. PCs demand instant fluency that can be disseminated by an on-line electronic mail system throughout a business.

These are real issues happening in offices today as American business struggles to regain its competitiveness. The following case studies are drawn from recent management applications of Work Force Education programs supervised by the authors.[2]

MANAGERIAL WRITING/TECHNICAL WRITING

Accounting firms began competitively marketing their services in the 1980s. As a result, the writing skills of CPAs have come under increased scrutiny by clients. The jargon and acronyms of the accounting profession often create an unintelligible audit report, document or "annual accounting letter" for the client's board of directors. Besides their technical inscrutability, these documents are often boring, with little variance in basic analysis from year to year. Few college schools of accounting offer students a serious business writing program. CPAs, until the current era, had little opportunity or inclination to practice improving their writing skills. More than one CPA admitted to the authors that being able to avoid writing projects in college (e.g., term papers) was one reason they chose accounting as a profession.

Writing as an unmet literacy or fluency issue has resulted in accounting firms' loss of clients to competitors. Accountants must now be able to produce financial reports that are individually written, clear, concise and punctuated with careful recommendations to improve corporate financial management.

Price Waterhouse, a "big-six" accounting firm, worked with the authors in offering its CPAs an advanced writing communications program. Individual CPAs were trained by a writing specialist with a background in financial reports. The 1:1 IIP tutorial was conducted onsite, with two 60-minute classes held each week for ten weeks. The key element in business writing training is for the executive to practice, not listen to a lecture on "good writing habits." We have repeatedly tutored managers who had already attended in-house public writing seminars. Even though some seminars are conducted over several sessions, there is little time to practice writing, critique the result and try again.[3]

A managerial writing trainer typified the traditional training approach:

Any one person can feel comfortable in the seminar just sitting there taking notes. The one announcement I make very early is that all speaking and writing in the seminar is voluntary. This allows people in the first minute to relax and know that they will not be embarrassed.[4]

A successful business writing Work Force Education program is not similar to management development in team building, project management, change management or other current executive development areas. The goal is acquisition, review and application of abstract, cognitive thinking skills for written communication. The test-tutor-test IIP format allows executives on a 1:1 or 1:5 basis extended, applied, confidential practice.

An individual CPA's written reports were studied by the trainer before the program. The accounting firm selected specific examples of "model letters" as course goals. These documents paralleled the firm's management perspective, tone and accounting philosophy. These training modules were designed to diagnose specific writing weaknesses and undertake individual skill improvements to attain the firm's writing standards. Personal allowances were made for the individual writing style of the CPA. This advanced written communication Work Force Education program is used as individual needs are identified by Price Waterhouse (Chicago) for continuing professional education.

The authors have assisted many other organizations with basic, intermediate and advanced managerial writing programs based on the IIP format. An executive in U.S. Gypsum's Electronic Data Processing (EDP) department was given training to improve her writing skills. A staff trainer at the Hartmarx Corporation was given a specialized tutorial to write in-house training programs. The program included proofreading and self-editing techniques. Other executives at the Santa Fe Pacific Corporation (railroad) and Carson Pirie Scott & Company (retailer) were tutored in programs that assessed their specific writing problems and incorporated practice with appropriate company job-related writing assignments.

The engineers of the international division at Continental Can were participants in a technical writing program. This professional education program resolved the growing problem of helping these technical professionals improve communication with other nonengineering staff.

A technical writing professional taught this IIP tutorial on a 1:5 basis to sharpen these engineers' writing skills for clarity, vocabulary usage (nontechnical), conciseness and organization. The principles of effective technical writing were practiced with typical business memos, reports and letters for internal use or client correspondence.

ENGLISH AS A SECOND LANGUAGE

During the past 20 years, large numbers of foreign students attended U.S. universities for their professional and technical education. Many have remained to work for American companies as mid- and upper-level management employees. On the whole, they have exceptional business/ technical abilities and read English well. But their ability to speak, understand and write in contemporary American English is often inadequate. The authors have worked with many organizations (W.W. Granger, Morton International, Tellabs, Inc., Continental Can) to help engineers or executives improve their interpersonal and group communication skills on the job. Specialized industry vocabulary and specific common written documents were included in the IIP tutorials.

Both American and Japanese companies are relocating Japanese and other foreign nationals for a "tour of duty" with a U.S. firm. In the case of Japan, the government operates Japanese schools in the United States for these executives' children while they live overseas.

Though the average overseas executive's prior foreign language training is considerably more advanced than that of his American counterpart, these businesspeople often arrive at an American company with an unacceptable English fluency level. The authors worked with several corporations (Motorola, Panasonic, Honda) in providing IIP tutorials for these managers and, in some instances, their entire families. Our ESL training increased proficiency in spoken English, identified pronunciation problems and dealt with related idiomatic business expressions.

FOREIGN LANGUAGES FOR BUSINESS

The world market has arrived for North America, Europe and Japan. Any company that hopes to remain an industry leader with a product or service for which there is international competition has to compete in this international business arena. Any company that needs to export its products or services had better get busy if it wants to remain healthy and profitable.

As the world marketplace continues to merge overseas corporations with their American operations, it is now necessary for American executives to function effectively in languages other than English. Few corporate training programs are geared to teach foreign languages applied to a specific industry's vocabulary and terminology.

Indramat is a Frankfurt, Germany, automotive engineering and manufacturing company with U.S. operations in Chicago's northwest suburbs. American engineers were prepared to use German for their telephone conversations and in written correspondence or to conduct face-to-face business negotiations with their Frankfurt counterparts at the company's headquarters. The training was given through small tutorial groups of five engineers led by a German-language trainer using appropriate IIP materials. Grammar, vocabulary and usage were specifically linked to content areas of automotive engineering and manufacturing. Twenty class modules were used, built one upon another, until the individual engineer reached the proficiency level required by his/her job assignment. This Work Force Education program was conducted over a two-year period with over 40 participating engineers. The authors will resume the program as Indramat hires new engineers who require German-language training.

Another international business application is the preparation of corporate marketing or management staff for overseas operations. Motorola had the authors conduct French-language training for overseas marketing assignments. This small-group tutorial, using IIP materials, emphasized those language skills needed to conduct negotiations in the electronic industry.

The sales manager of NutraSweet worked in South America and spoke excellent Spanish. He needed to rapidly acquire advanced Portuguese-language abilities. Because of tight scheduling and travel, classes were conducted on a 1:1 basis and were made extremely flexible. The IIP curriculum also made use of specialized Portuguese-language training tapes to be used while traveling.

In similar circumstances, other NutraSweet marketers learned Spanish for their South American operations. One manager was even trained in Chilean-dialect Spanish. All of these foreign-language Work Force Education programs necessitated precise individualization for the company's products and a shortened time frame to achieve job-required fluency.

A vice president of international sales at Newly Weds Foods received 1:1 French-language training to assist in business negotiations. Although this executive also used a French interpreter, he had felt out of touch when French was being spoken. Europeans in business can generally speak some English. However, many will naturally begin a business discussion in their own language. They believe that since you are in their country, any foreign business representative should at least make an attempt at using their language and following accepted local business customs. Americans traveling abroad have often told us that if they make a sincere effort to use the local language, even imperfectly, their hosts will use enough English to successfully conclude the negotiations. However, greater foreign-language fluency brings enhanced long-term business results.

SPEED-READING/BLUEPRINT READING/PUBLIC SPEAKING/DIALECT ENHANCEMENT

Requests for managerial Work Force Education programs have included a speed-reading program for a senior executive at Northern Trust Bank. The volume of reports that need study by top managers has grown substantially. Speed-reading techniques can be useful when the individual possesses advanced vocabulary and comprehension skills. The 1:1 IIP program included techniques that strengthened peripheral vision, used subvocalization and improved time management related to reading business reports.

A blueprint reading program was conducted at Schless Construction, a civil construction firm. Flexible scheduling, on-site instruction and a shortened training period were the principal factors that favored an IIP tutorial versus traditional instruction at a local adult-education program. A civil engineering instructor individualized the training to meet the specific blueprint reading needs of the employees.

As an executive climbs the corporate ladder, job-performance abilities may grow faster than the individual's ability to communicate at an advanced level. It takes both specialized training and practice for many business persons to become more aware of proper speech, dialect, syntax, diction or vocabulary. The authors have provided many specialized speech dialect/communication programs by training already effective managers to improve their interpersonal communication skills. These individualized IIP programs feature a review of grammatical usages, verb tenses, pronunciation skills, business vocabulary and written punctuation. In several cases, speech therapists were used to improve personal dialect and enunciation abilities.

CONCLUSIONS/RECOMMENDATIONS

The need for Work Force Education programs for managers and professionals will increase as businesses become more technically complex and international in scope. Time is money. Classroom training is expensive for any executive, since it reduces time-on-task. Changes in business practices are accelerating. The work done by middle managers in the past decade does not disappear. It is pushed up and down the chain of command. The PC has brought an information explosion right to the executive's desk. IIP tutorials offer the following advantages to cope with these issues:

- By selecting a more highly individualized training medium on a 1:1 or 1:5 basis, you may now schedule private, confidential training only for those who really need it. Gone are the days when all managers must be given the exact same training. With an IIP training format, you will not publicly embarrass the executives who need further educational development, either to do their job or for promotion.
- "Flexibility" is the name of this training approach. Too often, the unexpected reduces a manager's commitment to his/her continuing professional/managerial education. With individualized training, rescheduling can be accommodated and business-educational goals achieved.
- The IIP cognitive-learning approach reduces the individual manager's time

spent learning new information. It has proven to be more efficient than traditional classroom instruction and offers the bonus of greater long-term retention.

- Continued professional education assumes a new identity in a Work Force Education environment. Individual executives' deficiencies can be dealt with much more openly. Senior management now possesses a new, powerful medium to reeducate managers at all levels—quickly, confidentially and right in the organization.

Work Force Education programs for managers will lead to the broadening of educational opportunities throughout the organization. In an era of tightened manpower, this is an important solution for the successful internal development of corporate human resources. Just about any topic imaginable can be offered using an IIP format that improves "managerial fluency," that is, the ability to get the job done well.

Do managers and professionals need Work Force Education programs? The authors' success with so many managerial skill-training programs has opened up new dimensions in achieving corporate competitiveness in the 1990s. We have pushed the "outer envelope" of corporate culture and gained admission with these unique training applications. We hope they will serve as an HRD model to stimulate new thinking within your own organization.

NOTES

1. Timothy D. Patterson, "The Global Manager," *World* 2 (1990): 13.

2. All case studies used in this chapter are confidential and are on file at the business offices of Imperial Corporate Training and Development, 10341 Lawler, Oak Lawn, Illinois, 60453-4714, (312) 881-3700, (708) 636-8852. Please direct phone or mail inquiries regarding this data to Dr. Edward E. Gordon, President.

3. Edward E. Gordon, "Assessing Training Alternatives in Today's Corporations," *Training Today,* December 1986, 8–9.

4. Geraldine Sprvell, "Teaching People Who Already Learned How to Write, to Write," *Training and Development Journal,* October 1986, vol. 40, no. 10, pp. 32–35.

8

Establishing a Corporate Work Force Education Policy

As we have seen, overwhelming evidence points to the immediate need for establishing basic skill training programs throughout American corporations and, many say, international businesses. But the naysayers remain in the majority. In late 1989, the *Wall Street Journal* reported a survey by the Society for Human Resources Management of Business on remedial training. Despite a small increase in Work Force Education programs, most organizations still see no need for basic reading or math programs. Of the surveyed companies, 74 percent did not offer any basic training and saw no reason to get involved. Almost half insisted they did not hire persons needing basic skill training. Other companies cited the great expense of a basic skills effort or said they lacked the necessary expertise. Some major companies have tried these programs, which failed to work. The major implication of this study was that most businesses "don't see the basic skills crisis as their problem yet."[1]

Work Force Education is a further development of the corporate training and development partnership that exists among labor, management, government and education. Workable training-education solutions, many already found in these sectors, need to be transferred to the workshop and office. While preparing a twenty-first-century work force, we must avoid the old rivalries between these groups. New "turf battles" will only delay the introduction of Work Force Education programs and further diminish American competitiveness.

Work Force Education is not literacy education per se but is the application of a wide variety of educational skills to the world of work. This HRD strategy affects all employees—managerial, professional and hourly. Work Force Education will move our economy from mass-produced goods that require lower educational standards to the specialized products and services of the twenty-first-century. It necessitates a massive HRD investment for higher levels of personal education performance on the job.

OBSTACLES TO PROGRAM DEVELOPMENT

Executives considering future manpower needs still assume that the so-called functional illiterate cannot be trained successfully for twenty-first-century technology. Their rationale remains that they will not hire a new employee incapable of passing a technical-training program. This approach originates with senior managers who equate Work Force Education with "school reform." Industry should leave this to the public sector. A corporation may engage in an "adopt-a-school" or other "school partnership" program, but the general view is that adult literacy remains a social problem to be solved by educators in the public schools, not within the business community. Many executives fear that a public admission that their corporation needs to address the workplace literacy issue will weaken their company's public image.[2]

Though American business has been battered by foreign competition, a deep nationalistic belief remains that America is "number one." Corporate pride deters a willingness to mobilize business in addressing this internal vulnerability and admitting that Work Force Education is now a necessity.

Cost is another major argument favoring nonaction. The federal Job Training Partnership Act (JTPA) and other government-subsidized literacy programs offer the convenient excuse that literacy is another "social problem" best solved by government-funded programs, not through individual business initiatives.

As a result of these arguments, relatively few companies are now preparing local Work Force Education programs. A recent study (1990) by the Commission on the Skills of the American Workforce found that less than 10 percent of businesses plan to increase output by reorganizing work that calls for better-educated employees. Only 15 percent worry about the present and future shortage of skilled workers. Less than 30 percent are planning any special programs for immigrants, women and minority youth, who will make up 85 percent of new workers. Over 80 percent seem more troubled by worker attitudes than by the basic skills gap in the workplace. On top of this general lack of concern by large corporations is the fact that smaller businesses of under 300 employees are doing even less to accommodate the Work Force Education crisis.

In our conversations with many corporate human resource directors and training managers, we often heard all of the above arguments reiterated. However, the final bottom-line rationale that delayed implementing new training/education programs had nothing to do with these conten-

tions. The "corporate culture" of the American boardroom had prohibited most CEOs from addressing the Work Force Education issue.
Education programs for hourly, nonexempt workers are thought to be almost anathema. An apparently bottomless pool of entry-level labor
throughout America's history has developed a corporate culture that
strategically chooses dumbed-down jobs and investment in high-tech labor-saving equipment that improves productivity. Any alternative long-
term strategic human resource strategy that invests in hourly employee
training/education has never been seriously considered as sound management policy by most CEOs.

However, the recent $300 billion U.S. annual productivity decline, aris-
ing from the failure of these policies, has now reached into almost every
corporate boardroom and many local businesses as well. For most large,
medium and small companies, the race has begun in implementing successful Work Force Education programs. American business must radically upgrade its worker education before the high-tech "workplace of
the future" drives many organizations into oblivion. The ever accelerating cost of an ever shrinking skilled/educated labor pool has already
driven many U.S. firms overseas. It has increased the foreign acquisition
of American businesses. Corporate bankruptcies are up, a result of the
inability of too many ill-educated workers to help their companies successfully compete in an aggressive world marketplace.

REFOCUSING CORPORATE BASIC SKILL ISSUES

Using these arguments, senior executives generally have resisted corporate policy formation for workplace literacy. Training and development managers need to adopt a new strategy that refocuses this
controversy on specific company problems involving productivity, operational cost, quality and profit. Though the federal government may provide limited "demonstration grants" for basic education, the scope of
this labor issue is too vast for government to fund a comprehensive solution. However, since 80 percent of the American work force for the year
2000 is now in place, general educational reform will have little impact
on business during the 1990s. We must remember that public education
remains a local and regional prerogative. Corporations cannot rely on
sweeping educational reforms to universally raise students' reading,
math and writing skills.[3]

The educational establishment of teacher unions, state/county/local
school boards, school administrator associations and higher education
teacher certification programs will reinforce opposition to general reforms that might raise workers' literacy standards. Schools see any significant change as a way around their bureaucratic control of jobs,
funding and political power.

Current funding of basic skills training by business and government remains insignificant. In 1989 the American Society for Training and Development (ASTD) reported the annual expenditures of all U.S. business for training and development exceeded $130 billion. Basic skills training accounted for only $500 million. Of the 20 percent of the U.S. adults who are functionally illiterate, only 1 percent are currently enrolled in a business or government-sponsored basic skills training program. As previously noted, the U.S. Department of Labor now estimates that the lack of Work Force Education programs throughout American business results in an up to $300 billion annual revenue loss due to poor worker productivity. All of our research indicates that this trend will continue well into the twenty-first century unless senior management changes its perceptions of the linkage between productivity and Work Force Education.[4]

The typical business faced with these issues cannot afford to idly wait and hope that workers' skills will somehow improve. Since these problems exist across most organizations, a task-force model is a sensible approach to begin the formation of Work Force Education policy. How will this measure ultimately gain senior management approval? It is our recommendation that you build your case on the following facts:

1. Foreign and domestic competition is becoming more intense. To compete, a company must have better quality products or services.

2. Skilled workers are disappearing. Retirements will continue to increase into the next century. New skilled workers for the factory or office are not being produced by America's schools. Society strongly encourages a college education. As a result, vocational education programs are shrinking. Immigration of foreign workers has changed from the technically literate worker of post–World War II Europe to Third World immigrants with little technical expertise. Many are not literate even in their own native languages.

3. Most offices, factories and operating plants today have significant skills problems. To compete, the American worker needs a higher level of skills acquired through better basic training. By the year 2000, basic skills at a senior high school level will be mandatory in most automated factory environments. These skills must be applied to operate complex machinery and computers. In the office, the same trend is occurring as computer software products demand more employee skills and application abilities. Even managers are now being challenged to employ these same automated tools at their desks. Increased international marketing is beginning to require extensive foreign-language education, a trend long resisted by American business but now becoming an increasing necessity. In contrast, the new European Community (EC) has established the goal that foreign languages become "an integral part of the training of managers and trainers. This applies above all to small and medium enterprises."[5]

4. The solutions to the Work Force Education problem are long-term, need to address the corporation both horizontally and vertically and will require expansion of training and development programs. Only a multifaceted response

will serve a company's current and future operations. A carefully thought-out program using the latest training and educational applications must replace current one-dimensional, simplistic training approaches.

5. Those organizations that choose to ignore the Work Force Education issue will see operating costs rise to unacceptable levels. Quality will lag behind other world-class products and services. Corporations that fail to keep pace with a literally smarter, faster competition face extinction, merger or acquisition in the early twenty-first century. The 1980s and 1990s have already begun this unalterable trend.

The operations and performance indicators for any industry or profession can be applied to specific business factors as you prepare your case for organizing a company-wide Work Force Education task force. Your organization of preliminary data will provide a strong base of facts to win approval for a task force strategy.

ESTABLISHING A WORK FORCE EDUCATION TASK FORCE

Organizing a successful Work Force Education task force presents two immediate problems: representation and direction. Broad-based information input will help ensure quicker acceptance of recommendations by senior management and later cooperation when implementing solutions across operating units. Each vital component of your business must be represented by a manager, director or professional representative of a key business function. Human resources will be present but must not have a solution prepared before all the facts are reported. A workable task force model will be limited to no more than eight to ten managers.

Direction of the task force will probably come from your human resources department. Once the goals and objectives of the project are agreed on, each member must be given wide discretion in the gathering of nonprejudicial information. Employing a specialized outside training/educational consultant will save your company time and help to accurately identify literacy problems related to specific jobs throughout the organization. A key consideration is selecting an individual consultant who has acquired broad business experience that is integrated into a specific background in Work Force Education issues and assessment.

Corporate America does not have the time or capital to reinvent basic skill training programs for adults. As we have already described, many key components to a training/education solution are already available in business communities across America. Your key role as an HRD manager will be to select a knowledgeable consultant who will adapt educational assessment and instruction programs to industrial and office staff applications. With the company Work Force Education task force orga-

Table 8.1
Work Force Education Task Force Agenda

Phase I	Target Productivity, Quality or Production Problems to Work Force Skills
Phase II	Prepare Work Force Education Program Alternatives
Phase III	Present Work Force Education Task Force Report to Senior Management
Phase IV	Gain Worker-Union Support
Phase V	Prepare Curriculum
Phase VI	Initiate Program
Phase VII	Ongoing Evaluation and Implementation

nized, you are then ready to construct a comprehensive Work Force Education policy. (See Table 8.1.)

PHASE I: TARGET PRODUCTIVITY, QUALITY OR PRODUCTION PROBLEMS TO WORK FORCE SKILLS

The task force must identify these problems at all job levels and operating sections. How are these issues driven by a need for improved basic skills?

1. Can you document these employee deficiencies?
2. What is the present cost to the business?
3. What is the future cost to the business?
4. Who composes the populations that need Work Force Education?
5. How large is each group?
6. What are the skill levels required for each targeted job?
7. How will you gain union and employee participation in the new program?

PHASE II: PREPARE WORK FORCE EDUCATION PROGRAM ALTERNATIVES

Attention must be directed to the following issues:

1. Select appropriate training-educational programs for each targeted group
2. What specific skills are needed?
3. At what grade level are the skills needed?
4. Determine the appropriateness and efficiency of each program, beginning with the most remedial instructional services and ranging upward to self-paced or computer-based training
5. When appropriate, prepare a task analysis for selected jobs to complete the above planning
6. Determine an evaluation system for each instructional program and a record-keeping system
7. Prepare a budget detailing typical alternatives at different company locations

PHASE III: PRESENT WORK FORCE EDUCATION TASK FORCE REPORT TO SENIOR MANAGEMENT

The report will point out specific operational problems and their related costs. You must present a clear, concise picture of past problems, present needs and future workplace consequences. Your documentation must demonstrate how a Work Force Education program will enhance corporate competitiveness and decrease operating cost. The plan presented must show broad participation of employees at all levels of the organization and probable costs. The report should include the following items:

1. Management: writing skills, foreign languages
2. Support Staff: grammar training, shorthand, typing, word processing/office software
3. Industrial Shop: reading, math, ESL, grammar training, blueprint reading

PHASE IV: GAIN WORKER-UNION SUPPORT OF WORK FORCE EDUCATION PROGRAM

In some instances, formal negotiations will be conducted with union representatives. Even if this is not necessary, informational sessions must be scheduled throughout the company to acquaint *all* employees with the Work Force Education program. Participation should be voluntary in the initial implementation phase. At first, expect some employees to be reluctant to enroll in the program. However, as fellow workers succeed in the program, others will begin to see this as a personal opportunity to ready themselves for the office or shop of the twenty-first century. Initial emphasis must be placed on the confidentiality of all programs. Job evaluations or promotions will not be tied to program test results. Less threatening evaluation procedures that are part of this program are available to accurately measure training results.

PHASE V: PREPARE THE WORK FORCE EDUCATION CURRICULUM

In preparing the curriculum, you should address the following questions:

1. What specific programs are to be offered at each company location?
2. Who will staff these programs?
3. Use in-house staff?
4. Use part-time staff?
5. Use external consultants?
6. Use local educational programs?
7. Where and when will the training be given?
8. Will it be offered on company or employee time?
9. What materials or equipment are required for each program?
10. A complete record-keeping system and testing/evaluation procedures should be in place for each phase of the program

PHASE VI: INITIATE THE WORK FORCE EDUCATION PROGRAM

Attention must be directed to the following components:

1. Conduct train-the-trainer programs for company training staff
2. Determine local program management
3. Orient part-time or outside consultants to organization and program responsibilities
4. A voluntary, trial program is a reasonable approach that will lessen employee stress and resistance and acknowledge personal needs

PHASE VII: ONGOING EVALUATION AND IMPLEMENTATION

Two central issues need your review:

1. How do supervisors rate participating employees' job performance before, during and six months after their enrollment in the program?

2. What local program modifications will be made based on instructors' and supervisors' evaluations?

Twelve months after the program has begun, a company can then begin to consider the permanent incorporation of the Work Force Education program into the training and development department. A key factor in making this decision will be a report back to senior management on how the program has begun to reduce the organizational problems documented earlier by the task force. Discounting other outside economic factors, operational costs will begin decreasing as quality improves and productivity increases.

COST JUSTIFICATION/IMPROVING THE BOTTOM LINE

Additional cost justifications that will indicate the success of a company's Work Force Education program may also include the following applications:

1. Decreased Hiring Costs. Before the program, how many interviews were conducted to fill a vacant job? How much did this personnel process cost your company? What are the current hiring standards (i.e., interviews to hires)?
2. Decreased Training Costs. Even if your company offered a new employee little, if any, new formal job training, informal on-the-job training (OJT) had to be given to every new hire. Since the Work Force Education program was initiated, can you document:
   a. a reduction in the turnover of new hires?
   b. a decrease in OJT time spent with a new hire?
   Is the total amount of these training cost reductions attributed to the Work Force Education program?
3. Employee accidents on the job can result from a failure to read or understand work rules or equipment operations. How many accidents have been reported over the past 12 months since the Work Force Education program began? Does this represent a decline when compared with the previous year? How much cost was saved because of fewer sick days? Lower workers' insurance claims?
4. Incremental employee costs versus services or products sold is a key company indicator. By your normal measures of employee productivity, the Work Force Education program should document increased operational efficiencies such as
   a. fewer employee work errors
   b. less time spent by supervisors answering basic questions
   c. higher production levels
   d. better employee troubleshooting abilities
   e. overall, more employee interest in job advancement
   f. more employee suggestions of practical, new solutions to job-related production concerns
   All of these factors add up to increased competitiveness, small operating mar-

gins and increased profitability. They are the realistic bottom line for Work Force Education.

5. What new equipment or work procedures have been introduced because of the employees' increased educational abilities? Does this increase production or reduce operating costs?

All of the above cost justification questions will accurately measure the success of Work Force Education. To document many of these issues, you will need to survey shop stewards, first-line supervisors or employee managers about short-term or long-term employee work changes they have observed. These surveys should be conducted immediately after the employee's training ends, 6 months later or up to 12 months after class attendance. HR managers should feel comfortable conducting these potential cost-reduction surveys because industry has long purchased labor-saving equipment based on some of the same assumptions. Now HR possesses a mechanism, with Work Force Education programs, that enables the employees to offer their higher education levels as a major contribution to introducing twenty-first-century, world-competitive operating standards, procedures and high-tech equipment.[6]

ALTERNATIVE PLANNING MODELS

Several other notable Work Force Education program planning models have been prepared by the U.S. Departments of Education and Labor, American Society for Training and Development (ASTD)/U.S. Department of Labor and the Business Council for Effective Literacy (BCEL). Detailed, step-by-step management manuals are available from all three agencies providing guidelines for setting up these employee programs. The programs generally complement each other and support the authors' recommended multiphased programmatic approach.

The Bottom Line: Basic Skills in the Workplace was prepared by the U.S. Departments of Education and Labor in 1988. Their training plan includes the following eight steps:

1. Determine the nature of the basic skills problems in your company
2. Design the training program
3. Set the program goals
4. Assess the available local resources
5. Recruit the trainees
6. Work with training and education partners
7. Build the curriculum
8. Evaluate the program

The ASTD/U.S. Labor Department joint program, *Workplace Basics: The Skills Employers Want*, offers a slightly different blueprint on how to establish and deliver a Work Force Education program. Their eight-step process includes:

1. Identify and assess problems
   a. Determine extent of the problems
   b. Form a company-wide representative advisory committee
   c. Analyze selected jobs
   d. Document employee performance problems
   e. Target population to be trained
   f. Build cooperation with workers and/or union
2. Build support
3. Propose a plan for management, union, worker approval
4. Perform a task analysis for selected employee jobs
5. Design the curriculum
   a. Performance based
   b. Functional work-context program
   c. Prepare evaluation instruments, daily record-keeping on each trainee
   d. Final implementation budget
6. Develop the curriculum
7. Implement the program
   a. Worker orientations
   b. Management orientations
8. Evaluate and monitor the training program

The Business Council for Effective Literacy prepared *Job-Related Basic Skills: A Guide for Planners or Employee Programs* in 1987. The guide offers both large and small companies the basic planning concepts and steps to take in deciding the purpose and content of a Work Force Education program.

1. Assess company resources and needs
   a. Funding
   b. Space
   c. Full/partial work-release time
   d. Skills/jobs
   e. Number of employees
2. Create a company-wide planning team
3. Select needed consulting partners to help provide services
4. Establish program goals
   a. Program operation
   b. Instructional outcomes
   c. Product outcomes

5. Select staff
   a. Program manager
   b. Program director
   c. Program teaching/training staff
6. Determine curriculum, teaching methods, materials, tests
7. Recruit the employees
   a. Non-job-threatening training program
   b. Avoid language or attitudes that denigrate low-skill employees
   c. Assure confidentiality
   d. Provide concrete incentives (e.g., on-site instruction, with 100% work-release time)
8. Test and screen
9. Keep accurate records
10. Select an appropriate training class site
11. Provide support services
    a. Child care
    b. Transportation
    c. Counseling
12. Evaluate the program
    a. Testing
    b. Anecdotal data from trainees or supervisors

A FINAL CAUTIONARY NOTE

All of these incremental Work Force Education plans have enough common elements to make them complementary in scope. There can be only one right operational plan for your organization. That plan must reflect the realities of the "business culture" within your organization. One additional suggestion is to start your Work Force Education effort with a "pilot program." This will make the trainees' participation voluntary and allow you to fine-tune consulting and/or internal staff relationships. Upper management can use the results of a pilot program to commit itself to a longer-term, company-wide training effort.[7]

As American business enters the twenty-first century, Work Force Education is not a remedy for all the strategic issues. However, it offers a mechanism that touches on the educational and training requirements of many groups throughout an entire organization. As a new, fundamental HRD concept, it will better prepare America to meet global competition and will reduce the impact of significant shortages of skilled manpower.

That global competition has many of the same Work Force Education needs as American business. What has been the response of overseas industrialized nations to the adult literacy gap? In the next chapter, we will review the extent of foreign literacy needs and how many countries have already heavily invested to stay even or pull ahead of their American business competitors.

NOTES

1. "Remedial Training Increases at Firms," *Wall Street Journal*, 7 November 1989, Sec. 1, 1.

2. G. F. Sanderson, "Innovative Training Programs," *Worklife*, 1986, 12–13.

3. John Hoerr, "Business Shares the Blame for Worker's Low Skills," *Business Week*, 25 June 1990, 71; Arnold Packer, "Preparing Workforce 2000," *Human Capital*, November/December 1989, 34–38; "Productivity Drop Is Biggest since '81," *Chicago Tribune*, 5 August 1988, Sec. 3, 3.

4. Mark Hornung, "How 'Conservative' Won Vouchers," *Craine's Chicago Business*, 13, 16–22 April 1990, 1; Merrill Goozner, "Thompson Sets Summit for Industry," *Chicago Tribune*, 3 April 1990, Sec. 2, 1; "Productivity Drop Is Biggest Since 1981," *Chicago Tribune*, 5 August 1988, Sec. 3, 3.

5. " 'LINGUA'—A Programme to Overcome Language Barriers in Europe," *Council of Ministers for Education of the European Parliament News (CEDEFOP News)* 4 (August 1989): 3.

6. Long-Term/Short-Term Surveys have been developed by the authors for their field-based company Work Force Education research. For more information, contact Dr. Edward E. Gordon, Imperial Corporate Training and Development, 10341 Lawler, Oak Lawn, Illinois, 60453-4714, (708) 636-8852.

7. *The Bottom Line: Basic Skills in the Workplace* (Washington, D.C.: U.S. Departments of Education and Labor, 1988); Anthony P. Carnevale, Leila J. Gainer, and Ann S. Meltzer, *Workplace Basics: The Skills Employers Want* (Alexandria, Va.: American Society for Training and Development, 1988); *Job-Related Basic Skills: A Guide for Planners of Employee Programs* (New York: Business Council for Effective Literacy, 1987).

9

International Focus on Work Force Education

Literacy is more than the ability to read, write and compute. The demands created by advancing technology require increased levels of knowledge, skills and understanding to achieve basic literacy. Literacy is a means of acquiring the understanding and ability necessary to improve living and working conditions.

International Council for Adult Education (1987)

American business managers grumble, "Why are only U.S. workers falling victim to the 'literacy gap' opened by advancing high-tech?" The answer may surprise you. America is not alone. In 1980 the European Parliament reported that the functional illiteracy rate among the member nations of the European Community (EC) (including Great Britain, France, Germany, Belgium, Denmark, Ireland and the Netherlands) stood at 4 percent to 6 percent. This means that 10 to 15 million European adults possess an educational-ability level lower than that of a thirteen-year-old student. The same report placed the functional literacy rate of southern Europe even lower, at an astounding 24 percent.

GRIM STATISTICS

Vélis (1990) has assembled an impressive United Nations Educational, Scientific, and Cultural Organization (UNESCO) study of Work Force Education problems in the industrialized nations of Europe and Canada. Country by country, region to region, he has documented the startling fact that our European trading partners are burdened with the same undereducated, contemporary work force. They are all struggling to catch up and stay competitive in the high-stakes trade race with America and Japan. (See Table 9.1.)

A British government study in 1987 uncovered over 6 million functionally illiterate adults. The *Guardian* headlines portrayed these figures as "Only the Tip of the Iceberg." But merely 100,000 adults were benefitting from some sort of Work Force Education in Britain at the time of this study.

A year later the French government determined that one French adult in five was functionally illiterate. However, Germany reported in 1989 that only 3 percent of its population was at this educational level (excluding East Germany).

Even the Swiss recorded (1987) that 50 percent of their army recruits were below functional literacy levels (approximately 17,000). In 1988 there were 20,000 to 30,000 native-born Swiss who could neither read nor write. Other northern European countries also have defined the size of their Work Force Education problems. Sweden (1984) has determined that 500,000, or 6 percent of its adult population, have functional literacy problems. A similar illiteracy rate of 6 percent can be found in Hungary (1989), where the school dropout rate stands at 26.6 percent. Of these dropouts, 20 to 30 percent cannot read elementary school textbooks (i.e., 3 million young adults).

In southern Europe the level of individual educational attainment is even lower. Portugal (1981) estimated that of its then 10 million inhabitants, 5 percent were illiterate under age 34, 6.2 percent ages 35–39, and 50 percent over age 60 had never achieved literacy. However, by 1989 only 17,000 adults were enrolled in any form of Work Force Education effort. Over 36 percent of Spain's population (1986) above the age of ten had either never attended school or left school before graduation, causing widespread functional illiteracy. In 1991 the Spanish government's response was the initiation of a $1.23 billion job-training and literacy program assisting 523,000 workers.

Italy recorded similar conditions (1986), with 23 percent of its adult population never attending school or leaving the classroom without their diploma. These same conditions were also found among 23.2 percent of Greece's adult population (1986).

The UNESCO study also reported widespread Canadian literacy problems. In 1983, 5.5 percent of the population over the age of 15 (850,000) had attended school for less than five years; 3.5 million (22.8%) attended five to eight years and 4.3 million (28.4%) received less than nine years of formal education. A later study (1989) by the Provence of Quebec showed no improvement in these statistics. One and a half million adults were found to be functionally illiterate, with only 15,000 enrolled in any literacy program. The survey also discovered that 77 percent of these adults never went near a library. More disturbingly, 38 percent saw no

Table 9.1
Rates of Illiteracy among Western Industrialized Nations

Nation	Illiterate Population % (Year)	Illiterate Population (Year)
Great Britain	4% – 6% (1982)	6M (1987)
France	4% – 6% (1982)	2.2 – 3.3M (1982)
Germany	4% – 6% (1982) 3% (1989)	2.5 – 3.9M (1982) 20M (1989)
Belgium	4% – 6% (1982)	400 – 600K (1982)
Denmark	4% – 6% (1982)	208 – 320K (1982)
Ireland	4% – 6% (1982)	132 – 198K (1982)
Netherlands	4% – 6% (1982)	560 – 840K (1982)
Switzerland	––––––	30K (1988)
Sweden	6% (1984)	500K (1984)
Hungary	6% (1989)	3M (1989)
Spain	36% (1986)	14M (1986)
Italy	23% (1986)	13M (1986)
Greece	23.2% (1986)	2.3M (1986)
Canada	22% (1988)	5M (1988)

Source: UNESCO, 1990

connection between raising their educational abilities and their jobs. Most (89%) did not consider higher personal literacy as being advantageous for improving their lives.

A later national Canadian study (1988) indicated that 5 million adults were functionally illiterate, or 22 percent of the entire population. The government estimated that Canadian industry lost over $10 billion as a direct cost.

By 1991 the Canadian National Literacy Secretariat was recommending a "Workplace Literacy and Basic Skills Program" based on the results of strong partnerships among labor, business, education and government. Several basic approaches seem to be emerging in the Canadian workplace. Local community college, school board or education/training consultants are helping industry formulate Work Force Education programs. Second, peer tutors are instructing other workers on a one-to-one or small-group basis. Finally, trade training programs are incorporating basic skills into their regular training efforts. However, the Canadian government, emulating its American cousin, has thus far failed to mandate national Work Force Education standards, reform public education or seriously help fund any of these training programs.

One of the major problems, according to UNESCO, faced by Europe, Canada and the United States in reducing these grim statistics is that it is still very difficult to find professional educators trained to teach adults. Higher education teacher-preparation programs are almost universally concerned with elementary and secondary education. Adult education is still largely ignored. Internationally, this remains one of the weakest links in the chain to establish effective Work Force Education programs.[1]

INTERNATIONAL INNOVATIONS FOR WORK FORCE EDUCATION

American business, then, is not alone, as the above statistics prove, in its dilemma over the low educational levels of its work force. There is not a single Western industrialized nation that sees its education and worker-training programs as up to the demands of twenty-first-century productivity. William E. Nothdurft, in a Brookings Institution study in 1989, found that the industrialized economies of Western Europe are struggling with the same Work Force Education issues. However, there is considerable evidence that several are succeeding in educating for higher worker productivity, making economies grow faster and lowering poverty rates and unemployment. What is a distinct reason for these results? A commitment has been made for human investment as a fundamental economic principle shared by business, labor and government. This has not always been the case in Europe's history.[2]

In 1851 a London industrial exhibition caused grave concern in the elegant boardrooms of some major English manufacturers. American products were stealing the show. They were mass-produced at high levels of quality with interchangeable parts and sold at a competitive price. These American products upset the British industrial companies' unassailable position of world economic dominance. The English conducted a personal fact-finding tour and learned that the American secret was not better machinery or process innovations but a higher level of basic worker education. The New England industrial heartland of the day boasted a 95 percent literacy rate, compared with only 66 percent in Great Britain. Over the next 150 years, England never closed this worker talent gap. This was a decisive contributing factor to Britain's long decline as the world's foremost industrial power.

The fundamental issue of global competitiveness has led to a contemporary European consensus on developing strong training/education systems, including specific preparation for work. Unlike Europe, America lacks a nationwide consensus on these issues of work force competencies and appropriate programs to ensure that school graduates are ready, willing and able to successfully enter and remain in the world of work. Even though the diversity of the work force in the United States dwarfs the problems faced by our European competitors, we share with Europe many common economic, political and cultural values. What follows are European country profiles that address the future challenge of Work Force Education.

SWEDEN

Fewer than 10 percent of all students who complete compulsory schooling at age 16 fail to continue at an upper secondary school for vocational training or university preparation. Unemployment for Swedish young adults aged 16–24 is only 5 percent. Why? Because the government overhauled the nation's entire secondary school system. It created a comprehensive, integrated basic and vocational educational program supporting an aggressive, national labor market policy emphasizing training and work experience.

The program works because Sweden, as a society, has adopted the "American work ethic." Work is recognized as the central element defining one's life, and education is the process through which meaningful work is found and retained.

At age 16, students choose one of 27 programs of study, ranging from liberal arts, nursing and accounting to process engineering, manufacturing and forestry. Throughout their upper secondary school experience, the line between education and job training is intentionally blurred. Work-life experiences are organized by vocational counselors at on-site company "industrial high schools." (Only 25% of all students pursue higher education in Sweden.) Ten to 20 percent of a student's time is spent in a work setting, growing to 60 percent by the third year of study. Many students will go to work for their "host" company but not all, nor are they obligated to join a particular company.

However, many Swedish young people drop out or choose not to go on to upper secondary school. Many of these are functionally illiterate due to learning problems never diagnosed. The "Youth Centre Program" was created for these young adults to strengthen basic skills and self-esteem and to provide a less-formal point of access to further education or work preparation.

Youth Centre offers a wide array of programs, including on-the-job training, vocational courses, basic remedial academic study, apprenticeship training and craft workshop, among many others. These alternative secondary school programs have yielded impressive results. About one-third of the students return to school; another third enter the labor market and pursue meaningful work careers. Ten percent register with the national employment service, pursuing work with the training already accomplished. Twenty percent move to the country to pursue farming or begin families. A very small number end up functionally illiterate and without useful job skill training.

LESSONS FROM SWEDEN

Several key Work Force Education concepts can be learned from Sweden's Work Force Education program. The focus on improving school-to-work transitions, reducing the dropout rate and instilling a meaningful work ethic is the creation of an educational system with an explicit and gradually increasing work experience component. This variation in the process of teaching (didactics) combines both important academic skills and technical-functional skills.

Sweden's model also reaches out to all young people, in particular the disadvantaged or disaffected. By offering a wide array of educational choices, it empowers students to choose their own futures and take ownership of their own solutions.

These two Work Force Education concepts have valuable applications for American business to solve some academic weaknesses. Motorola related to the authors how it has become necessary, in the practicalities of the marketplace, to "retrain" new engineers after they are hired. Motorola found that their engineers designed the most sophisticated high-tech electronics available anywhere in the world. However, it was impossible to manufacture these products because of their noncompetitive cost and complexity. It became necessary for Motorola to reeducate its engineers in the practical engineering needs of the manufacturing marketplace. If the Swedish model of education had been available to

Motorola, new engineers on their first day of full-time employment would arrive with the latest in engineering theory. They would also possess considerable mastery, from prior experience, of what Motorola needs to manufacture competitively for the international electronics marketplace.[3]

The federal Job Training Partnership Act (JTPA) annually spends billions of dollars attempting to offer the high-risk, unemployed, low-skilled adult a means to entry-level employment. Many of these are older adults who are functionally illiterate school dropouts with few job skills, weak work-ethics and low personal self-esteem. Social science research overwhelmingly indicates that it is very difficult to achieve a permanent life-style change for the older adult in this high-risk population. America would be better served if it were to use these Work Force Education funds for students still in school. We must consider the Swedish model as a more creative system that offers many potential career choices rather than the present, almost exclusionary U.S. college-preparatory educational system. The Youth Centre programs in particular are ideally suited for problematic students. Too often these young adults "fall between the cracks" of American secondary education and drop out, or are ill served by generally inferior postsecondary vocational-technical education programs.

GERMANY

The Work Force Education needs of Germany, unlike the needs of other Western industrialized nations, are focused, for the most part, on older, low- or narrowly-skilled workers in traditional heavy industries. Germany has the lowest level of young adult illiteracy and unemployment in Europe because of the post–World War II "Dual System" of education based on apprenticeship and vocational training.

In 1986, of the over 1 million high school graduates, 210,000 began university studies. The greater majority (685,000) entered industry after having received extensive vocational training. During primary-school years, all children are given some tactile-skills education along with their standard academic instruction. Using students' average grades and teacher recommendations, parents and students are counseled to select from one of two kinds of secondary school. The "Hauptschule," which prepares young people for trade apprenticeships, or the "Gymnasium," where students pursue a classical education for university admission.

This decision is not final. Students may change from one program to another. Germany, like the United States, has begun to feel the social pressure for children to pursue formal professional education rather than the technical-vocational track. However, the German system offers many more educational opportunities. The Gymnasium student pursues studies until age 19, a more rigorous education than found in most American high schools. The Hauptschule student completes school at age 16–17. They may take another "bridge" of a few years to a university-prep grammar school or go directly on to one of several higher technical-vocational schools and colleges. However, most complete their compulsory education at age 15–16 and choose to pursue an apprentice-ship from approximately 480 state-recognized occupations.

For most trades, this apprenticeship lasts three years. The student works four days a week for pay under the guidance of an approved in-structor. One day a week he/she attends a local state-run vocational school (Berufschule) specializing in that trade. Pressure has been build-ing in recent years to increase this to two days, to teach more academic skills.

At the conclusion of these three years, and after passing a nationally administered written examination and a practical examination, the ap-prentice becomes a "journeyman." These credentials allow the young adult to work anywhere in Germany. After working three more years and completing courses in business management, technology and law, a journeyman takes the examination to become a "master." A craftsman may not operate any business in Germany without a "master's" license. This dual system has served Germany well with highly literate, techni-cally capable workers for many varied industries.

Consultation, involvement and partnership are the watchwords that make this Work Force Education system function. Industry, unions and government work together to formulate the content of these vocational-technical education curriculums. Industry is very heavily involved, both with staff time and with money. This makes sense for German business because it is part of their "national corporate culture." Everyone is doing it. If a student-apprentice decides not to take a job at the business that has helped educate him/her, an equally qualified entry-level worker will take that job spot. The business is assured that this new worker has been just as well prepared by another competitor who has held up its end of this "dual-system."

Unions also work as national partners in this system. Instead of tightly regulating a limited supply of apprenticeships, there exists much greater flexibility in allowing enough apprentices, journeymen and masters to maintain high quality and constant innovations that "smarten up" their products.

The number of low-skilled jobs in Germany, as elsewhere, is swiftly declining. Many German businesspeople complain about a perceived decline in vocational school graduates. But vocational counselors argue that parents and society pressure young people to attend the university, not enter a technical-vocational field. Students branded as "failures" have little motivation and low expectation to excel in the dual system.

Unfortunately, this system was not designed as a remedial education program. The solution may result in more time spent in school with less spent on the job. It remains to be seen how supportive industry will be for a fundamental shift away from applied, on-the-job learning for those students lacking basic skills or personal motivation.

LESSONS FROM GERMANY

Educational competencies in reading, writing, math and problem solving are fundamental requirements for successful vocational-technical training. Even if the secondary school has done an adequate job educating an entry-level worker, accelerating high-tech changes will probably require all workers to enroll in educational skill-upgrade programs at work (e.g., quality assurance, statistical process control).

Second, "streaming" students through vocational versus university-bound programs is beginning to create as many problems in Germany as already exist in the United States. The Swedish multiple school-education model seems to make more sense, by helping students who will not do well with more traditional educational tracks.

Finally, the participation of the employers and unions in partnership with the government is essential to make the dual system work. Financial commitment by all parties is also critical. In 1985 approximately 500,000 German companies provided on-the-job training at a cost of roughly $30 billion. These partnerships are found in all economic sectors: commerce, craft trades, the service sector, agriculture, doctors, architects, pharmacists and in the public sector.

By combining academic instruction and an on-the-job work experience/training, Germany is better able to use all of its young people's talents, aptitudes, interests and abilities. In the United States, vocational-technical education at the secondary level has been declining since the end of the Second World War (1945). Even though many community colleges now offer these programs, there remains a lack of serious commitment by most businesses to train apprentices on the job. Educators have also shunned combining the classroom with the office or workshop, viewing it as "un-American" and not offering the opportunity of a college education to everyone. This ignores the economic reality that the severe shortage of highly trained technical workers is seriously constraining American industries' ability to keep pace with state-of-the-art technology. Many college-educated, white-collar, entry-level employees have few motivations for work other than financial considerations. Their personal aptitudes and long-term standards of living might have been better served if a regionally adapted "dual system" operated across the United States.

It is also interesting to note that American business spends about the same amount in training its workers (over $30 billion, according to ASTD) as German business invests in the "dual system." The fundamental difference is that Germany spends the funds at the front end, on earlier worker job preparation, whereas American companies try to play "catch-up" by offering older adults isolated, in-house programs that are not usually offered with high educational standards in mind.[4]

FRANCE

In 1982 the French government created an experimental system, "Missions Locales," consisting of local task forces for helping young adults make the transition from school to work. The Missions Locales program integrates social, economic and educational services offered by a number of private and public agencies. These services include job training, work experience apprenticeships, adult literacy education, counseling services, health and welfare, housing and transportation assistance.

In 38 Missions Locales, a high-tech training program is operated in conjunction with 125 commercial and industrial firms and 75 agricultural companies. No matter who are the partners, the main purpose of the Missions Locales program is to establish or reinvigorate local job-training and education programs for the young potential entry-level worker.

By 1987 approximately 170,000 of France's 400,000 underskilled youth actively participated in Missions Locales around the country. In this group, 10 percent had graduated from high school but were functionally illiterate. Seventy percent had no diploma at all or had graduated with a very poor academic record. The balance of these young adults had drug, alcohol or other personal problems.

To improve the school-to-work transition process for these students, the Missions Locales offer three basic local programs:

1. *Public/Community Works Projects* (TUC). Job training is provided for individuals ages 16 to 25 through a combination of work experience and vocational training. Government and industry share the cost of the program by paying less than minimum wage but providing meaningful professional training.

2. *Private Company Internships* (SVIP). Young, entry-level workers work full time for three to six months and receive training one week per month. Wages are higher than the TUC program and are paid by a corporately supported foundation and labor unions. The state pays the Social Security taxes.

3. *Professional Job Training.* Individuals develop a "training itinerary" that enhances their skills and provides enough work for their immediate financial needs.

The Missions Locales program has increased public recognition that France's school system produces too many poorly educated or technically trained youth in order to satisfy the needs of France's growing high-tech economy. Unless these conditions change by 1992, France will not be able to compete successfully in the new European Community or in global markets. To avoid this catastrophe, in 1987 France's High Committee on Education and Industry Relations established the goal of increasing the number of students attaining higher technical qualifications from 80,000 to 160,000 per year. It remains to be seen if France can achieve this goal and continue to broaden its other Work Force Education programs.

LESSONS FROM FRANCE

1. Local programs are preferable to national solutions. A national program cannot hope to accommodate local economic conditions. These efforts offer a much wider range for experimentation that other communities may copy.
2. A program may have a specific aim but still needs integrated social services. The delivery of education, counseling, job training, etc., is best organized where the student lives in the local town or city.

Across from Manhattan in New York City, the Jersey City Public Schools have entered into a joint educational partnership with Merrill Lynch. The Financial Industry Readiness Skills Training (F.I.R.S.T.) Program has striking similarities to the Missions Locales. The purpose of the F.I.R.S.T. Program is to provide inner-city, minority students with the basic knowledge and skills required to succeed in the financial services industry. In 1992, Merrill Lynch will open an operations facility in Jersey City. They see it as vital that a pool of well-rounded students are ready for possible career opportunities in the financial services industry.

Merrill Lynch offers high school students special courses so that they can apply for internships at any of the financial services firms in the Jersey City Waterfront area. A Mentoring Program was established to provide positive role models for students, encouraging open discussions on corporate work issues and workplace relationships.

The local superintendent of schools has called on other companies in New Jersey to emulate this example and provide students with courses dealing with their own industries. Plans are now under way to establish a special commercial high school that will offer this expanded involvement by Merrill Lynch and other companies in preparing inner-city, minority youth for the world of work.[5]

GREAT BRITAIN

England's Prime Minister John Major and Princess Diana have something in common. They, like 67 percent of all British youth, left school at age 16 and rarely darkened a classroom door again. Only 16 percent of compulsory school graduates go on to Oxford, Cambridge or the handful of other British universities (compared with 57 percent in the United States).

Few school-leavers rise as high as Major or Princess Diana. As a group, they are helping Britain lose the economic competition with better-schooled nations. Hilary Steedman, a researcher at Britain's National Institute of Economic and Social Research, believes that Great Britain is "far behind other countries" in training students for the job market. "It's our most serious problem." According to a recent study (1991) productivity per worker is 22 percent higher in France and 45 percent higher in Germany and the Netherlands.

In 1981 the British government embarked on a Youth Training Scheme (YTS). These new training initiatives sought to create opportunities for employed and unemployed adults to expand, update or strengthen their skills. They provided trainees a certified standard of skills and encouraged young students to pursue formal education or training until at least age 18. The YTS program provided an average 25-week off-the-job training over a two-year period. It combined this component with on-the-job training and planned work experience. It was the intent of YTS to lead toward recognized vocational qualifications. Trainees received a small training stipend and direct contact with the realities of the workplace. In 1989, 450,000 students were enrolled in YTS.

In addition to this program, in 1983 the Thatcher government introduced the Technical and Vocational Education Initiative (TVEI) aimed at increasing the creativity and problem-solving skills of students ages 14 to 18. At local schools, managers and executives act as curriculum advisors, tutors and student mentors. An actual work experience is a central component of all TVEI programs. Special vocational-technical courses were also introduced: craft and design technology; art, design and graphic communications; business studies and information technologies; and technology sciences.

By 1987, TVEI programs were under way at nearly all "local education authorities" (i.e., school districts) in England, Scotland and Wales. By 1992 the government plans to make the program universally available in all secondary schools and for all students.

LESSONS FROM GREAT BRITAIN

1. A school-business connection is essential to improve the relevance of education and technical training. It assures students that an actual job exists for them in the working world when they complete their education.

2. The ideological differences between the Conservative and Labour parties in Britain were overtaken by the convergence of local concerns that bridged the

ideological/political chasm. The local school officials, parents, businesspeople, unions and others succeeded in school reforms that achieved the different aims of the partners while benefitting the community as a whole with Britain's version of Work Force Education.

In the United States we have yet to clearly formulate a nationally mandated school-reform program. Britain had to take this difficult step or face industrial oblivion. Yet once taken, the British program was at the local level so that practical partnerships were formed between business-education-union and community. Maybe America can take this page from British Work Force Education reform. Can we establish a new national agenda educating everyone for profitable twenty-first-century employment? This mandate should give local communities the power to interpret Work Force Education in a realistic manner that profits everyone.[6]

CONCLUSIONS FROM EUROPEAN WORK FORCE EDUCATION MODELS

No matter how substantial a commitment corporate HR makes to local in-house Work Force Education programs, businesses will never by themselves change the abilities of most entry-level workers. International economic competitiveness demands the creation and maintenance of a world-class universal educational system. American business recognizes that remediation of workers, once they get on the job, is far more difficult than creating and supporting a twenty-first-century educational system that assures a steady supply of workers for all levels of research, commerce and industry.

A key component to this new school era will be the use of work-related experiences and of classroom education that keeps pace with technological change. This does not mean that all American high schools and colleges must abandon a "classical" education for "real-world" courses. European models of education reform do not call for any society to swing entirely away from one model to another. If we do desert the liberal arts education model in favor of Work Force Education, America will only again duplicate its present erroneous societal fixation on college-preparatory programs as the only respectable goal for our best and brightest youth. Our current intolerance of technical/vocational/craft careers for students must not be replaced by scorning the equal educational value of history, literature or political science.

The truth is that our children in the next millennium will need greater educational diversity. We must educate the mind to seek new ideas from the liberal arts while we offer students greater opportunities to develop the practical skills and craft aptitudes that will give form and substance to the rapid technological changes coming in the next 100 years. This balanced educational policy of the theoretical and the practical may well determine America's international competitive future.

Behind any national mandate in the schools for Work Force Education, we must develop universally recognized skill credentials that will change with the times. The private, regional accreditation associations in higher education (e.g., the North Central Association of Colleges and Schools) may serve as a model to develop new private, universally recognized accreditation of local programs. They will assure students of their employability and guarantee employers the availability of properly prepared entry-level workers.

Work Force Education and updating schools for the twenty-first century will require ongoing, vigorous partnerships between the public and the private sectors. As we enter the next millennium, global change will continue accelerating in world society and technology. There are no easy "quick fixes" in creating and maintaining an educated global society. The public must demand, in all advanced societies, long-term investment in human capital to heavily finance an increasing variety of Work Force Education programs.

Because of future quantum leaps in the power of technology, investment in heavy industry will gradually wane. Corporate investment in human learning will become the foundation for a "second American century" as a world power. Technology has already freed mankind from more and more of its past heavy labors. The twenty-first century will witness business and government's focus on the development of a child's mind to build, to think, to lead a global competitive society.

This will not come about easily or cheaply. In most European countries, a large investment is now being made by the taxpayers and by business in additional postsecondary compulsory school training. As we noted earlier, the United States spends more than almost any other country on its university and college educational programs but comparatively little in the postsecondary technical-vocational arena. The concept of apprenticeship education is vital to the future of almost every American business. We must immediately decide how to locally offer successful business/education-sponsored youth-training programs.[7]

Neither Japan nor Europe has any inherent technological advantage or production system that cannot be duplicated in the United States. Both Japan and Europe have earned their global competitive edge by making sustained and significant investments in the education and skills training of all their citizens. Is it not time for America to do the same?

NOTES

1. Jean-Pierre Vélis, *Through a Glass, Darkly: Functional Illiteracy in Industrialized Countries* (Paris: UNESCO, 1990), 14, 31, 32, 35, 36, 39, 40, 44, 49, 62, 63, 64, 65, 66, 68, 78, 79, 103, 106, 107; "Spain's Job Training Plan," *Wall Street Journal*, 17

December 1990, 16; Sue Waugh, *Workplace Literacy and Basic Skills* (Ottawa, Ontario: National Literacy Secretariat, 1990).

2. William E. Nothdurft, *School Works* (Washington, D.C.: Brookings Institution, 1989), 1, 4, 6, 7, 12, 13, 14, 17, 18, 19, 25, 27.

3. "Integrating Skills and Content Areas in Education and Business" (Presentation by Motorola, Inc., American Society for Training and Development Program, Round-Table Forum, DePaul University, Chicago, February 1988).

4. All of our comments on Germany are based on information regarding the Federal Republic of Germany (West Germany). At the time of our writing (1990–91), information was not available (at least in English) on the Work Force Education position of a reunified Germany; Nothdurft, *School Works*, 29–43; Tom Peters, "West Germany's Unsung Economy Hums along amid Labor Harmony," *Chicago Tribune*, 23 July 1990, Sec. 4, 6; William Pfaff, "Germany's History: A Lesson for the Future," *Chicago Tribune*, 12 August 1990, Sec. 4, 3; "Vocational Training," *Public Information Document #28* (Bonn: Press and Information Office of the Federal Government, Federal Republic of Germany, 1987); David C. Rudd, "School Days Never End, Workers, Companies Find" *Chicago Tribune* Sec. 7; 17 February 1989, 1, 16.

5. Nothdurft, *School Works*, 45–55; Dave Spieghts (Editor, *Report on Literacy Programs*), "Literacy Challenge Facing Corporate America" (Presentation given at Workplace Literacy and Education Solutions Conference, Chicago, Ill., 19 March 1991).

6. R. C. Longworth, "Britain May Need More Schooling," *Chicago Tribune*, 27 January 1991, Sec. 1, 4; Nothdurft, *School Works*, 57–73.

7. Nothdurft, *School Works*, 83–93.

10

Work Force Education in the Twenty-First Century

Economic rivalries between North American, European and Asian markets in the global arena will move us farther down the path of economic restructuring. Denationalization means freer markets worldwide; however, individual national competitive advantage requires greater productivity. This is occurring at a time when demographic trends worldwide suggest a shortage of experienced, literate workers. If the world were a global village of 1,000 residents, the village would have 700 illiterate persons.[1]

Human resources must improve to compete in the world marketplace of advanced technologies. Our research leaves little doubt that Work Force Education will be decisive in mastering this strategic challenge. Internationally, those industries that invest the most in education today will remain very competitive in the world arena. Corporate support of long-term educational reform alone is an insufficient strategy to reach this goal. In the short term, corporate policy must encourage increased linkages of the educational system to industry and stimulate business efforts at Work Force Education.

Goldstein and Gilliam (1990) in their review of "Training System Issues in the Year 2000," point out that dramatic demographic shifts in the working populations will further raise expectations for future training programs to maximize the potential of every person. Research has already begun to identify abilities that workers need in order to perform more cognitively complex jobs. Educational opportunities will have to be broadened, since the twenty-first century will witness the rapid technical obsolescence of professionals and managers who previously had very advanced education and training. Some estimates are that the engineer's education has a half-life of five years (in 1980, the estimate was ten years). If job requirements are shifting so quickly, it may become necessary for HR managers to determine Work Force Education programs for organizational jobs that do not yet exist.

In future years, many corporations will consider siting decisions less on tax abatements or new roads. William Kolberg, president of the National Alliance of Business, sees companies more interested in the quality of an area's work force. "Those states that develop better systems for preparing their youth for work will attract employers in the future," Kolberg insists. "Those that don't, won't."[2]

VOCATIONAL/INDUSTRIAL EDUCATION PARTNERSHIP

We must recognize that a system for technical, vocational and specialized training has become a priority in any national economy. National trade deficits belie the notion of a prosperous "service economy" without a dangerous dependence on imported industrial goods. As we have already reviewed, a "dual system" of vocational/industrial education works well to varying degrees in Britain, Germany, Japan, Korea, Switzerland, Sweden, France and other foreign economies. Their industries do not suffer from a shortage of highly skilled, literate manpower.

Unlike the United States and Canada, other nations have developed respected high-quality forms of postsecondary technical education that exist beside the university. Our research shows that the majority of industrial trainees remain with the company where they received their basic industrial education through a business partnership with a local technical university or vocational trade school. To further broaden these opportunities, companies must forge closer ties with professional societies and trade associations.

This dual system already exists in America's aerospace and pharmaceutical industries, where firms and educators work closely together. During the decade of the 1990s, it will become increasingly less difficult for any American corporation to establish an in-house training/apprenticeship program with public and private postsecondary institutions. Work Force Education skills—with improved personal attitudes of punctuality, accuracy and reliability—must be embedded in basic industrial education. Further adaptation and adoption of these training/educational programs will improve quality, lower cost and produce a more highly motivated work force.

The clear message is that we must find ways to educate all present and future workers for the American economic system to grow and function. Joint, cooperative Work Force Education programs, including the business community, labor, educators and government at all levels, are required if minimal worker needs are to be met for the year 2000 and beyond.

Sarmiento and Kay (1990) issued *Worker-Centered Learning: A Union Guide to Workplace Literacy* for the AFL-CIO Human Resources Development Institute. They recognize Work Force Education as one of labor's real bread-and-butter issues. The guide is designed for use by union local representatives to gain an understanding of workplace literacy, to design a worker-centered program and to locate places to get more information. The authors believe, "The climate today—among educators, the government, employers, schools and community groups—is supportive of new workplace literacy initiatives."

Unions have historically responded to community development issues. In the nineteenth century, they provided a forum supporting the establishment of universal public schooling and vocational education. They now offer curriculum input for Work Force Education by emphasizing the life needs and personal interests of employees rather than by simply training workers in narrow job skills. Our research shows that this broader curriculum content is more successful in promoting and retaining an adult's motivation while participating in a Work Force Education program.[3]

U.S. apprenticeship programs have received a new lease on life in the 1990s. Even though 70 percent of the 300,000 current apprentices who are registered with the U.S. Labor Department are associated with the union building trades, this is beginning to change. America's apprenticeship system is expanding to include service jobs such as computer programmer, customer service representative, bank teller, laboratory technician, commercial designer and chef, among other jobs.

The Federal Apprenticeship 2000 Program concentrates on workers 16 to 25 years old who do not go on to college. That is about 50 percent of all high school graduates. The $10.5 million program acts as a conduit to encourage U.S. employers to introduce apprenticeships. Employers then hire apprentices for jobs. Apprenticeship programs offer "work-based learning." This means that young adults earn while they learn in a structured program that combines classroom instruction with specific on-the-job training experiences.

James Van Erden, director of the Labor Department's Office of Work-Based Learning, states, "What we're looking at is how to better link theoretical instruction with the practical, as is done in most European countries and Japan." In 1991, some 100 American cities had outreach programs to recruit women and minorities for apprenticeship training.[4]

However, the United States has a long way to go. Only 27 percent of all secondary students in America who major in a technical area ever work in a related field. The Carol D. Perkins Vocational and Applied Technology Act of 1990 may become an important step in redirecting vocational education by integrating vocational and academic education. For now, according to Rosenstock (1991), current high school vocational programs are often "literally and figuratively in the basement of the school. They have become a 'dumping ground,' and both the students and the teachers in these programs have the lowest status in the school."

The Perkins Act seeks to combine apprenticeships with academic learning. Vocational education is another way to learn the same academic concepts and skills that college preparatory students now learn. Students must learn thinking abilities, creativity and problem solving whether the focus is high-tech or academic. Students have many types of intelligence: artistic, kinesthetic, social, linguistic and logical. Elementary and secondary education must offer programmatic alternatives that make the best use of individual students' aptitudes and directs them toward purposeful careers.

The Perkins Act has the potential as a powerful tool for local school restructuring. However, the key is collaborative partnerships between local businesses and schools, by creating internships and apprenticeship programs that tie together classroom and job-training experiences. Educators now agree (Gray, 1991) that the reform of vocational education can become a mainstream issue in the reform of U.S. high school education. This is a tantalizing challenge for business and union leaders. You can now assume an activist role in local communities and provide needed leadership in an educational revolution focused on offering real vocational choices for students and parents.[5]

Can there be any doubt that a fundamental cause of America's current decline in technology and innovation is a faltering educational system? However, the continuing high rate of functional illiteracy of plant workers and managers mandates corporate Work Force Education. A Work Force Education program must first improve basic skills before proceeding to advanced technical training. Only then will worker competitiveness improve.

CORPORATE CHILD-CARE FACILITIES AND WORK FORCE EDUCATION

Literacy research encompasses a "family literacy approach." This is an effort to improve the parenting and basic skills of adults in order to foster their children's learning. We now know that a direct relationship exists between a nonreading parent and a potential illiterate child. The range of family literacy programs includes tightly structured settings where parents and preschool children are taught by adult literacy instructors and early childhood teachers.

A less formal program makes the adult's improved reading ability a reading role model for the children. Other informal interventions cover literacy events or information. These planned weekend activities for working or unemployed parents and their children include storytelling, puppet shows, book fairs or the use of computers. Parent self-help books on literacy and child-rearing offer tips on beginning family literacy experiences during the first year of a child's life.

A business issue just beginning to be addressed is the role of family literacy in the workplace. Nearly half of all mothers with children under age six now work outside the home. By the year 2000, 80 percent of American women will be employed. Two-thirds of the new entrants into the work force in the decade of the 1990s will be women. Because mothers are their children's first teachers, on-site child-care programs that incorporate parent-child learning activities will become a reality.

In 1989 IBM began tutoring adults in basic skill areas at its downtown Chicago corporate headquarters using volunteer IBM employees. Plans are now under way to link this basic skills training to an early childhood program. Other Chicago corporations have expressed an interest in establishing this family literacy program model.

During 1990, the National Center for Family Literacy in Louisville, Kentucky, began informational seminars and training sessions for family literacy providers. These programs for administrators and teachers offer training in planning, instructing and leading parent groups.

Fathers can also find themselves in the classroom. "Learning to Live through Literacy" is a program started by Bonnie Gordon, of the Milwaukee Family Court Commission and the University of Wisconsin-Milwaukee. Unwed fathers are ordered into literacy training programs after determining that their reading and writing skills are too poor to enable them to get and hold decent jobs. A clear correlation exists between low literacy and unwed fatherhood. Men ages 18 and 19 with weak reading, writing and job skills are three times as likely as those with average skills to have children out of wedlock. In 1986, 23 percent of all live births were out of wedlock. The Milwaukee program has as its goal assisting these fathers to become employable and capable of paying child support. Welfare-reform laws in many states permit a judge to order job or skill training to help unwed fathers make their support payments. There is no reason why "family literacy programs" cannot include fathers as well as mothers.

To support family literacy programs, the U.S. Congress created the Even Start Program in 1988. This program will provide some $50 million a year for parent-child literacy between 1988 and 1993. Combining literacy training and a day-care component makes good economic sense for retaining employees. If corporations want women to stay, Adduci (1989) believes, "they must be aware of women's family responsibilities." HR departments need to design family-friendly benefits to meet the diverse needs of a new work force. If women are not forced to choose between family obligations and economic necessity, more employees will be better able to meet company goals and satisfy their own personal needs as well.[6]

Work Force Education programs will help women best, according to Lori Strumpf, president of the nonprofit Center for Remediation Design, if they adopt a family literacy policy. "In training single mothers, services must be integrated into a program which has education and employment at its core, and must include child care services, optimally on-site, but certainly within the community, and training in parenting."[7]

FOREIGN-LANGUAGE LITERACY FOR BUSINESS AND GLOBAL COMPETITION

As we noted earlier, corporate Work Force Education in foreign languages is already a reality in American business. Our research points to an acceleration of this trend as Europe and Asia organize strong regional trade blocs. The European Community (EC) has established as an important goal multilanguage corporate training programs. Many foreign business leaders predict that English will become even more necessary as a common denominator among European and Asian businesspeople. However, foreign executives also see a need for different cultures to develop a better understanding of each other, including a familiarity with other languages.

American executives have never been well trained in foreign languages. Most U.S. international businesses hire foreign managers to circumvent the issue. This is now rapidly changing. To ensure broader and deeper market penetration, American businesses will establish more operations abroad and establish foreign business culture and foreign-language education programs. There is little choice. The United States is already falling behind. According to the General Agreement on Tariffs and Trade, a new unified Germany overtook the United States as the world's leading exporter in 1990. The value of German merchandise exports was $421 billion, compared with $394 billion for America.

Language literacy will assume an international character with increased instruction in Japanese, Chinese, Russian, French, German, Spanish, Portuguese, Italian, Greek and Arabic. The specific corporate service or product will act as a determinant of foreign language needs. Vocabulary, grammar, syntax and industry idioms will become increasingly relevant to the negotiation of a contract, the design of equipment specifications or the cultural considerations of a foreign business partner.

Who will need to become literate in a foreign language? In the past, only top executives have been given consideration. This has begun to change. The farther down the rank hierarchy, the more important for the employee to know the local language. Executives in management, marketing, engineering, human resources and international relations all have distinct foreign language needs. Even internal business communications will require these skills between headquarters and subsidiaries abroad. This is particularly true if the American company is foreign-owned. Rapid, accurate responses in the appropriate foreign language to telexes, letters, faxes and telephone communication are important problem-solving tools or effective mediums for negotiations.

As American companies become more global, service industries supporting banking, accounting and consulting will become more internationally oriented. However, ASTD reported in 1990 that 70 percent of American executives sent overseas were given no advanced training or preparation. Training for staff who are residents in the United States but who are engaged in international business is probably even less prevalent. We are relatively illiterate in international affairs because we do not commit the resources to be otherwise. Foreign languages, national business cultures and international business experience will become crucial to the leaders and workers of American companies for success in the twenty-first century.[8]

EDUCATION OF THE FOREIGN WORKER

By the year 2000, 1.5 billion people will speak English around the globe. However, new waves of recent immigrants do not put it in that light. Few speak English; many are not literate even in their own native tongue.

The teaching of English as a Second Language (ESL) is becoming more prevalent throughout both service and industrial sectors of American business. Foreign business executives on a "tour of duty" with an American partner arrive in the United States with varying degrees of English literacy. Writing and reading abilities may be far stronger than their verbal communication skills. Standard "American English" and the colloquial expressions of our culture defeat even the well-prepared foreign executive. Dialect is another problem that results in strained relations with fellow workers. A lack of understanding of "American business culture" often adds to language confusion.

The increasing numbers of foreign workers throughout the service sector and manufacturing will raise issues of quality, productivity, safety and customer service. This is particularly true in the entry-level labor market, which has been depleted by the "baby-bust." ESL will become an increasing dimension of Work Force Education well into the twenty-first century.[9]

JOINT ACTION FOR WORK FORCE EDUCATION

Twenty-five to eighty million American workers must upgrade their basic skills by 2001. *Training America: Learning to Work for the 21st Century*, a report by the American Society for Training and Development, characterizes this work force as ill-equipped to do business. "The United States will lose the battle for international markets in the next century unless employers, educators and government officials act together now to bolster America's ability to learn." The groundbreaking *A Nation at Risk*, issued by the U.S. Department of Education in 1983, concurred when it stated, "Our once unchallenged preeminence in commerce, industry, science and technological innovation is being overtaken by competitors throughout the world."[10]

Our research clearly shows that education and training provide the single greatest mechanism to upgrade industry. Improvement in general public education is an essential economic, not just a social policy priority.

One hundred years ago, as America approached the twentieth century, business and union leaders embarked on the task of introducing sweeping educational reforms. What motivated them was the realization that America could not compete with a rapidly industrializing Europe unless the average worker was literate and had vocational skills.

Tremendous opposition to mandatory public education was overcome through a working partnership among progressive educators, union apprenticeship/vocational training programs and business leaders. It was not an accident of history that universal tax-supported education was mandated throughout America between 1890 and 1920. Advances in the factory and office required all workers to possess skills that had not been needed in an earlier age. Machine-driven assembly lines, typewriters, precision tools and dies, uses of electricity, structural skyscrapers and the modern business letter were only a few aspects of this revolutionary "new technology" and modernization of the early twentieth century. A realistic partnership between business and labor set a political agenda that enacted into law the first American educational revolution.

What are today taken for granted as the attributes of public education were the components of this revolution: vocational high schools and trade schools, mandatory attendance until the age of 16, a 180-day school year, expanded state financial support of local public school districts and a demand for better qualified teachers.

Since that time, American business has mainly been satisfied with a public school system that met its basic labor needs. Overall, American education reached more people and offered them the opportunity of education at a level never before equaled in history. Illiteracy fell from 20 percent in 1870 to only 2 percent by 1990. Even if the level of functional literacy (about the fourth-grade level) remained unchanged at 20 percent for the same time period, American business had sufficient "standardized labor jobs" to profitably employ workers who were only minimally educated.

Since 1975, the business environment has undergone rapid redevelopment characterized by personal computers in the office, robotics, computer-driven assembly lines, global competitiveness, new quality concerns and an aging and shrinking work force. Almost unexpectedly to some in business, the American worker has become ill-educated, inept, functionally illiterate and incapable of operating in either the factory or office of the future. Have current technology and the demands of the marketplace outpaced the schoolhouse's ability to educate our children?

A renewed sense of corporate responsibility by business leadership needs to begin a second American educational revolution. The twenty-first century demands a far different school environment from that created 100 years ago.

Time and again, foreigners coming to America have portrayed our national diversity as a great strength or a colossal weakness. America's schools are the most diverse in the world. Current trends in educational reform point to the need for even greater experimentation. Our schooling process preserves a unique American heritage, a belief in the promise of the future, a better tomorrow. This our schools have always offered. They need to do it again. Corporate responsibility necessitates accelerating the educational reform process. Kaestle (1990) believes that school reform will never achieve universal literacy, effective character education or an adequate number of technically prepared entry-level workers. Schools are rather "inert institutions." They have had limited money and time to devote to societal changes.

However, we are cautiously optimistic. The Brookings Institution, in its 1990 study of American School reform, reminds us that the first great wave of American school reform was achieved during the Progressive political era (1890–1914), which was characterized by Theodore Roosevelt, "trust-busting" and the passage of the Pure Food and Drug Act. The Progressives succeeded because they had widespread national public support and the resources of powerful social groups mobilized for change.

Once again, many diverse groups in America are demanding basic school reform. Here is a potential scenario of how general school reform may unfold:

- *Stage One (1983): A Nation at Risk* begins a period of criticism and dissatisfaction over schooling.
- *Stage Two (1985–88):* The Carnegie Commission and others issue reforms centered on more of the same, reforms that only tinker with the system: spend more money, reform curriculum, change teacher training, establish local school councils, etc.
- *Stage Three (1989–90):* Individual states, cities or regions initiate radically different educational structures that depart from past contemporary practices: Min-

nesota's Choice Program, Wisconsin's Voucher System for Milwaukee's inner-city minorities, Chicago's "Corporate Community School," etc.

- *Stage Four (1991–95):* Business leaders and revisionist educators research and apply selected new educational models and publish their successful findings. Public awareness and support increase for adopting broad systemic change.

- *Stage Five (1995–2000?):* Politicians, businesses, unions and educators begin backing new education models "popular" with local communities. New laws are passed establishing significant school reforms.

- *Stage Six (2000–2010?):* Professional educators begin supporting selective new reform models.

- *Stage Seven (2010–20?):* Local, significantly changed school programs are enacted across the entire United States.

Must educational reform for a twenty-first-century America take this much time? The Brookings Institution offers us the following hope:

Bold executive leadership and broad popular support, especially if combined with the concentrated power of a unified business community—which, in effect, might reassume the historical role it played during the Progressive era as the political vanguards of reform—could succeed in overturning the established order and creating a new system of public education.[11]

We must also realize that general national educational reform will not happen overnight and that, even when it is accomplished, the public schools alone will be insufficient to ensure industrial competitiveness. Of equal importance is quickly establishing corporate policy to flexibly link the educational system to business. As James K. Baker, chairman of the U.S. Chamber of Commerce and chairman and CEO of Arvin Industries, reminds us, "Education is our business." He cites a national Roper poll that three out of four Americans expect business to take the lead, "to examine community school systems and recommend actions to correct the problem." Corporate management must include Work Force Education in the training and development environment. The realization of these twin objectives, general educational reform in the long term and Work Force Education in the short term, will help America regain a competitive advantage for every business sector.[12]

We are now engaged in the beginning of a global economic race. America's future and the history of the twenty-first century will be largely determined by the outcome. The United States is still better equipped than any other nation to win the race. First, however, all Americans must recognize the importance of the task. We must ponder its magnitude and then resolve to accomplish it. Work Force Education will support economic expansion, further economic diversification and allow America to once again regain its lead among the global industrial nations.

The time for action is now. The need is immediate. Work Force Education is the solution.

NOTES

1. "Business Facts." *Chicago Tribune*, 26 April 1990, Sec. 3, 1.

2. Michael E. Porter, *The Competitive Advantage of Nations* (New York: Free Press, 1990), 627–28; Irwin L. Goldstein and Patrice Gilliam, "Training System Issues in the Year 2000," *American Psychologist* 45, no. 2 (February 1990): 134–43; "NAB President Says Local Workforce Quality Will Dictate Future Plant SIte Decisions," *Report on Literacy Programs*, 20 September 1990, 146.

3. Hans A. Schieser, "Educating America's Labor Force to Meet a Global Competition," *Training Today*, February 1987, 8–9; Harry Wray, "Educational Differences: Are Japanese Schools Better Than American Schools?" *Speaking of Japan*, September 1989, 13–19; Constanza Mostana, "Pilsen-Area Program Offers Shot at Success," *Chicago Tribune*, 15 May 1990, Sec. 2, 1, 6; idem., *Policies for Transition: Transition of Young People from Education to Working and Adult Life* (Brussels: IFAPLAN—Commission of the European Community, 1984); idem., *Education for Enterprise: Transition of Young People from Education to Working and Adult Life* (Brussels: IFAPLAN—Commission of the European Community, 1986); Anthony R. Sarmiento and Ann Kay, *Worker-Centered Learning: A Union Guide to Workplace Literacy*. (Washington, D.C.: AFL-CIO Human Resources Development Institute, 1990).

4. Carol Kleiman, "Apprenticeships Get New Lease on Life in Service Jobs," *Chicago Tribune*, 3 February 1991, Sec. 8.

5. Larry Rosenstock, "The Walls Come Down: The Overdue Reunification of Vocational and Academic Education," *Phi Delta Kappan* 76, no. 6 (February 1991): 434–36; Kenneth Gray, "Vocational Education in High School: A Modern Phoenix?" *Phi Delta Kappan* 76, no. 6 (February 1991): 437–49.

6. "Literacy Begins at Home," *Business Council for Effective Literacy* 19 (April 1989): 1, 4–7; Merrill Goozner, "Literacy Quest Brings Together Cabrini and IBM," *Chicago Tribune*, 3 October 1988, Sec. 1; Steven B. Silvern and Linda B. Silvern, *Beginning Literacy and Your Child* (Newark: International Reading Association, 1989); "National Center for Family Literacy Offers Seminars, Starts Computer Effort," *Report on Literacy Programs* 2 (3 May 1990): 69; James L. Ketelsen, "Managing the Changing Workforce," *Chicago Tribune*, 20 October 1990, Sec. 1, 13; Carol Kleiman, "Child Care a Key Cause of Women Leaving Jobs," *Chicago Tribune*, 14 January 1991, Sec. 4, 3.

7. *Literacy and the Marketplace: Improving the Literacy of Low-Income Single Women* (New York: Rockefeller Foundation, 1989).

8. Carol S. Fixman, *The Foreign Language Needs of U.S.-Based Corporations* (Washington, D.C.: National Foreign Language Center at Johns Hopkins University, 1989); Michele N. K. Collison, "Fascination with Business and the Orient Fuels Enrollment in Asian Languages," *Chronicle of Higher Education*, 17 February 1988, A35; Glynn Mapes, "Polyglot Students Are Weaned Early off Mother Tongue: EC Schools Teach Britons, French, Germans, Dutch to Be Future Europeans," *Wall Street Journal*, 6 March 1990; "Germany Tops U.S. in Exports," *Chi-*

cago Tribune, 26 March 1991, Sec. 3, 1; "Why Aren't American Firms Training for Global Participation?" *Management Development Report (ASTD)*, Summer 1990, 1.

9. Joseph Oberle, "Teaching English as a Second Language," *Training*, April 1990, 61–67; Marja Mills, "Workers Learn to Talk Shop—in Two Languages." *Chicago Tribune*, 5 June 1989, Sec. 4, 3.

10. *Training America: Learning to Work for the 21st Century* (Washington, D.C.: American Society for Training and Development, 1989); *A Nation at Risk: The Imperative for Education Reform* (Washington, D.C.: U.S. Department of Education, 1983), 5.

11. Anne Lowrey Bailey and Kristin A. Goss, "Companies Give More to Schools, Insist on Accountability Tests," *Chronicle of Philanthropy*, 12 December 1989; David Kearns, "Improving the Work Force: Competitiveness Begins at School," *New York Times*, 17 December 1989; Carl F. Kaestle, "The Public Schools and the Public Mood," *America Heritage*, February 1990, 20–26; John E. Chubb and Terry M. Moe, *Politics, Markets, and America's Schools* (Washington, D.C.: Brookings Institution, 1990), 226–27.

12. Porter, *Competitive Advantage*, 628; James K. Baker, "Future Technology and U.S. Competitiveness" (Address to the City Club of Chicago, 26 March 1991).

11

A Game Plan for Work Force Education

Business groups, Washington think tanks, national unions, government agencies and local community coalitions have issued a blizzard of national reports on Work Force Education. We know that America faces a serious socioeconomic disaster. This book and others offer a menu of practical training and educational solutions.

How low must the U.S. economy sink before business leaders will overcome the corporate culture that denies training to hourly workers, before elected officials will forget their own parochial political interests and before educators will stop protecting their outdated bureaucracy from change? We know that America needs a second education revolution similar to that of 1890–1914, which established our present school system and underpinned U.S. economic growth during the twentieth century. But "revolutions" take time. The critical question for American Work Force Education remains, "What can be done now?"

Work Force Education programs offer a $300-billion incentive for America's GNP. HR managers will determine their companies' share in this profit enhancement largely from better employee productivity and a sharper competitive edge. Here is your game plan for a successful Work Force Education program.

STEP ONE: ESTABLISH COMPANY TASK FORCE

By assembling a team of managers across the organization, you will clearly identify operational problems linked to Work Force Education. These become revenue loss issues as you show how they retard achievement of current goals and objectives of the company. A Work Force Education program becomes productivity/quality/competitiveness solutions that translate into an improved bottom line and better long-term profits. For each business, this formula will differ. Some may see immediate financial results. For many American businesses during the next decade, Work Force Education will be the critical factor that will determine if they remain viable against tough international competition. The alternatives for many will be corporate bankruptcy or foreign ownership. Both have already begun accelerating throughout the U.S. economy.

STEP TWO: MULTILEVEL PROGRAMS

Incorporating Work Force Education into your company's overall training and development program follows a well-established training and development concept. Multilevel programs are necessary to train and develop managers and workers. At the most basic level, a Work Force Education program will use small-group tutorials to diagnose adult learning problems and teach reading, math or ESL. One-to-one tutoring will be used selectively for maximum individual learning acceleration beyond the basics.

Traditional large-group classroom instruction will follow for those at the seventh-grade level of skill applications and without specific learning disabilities. CBT and interactive videodiscs will be used to supplement the classroom teacher.

Support staff training will use these same training modes. Office skills will be the focus: grammar training, typing, shorthand and computer/software literacy.

Management development and Continuing Professional Education will use both the 1:1 and small-group tutorial format for writing skills, foreign languages and ESL. The 1:1 option will be particularly helpful to shorten a manager's preparation for a key assignment or a promotion. Leadership abilities can be enhanced with interpersonal skill training, speed-reading, public speaking or clearer speech articulation.

STEP THREE: MONITORING RESULTS

Program usefulness must rest on multiple measurements of educational results and their impact on business operations. A means can be found to use standardized pre/posttesting without violating employee confidentiality or work rules. Managers and supervisors will be surveyed on employee work changes before, during and after enrollment in the Work Force Education program.

Participants will be encouraged to write preprogram goals and record postprogram personal achievements that they see and experience. Each company will be able to determine specific industrial production/service measures that reflect, without overstatement, the Work Force Education difference in operating divisions.

STEP FOUR: MAKING PROGRAM MODIFICATIONS

A train-the-trainer Work Force Education program can become part of your overall training strategy. Once you have established the credibility of these programs, train-the-trainer—using a small-group mastery learning approach—will better enable you to reach larger numbers of employees. Cross-training, using volunteer peer tutors, may also help support other instructional classes. In both instances, subject-area experts in reading, math, writing or L.D. areas must be used to train, monitor, retrain and sometimes offer training interventions for either company trainers or volunteer trainers.

Local community colleges should be encouraged to offer on-site traditional classroom instruction for adults who have no learning disabilities and who are at or above the seventh-grade level of educational skills. Colleges will also be able to teach GED classes for adults to complete their high school education. If your locale is without a community college, recruit local part-time teachers with appropriate educational expertise and adult-teaching experience. They can then establish these in-house classes.

New programs may be added for Work Force Education as your company's market and job force evolve. Assembling a new program means recruiting part-time or full-time educational specialists who can work with your training staff in design and/or instructional activities. We have shown you how to develop a wide variety of program topics, for large groups down to solo training applications.

STEP FIVE: RECRUITING "LEARNING EXPERTS"

Finding this new breed of Work Force Education tutor/trainers may seem like a daunting prospect. However, if you check the background of many corporate trainers, you will be surprised how many have already migrated from the ranks of schoolteachers.

This does not mean that every prospective teacher will be successful in your Work Force Education program. Successful teachers/trainers have proven knowledge of the content and instruction methods unique to the course topic. They can demonstrate professional mastery through successful undergraduate and graduate courses, state teaching certificates and/or years of teaching experience similar to your in-house training requirements. Teachers must also have experience with adult learners. To help understand these areas, educational terminology, acronyms, "trade jargon," and the like, read one or more of the educational psychology books listed in Chapter 3. Of if you prefer, hire an educational consultant to advise on recruitment activities.

If you have not already noticed, we have made a clear distinction between "tutors" and "teachers." The educators you hire have generally been prepared to teach large groups, not tutor on a 1:1 or 1:5 basis. Teachers can be trained to become tutors by your training department, or you can recruit only tutor-educators for your program.

In either instance, you will require the help of a trainer/educator to ultimately direct these classes, both as a trainer and an administrator. The size of your need will dictate finding a part-time/full-time employee or using an independent consultant. The central issue will be locating a professional with a broad training and educational background and knowledge of learning theory, course design, assessment and train-the-trainer. Many professionals from school systems have acquired these experiences in adult education. They possess a master's degree or doctorate in educational psychology, reading, learning disabilities or ESL. These professionals will be increasingly available to businesses as the decade of the 1990s advances. They come to you interested in establishing the innovative adult programs resisted by the educational establishment.

PREPARING FOR THE YEAR 2000

The next move is yours! Human resources and training and development are the natural home of Work Force Education. The decade of the 1990s for American business has become a productivity marathon. The prime contestant, human resources, must win senior management's recognition of its capacity to fully develop the presently ill-prepared work force through new, powerful in-house educational programs. At present, the favored adversary, onrushing high technology, already has senior management's budgetary support. Business high tech will relentlessly demand ever-higher educational attainments by almost all workers and managers.

We have presented an HR game plan to enter and win the twenty-first-century international productivity marathon. The American economic advantage can be refueled through Work Force Education programs. Developing individuals to their maximum capacity has long been part of our American heritage. It now also makes good business sense. Work Force Education is an essential component for a broad competitive revival throughout America. If it is accomplished, we foresee the unleashing of stronger human resources that will reenergize America's technology and quality service at home and around the world.

Appendix 1

Guidelines for Education Software Selection

Comprehensive selection criteria must be applied before making an informal selection from the proliferating Work Force Education software. The following checklist is from the Adult Literacy and Technology Project, funded by the Gannett Foundation (1987–90). It is now forming into a professional organization that will be coordinated by Dr. Terilyn Turner, Adult Literacy Special Needs, St. Paul Public Schools, 265 Metro Square Building, St. Paul, MN, 55101. (612)-293-5220. It represents one of the most thorough and exact "yardsticks" available, one that publishers are already following as new software is introduced to the market. The Project also offers annual software-evaluation guides and a quarterly newsletter.

I. Educational Content
   A. Educational Content
      1. All content is factually accurate
      2. All punctuation, spelling and grammar is correct, except when instructional strategies require the presentation of incorrect material
      3. Responses to learners are appropriate, positive and nonjudgmental
      4. The skill levels (reading, typing, etc.) required to operate the program are commensurate with the skill levels being taught or practiced
      5. Instructions are clear, concise and complete
      6. The objectives of the instruction are explicitly stated or read to the learner
   B. Technical Features
      1. The intended users can easily and independently operate the program
      2. The program is reliable in normal use
      3. The software is free from programming errors and runs efficiently with minimum delay time
      4. The program operates as specified in the instructions

5. The screens are well formatted with appropriate use of color and graphics
6. All sound is under the control of the teacher or the learner except when the sound is an essential element of the instructional strategy
7. The pace of the program can be controlled by the teacher or the learner unless pacing is an essential element of the instructional strategy
8. Expected learner responses for program operation are consistent throughout
9. Unanticipated learner input does not disrupt program operation
10. Maps, graphs and other illustrations are clear and simple to interpret
  C. Support Materials
1. All punctuation, grammar and spelling are correct
2. Documentation includes at least the following elements:
   (a) Description of the hardware requirements
   (b) Procedures for installing software
   (c) Instructions for use
II. Desirable Attributes
  A. Educational Content
1. The program contains multiple levels of difficulty, which may be selected by the learner or the teacher
2. Motivational devices are appropriate to the content and skill levels being taught or practiced
3. The interest level and the vocabulary are well suited to the intended learners
4. The program provides useful responses to learner errors
5. The learner remains in control of the program and is actively involved in the learning process
6. The instructional design is based on appropriate learning strategies
7. When appropriate, the program branches to harder or easier content based on learner responses
8. Any game format utilized for instruction, reinforcement or motivation is appropriate and enhances the overall instructional design
9. Where simulations are used, the models and data are valid and not oversimplified
10. The program represents an effective use of the computer
  B. Technical Features
1. Instructional content can be adapted to include individualized word lists, problem sets, etc.
2. Program operation requires minimal teacher intervention
3. Content is presented in random sequence, when appropriate
4. A menu allows learners to directly access specific parts of the program
5. Learners can correct responses before they are accepted by the program
6. Learners can access operating instructions or HELP screens from any part of the program
7. Learners can bypass instructions at will
8. Learners can exit from any point in the program through an established escape sequence

9. Colors are selected for maximum discrimination when used on non-color screens
10. If record-keeping modules are included, they are protected from unauthorized access
11. If there is a record-keeping component, a minimum of 40 students can be accommodated

C. Support Materials
   1. Documentation includes at least the following items for teacher and student use:
     (a) Content descriptions in terms of specific objectives or skills to be acquired or practiced
     (b) Prerequisite learner skills
     (c) Expected time needed for successful execution of the program
     (d) Expected learner outcomes
     (e) Suggestions for integrating the program into the curriculum
     (f) Suggestions for use in various instructional settings
     (g) Suggested classroom activities
     (h) Lists of any books, equipment or other materials required for use with the program
     (i) Pictures of representative program screens
     (j) Sample program runs

III. Indicators of Excellence

A. Educational Content
   1. The program utilizes innovative approaches and encourages creativity on the part of the learner
   2. The learner is encouraged to use higher-order thinking skills such as application, analysis, synthesis and evaluation, where appropriate
   3. Alternative methods of presenting the content are used and are based on learner response
   4. The program provides for open-ended, natural-language responses
   5. The program presents material not easily provided by other methods or engages the learner in experiences not readily duplicated in the real world
   6. The program presents ideas and theories in a manner that makes them accessible to learners at earlier grades than suggested by the traditional curriculum

B. Technical Features
   1. The program provides for various learning modalities—auditory, kinesthetic, visual—where appropriate
   2. The program uses other technologies, such as speech synthesis, videotape, videodisc or audiocassette, when appropriate, to enhance the learning experience
   3. The program makes use of alternative input devices—voice, light, pen, mouse, graphics tablet, etc.—when appropriate
   4. The learner can exit the program from any point and return directly to that point from the beginning of the program, with previous work, or record of progress, intact
   5. The learner can go back through the program on demand to review responses and content

6. The program can print appropriate instructional segments, performance records, learner-created materials, etc.

C. Support Material

1. Teacher and student materials should

   (a) Describe the specific learning theories employed in the instructional design
   (b) Suggest a broad range of classroom applications
   (c) Contain masters for transparencies and learner materials
   (d) Include well-designed pre- and posttests, as appropriate
   (e) Correlate the material to standard textbook series, curriculum frameworks and standards, as appropriate
   (f) Describe learner outcome obtained from field testing in a variety of settings
   (g) Identify previous work and background qualifications of the author(s)

IV. Specific Considerations in Selecting Software for Disabled and Reluctant Readers

A. The following are specific features to be considered when selecting software for learning-disabled readers. Look for software or programs that

   1. Enable educational specialists to develop specific hardware peripheral devices that will enable students to communicate
   2. Allow students to work independently
   3. Have future vocational applications
   4. Teach activities of daily living skills or real-life situations, such as checkbook accounting, spreadsheet budgeting, word processing and running a business
   5. Stress basic skills in math, reading, spelling, social studies and general information
   6. Allow students to learn by manipulating real objects, such as coins, clocks and so on
   7. Can be run with minimal movements, such as keyboard strokes or paddles
   8. Utilize voice synthesizers and read aloud the information that is presented on the screen
   9. Incorporate voice and sound and can utilize headphones
   10. Use high-resolution graphics and large-sized print
   11. Can be used as rewards—game-type programs such as checkers, board games, memory span, etc., which students can eventually use in their leisure time

B. High-interest software is the key to getting reluctant readers to want to read and should contain the following qualities for motivation:

   1. Stimulating content to capture their imagination and interests
   2. A quick pace to sustain their attention
   3. Appropriate use of color, graphics and animation to provide visual stimulation

Appendix 2

Adult Software
Publishers/Distributors

The following "Index of Workplace and Adult Basic Skills Software" was prepared by Eunice N. Askov and the Institute for the Study of Adult Literacy at Pennsylvania State University (204 Calder Way, Suite 209, University Park, PA 16801, 814-863-3777. We thank the authors for their reprint permission.

In this matrix, software titles are listed in the far-left column. The next column indicates whether the program can be customized (i.e., allows insertion of special vocabulary by the teacher) or has a mini-authoring system (i.e., permits teachers to prepare their own lesson).

The Assessment and Skills column may be useful in several ways. First, the software may pertain to basic literacy or informational content. Second, the program may offer basic skills taught in a job context. Finally, specific job-related skills refer not to basic skill material but to metal types for steelworkers or to housekeeping supplies for maids, etc.

The numbers in the far-right column correspond to the numbers listed by the software publishers on the following page. The Pennsylvania State Literacy Institute does not endorse any of these products but assembled the matrix for adult literacy practititioners to receive the best return on their investment.

1. AAVIM
   The National Institute for
     Instructional Materials
   120 Driftmier Engineering Ctr.
   Athens GA 30602
   404-542-2586

2. Academic Therapy Publications
   20 Commercial Blvd.
   Novato CA 94949-6191
   800-422-7249

3. Aquarius International
   PO Box 128
   Indian Rocks Beach FL
     34635-0128
   800-338-2644

4. BLS, Inc.
   2503 Fairlee Rd.
   Wilmington DE 19810
   800-545-7766

5. Career Aids
   20417 Nordhoff St.
   Dept. Z9876
   Chatsworth CA 91311
   818-341-2535

6. Conduit
   The University of Iowa
   Oakdale Campus
   Iowa City IA 52242
   319-335-4100

7. Conover
   PO Box 155
   Omro WI 54963
   414-685-5707

8. Continental Press
   520 East Bainbridge St.
   Elizabethtown PA 17022
   800-233-0759

9. Davidson & Associates, Inc.
   3135 Kashiwa St.
   Torrance CA 90505
   800-556-6141

10. Design Ware
    185 Berry St.
    San Francisco CA 94107
    800-572-7767

11. Educational Activities, Inc.
    PO Box 392
    Freeport NY 11520
    800-645-3739

12. Educational Technologies, Inc.
    1007 Whitehead Rd. Ext.
    Trenton NJ 08638
    609-882-2668

13. Educulture, Inc.
    1 Cycare Plaza
    Suite 805
    Dubuque IA 52001-9990
    800-553-4858

14. EMC Publishing
    Changing Times Education
      Serv.
    300 York Ave.
    St. Paul MN 55101
    800-328-1452

15. Focus Media, Inc.
    839 Stewart Ave.
    PO Box 865
    Garden City NY 11530
    800-645-8989

16. Hartley's Courseware, Inc.
    Box 419
    Dimondale MI 48821
    800-247-1380

17. Houghton Mifflin
    PO Box 683
    Hanover NH 03755
    603-448-3838

18. Ideal Learning, Inc.
    5005 Royal Lane
    Suite 130
    Irving TX 75063
    214-929-4201 (TX)
    612-445-2690 (MN)

19. Institute for the Study of
      Adult Literacy
    Penn State University
    College of Education
    204 Calder Way. Suite 209
    State College PA 16801
    814-863-3777

20. Island Software
    Box 300
    Lake Grove NY 11755
    516-585-3755

21. Learning Unlimited Corp.
    6512 Baum Dr., No. 11
    Knoxville TN 37919
    800-251-4717

22. Marshmedia
    PO Box 8082
    Shawnee Mission KS 66208
    816-523-1059

23. MECC
    3490 Lexington Ave. N.
    St. Paul MN 55126
    612-481-3500

24. Micro Power & Light Co.
    12810 Hillcrest Rd.
    Suite 120
    Dallas TX 75230
    214-239-6620

25. Milliken Publishing Co.
    1100 Research Blvd.
    PO Box 21579
    St. Louis MO 63132-0579
    314-991-4220

26. Mindscape, Inc.
    Educational Division
    Dept. D, 3444 Dundee Rd.
    Northbrook IL 60062
    800-221-9884

27. Morning Star
    PO Box 5364
    Madison WI 53705
    800-533-0445

28. Optimum Resource, Inc.
    10 Station Pl.
    Norfolk CT 06058
    800-327-1473

29. Queue, Inc.
    562 Boston Ave.
    Bridgeport CT 06610
    800-232-2224

30. Scholastic, Inc.
    PO Box 7502
    2931 East McCarty St.
    Jefferson City MO 65102
    800-541-5513

31. Softwriters Development Corp.
    4718 Harford Rd.
    Baltimore MD 21214-9968
    800-451-5726

32. South-Western
    5101 Madison Rd.
    Cincinnati OH 45227
    800-543-7007

33. Spin-A-Test Publishing Co.
    3177 Hogarth Dr.
    Sacramento CA 95827
    916-369-2032

34. Sunburst Communications
    39 Washington Ave.
    Pleasantville NY 10570-2898
    800-431-1934

35. Teach Yourself by Computer
      Software, Inc.
    349 W. Commercial St.
    Suite 1000
    E. Rochester NY 14445
    716-381-5450

36. Teacher Support Software
    PO Box 7130
    Gainesville FL 32605-7130
    800-228-2871

37. Ventura Educational Systems
    3440 Brokenhill St.
    Newbury Park CA 91320
    805-499-1407

Index of Workplace & Adult Basic Skills Software

Software	Customize	Mini-authoring systems	Math	Reading/Decoding & Structural Analysis	Reading/Comprehension	Writing/Grammar	Writing/Composing	Vocab./Spell. & Meaning	Problem-solving	Complete B. Skills Prog.	General B. Skills Content	Workplace Basic Skills	Job-Domain Related	Job Search/Career	E.S.L.	Drill & Practice	Tutorial	Simulation	Games & Puzzles	Apple	I.B.M.	Tandy	Commodore	TRS-80	Macintosh	Publisher/Distributor
	Teacher/Tutor Tools		Assessment & Skills								Content					Instruction Method				System Requirements						*
ABS										●	●						●			●	●	●				21
Adult Education - Math			●								●									●	●					4
Adult Education - Reading					●						●									●	●					4
Agricultural Math Tutor			●									●					●			●						1
All About Your Body								●					●							●						15
Angling for Words in Bits & Bytes				△							●					●				●						2
Base										●	□						●			●	●					12
Basic First Aid and Illness													●							●						3
Basic Language Units: Parts of Speech						●					●									●	●	●				8
Basic Grammar Units: Sentences						●					●									●	●	●				8
Basic Math Competency Skill Building			●								●						●			●	●					11

△ Teacher required □ Basic Skills keyed to jobs, but content generic

Index of Workplace & Adult Basic Skills Software

Title	Teacher/Tutor Tools: Customize	Mini-authoring systems	Math	Reading/Decoding & Structural Analysis	Reading/Comprehension	Writing/Grammar	Writing/Composing	Vocab./Spell. & Meaning	Problem-solving	Complete B. Skills Prog.	General B. Skills Content	Workplace Basic Skills	Job-Domain Related	Job Search/Career	E.S.L.	Drill & Practice	Tutorial	Simulation	Games & Puzzles	Apple	I.B.M.	Tandy	Commodore	TRS-80	Macintosh	Publisher/Distributor
Basic Skills in Math			●								●									●						5
Bones and Muscles: A Team to Depend On													●							●						30 22
Career Arithmetic			●									●								●				●		4
Computational Skills Program			●																	●	●					17
Cooking & Baking Series			●		●							●				●	●			●	●					3
Create Lessons	●																			●						16
Create Lessons - Advanced	●																			●						16
Create - Medalists	●																			●	●					16
Crossword Magic	●					●		●			●									●			●			30
Diascriptive Language Arts Development											●						●			●	●	●		●		11
Diascriptive I, II, III Reading					●			●			●									●	●	●	●	●		11

172

Index of Workplace & Adult Basic Skills Software

Software	Teacher/Tutor Tools		Assessment & Skills								Content					Instruction Method				System Requirements						Publisher/ Distributor
	Customize	Mini-authoring systems	Math	Reading/Decoding & Structural Analysis	Reading/Comprehension	Writing/Grammar	Writing/Composing	Vocab./Spell. & Meaning	Problem-solving	Complete B. Skills Prog.	General B. Skills Content	Workplace Basic Skills	Job-Domain Related	Job Search/Career	E.S.L.	Drill & Practice	Tutorial	Simulation	Games & Puzzles	Apple	I.B.M.	Tandy	Commodore	TRS-80	Macintosh	
EA Core Vocabulary Worksheet Generator	●							●			●								●	●						11
ESL Writer	●						●								●					●	●	●				30
Exploring Career Options					●									●						●						29
E-Z Pilot II Authoring System		●																		●						16
Food For Thought													●							●	●					34 29 22
Foreign Language Vocabulary Games	●							●			●				●				●	●	●					29
Game Power for Phonics, Plus				●				●			●				●				●	●	●		●	●		33
Gapper Reading Lab	●				●			●			●									●						13 29
I Love America Series/U.S. Cities			●							●			●			●				●						20
Ideal Learning Curriculum											●									●						18
Improving Your Vocabulary Skills								●			●									●	●					29

Index of Workplace & Adult Basic Skills Software

Software	Publisher/Distributor	Macintosh	TRS-80	Commodore	Tandy	I.B.M.	Apple	Games & Puzzles	Simulation	Tutorial	Drill & Practice	E.S.L.	Job Search/Career	Job-Domain Related	Workplace Basic Skills	General B. Skills Content	Complete B. Skills Prog.	Problem-solving	Vocab/Spell. & Meaning	Writing/Composing	Writing/Grammar	Reading/Comprehension	Reading/Decoding & Structural Analysis	Math	Mini-authoring systems	Customize
Individual Study Center	35										●														●	●
Interpreting Graphs	6						●	●	●					●				●						●		
Introduction to the Business Office	13						●							●												
Keyboard Cadet	5						●							●												
Key Game	36		●	●			●				●					●			●							[•]
Language Arts: The Rules	27						●				●					●			●							●
LEA-1 Functional Lit. Using Whole Language	11		●		●	●	●					●								●						
Learning to Write	13					●	●					●				●					●	●				
Learning Ways to Read Words	13	●				●				●		●							●				●			■
Letter Man	5					●	●							●												
Lucky 7 Spelling Games	13, 29					●	●	●								●			●							●

Legend: ■ Need extra management system · [•] Need extra Utility disk

Index of Workplace & Adult Basic Skills Software

Software	Customize	Mini-authoring systems	Math	Reading/Decoding & Structural Analysis	Reading/Comprehension	Writing/Grammar	Writing/Composing	Vocab./Spell. & Meaning	Problem-solving	Complete B. Skills Prog.	General B. Skills Content	Workplace Basic Skills	Job-Domain Related	Job Search/Career	E.S.L.	Drill & Practice	Tutorial	Simulation	Games & Puzzles	Apple	I.B.M.	Tandy	Commodore	TRS-80	Macintosh	Publisher/Distributor
Lucky 7 Vocabulary Games	●							●			●								●	●	●					13
Make - A - Flash	●							●												●						36
Math Facts			●								●									●						27
Medical Terminology: General Terms												●				●	●			●						13
Micro-Computer Simulations in Business	✷												●			●	●			●	●	●		●		32
M_ss_ng L_nks					●						●								●	✷	●	●	●	●		34
Nursing												●								●	●					3
Penn State Adult Lit. Courseware	▲							●								●			●	●	●					19
Prevocational Math Review			●					●				●				●	●			●	●					1
Print Your Own Bingo Plus	●																			●						16
Print Your Own Calendar	●																			●						16 / 30

▲ Module 3 & 6 only

✷ Only customize Apple software

175

Index of Workplace & Adult Basic Skills Software

Software	Customize	Mini-authoring systems	Math	Reading/Decoding & Structural Analysis	Reading/Comprehension	Writing/Grammar	Writing/Composing	Vocab/Spell. & Meaning	Problem-solving	Complete B. Skills Prog.	General B. Skills Content	Workplace Basic Skills	Job-Domain Related	Job Search/Career	E.S.L.	Drill & Practice	Tutorial	Simulation	Games & Puzzles	Apple	I.B.M.	Tandy	Commodore	TRS-80	Macintosh	Publisher/Distributor
Project Star										●	●									●						16
Read - A - Logo			●					●			●				●					●						36
Retailing Series					●							●								●	●					3
Rov-A-Bot									●				●							●						11
Rules of the Road								●			●	●								●						4
Skills Bank II										●	●									●	●					31
Spelling for Careers in Business								●				●								●						3, 14
Spelling for Careers in Medicine								●				●								●						3, 14
Soft Text: English						●					●									●						8
Soft Text: Math			●								●					●				●						8
Soft Text: Word Study								●			●									●						8

Index of Workplace & Adult Basic Skills Software

Software	Customize	Mini-authoring systems	Math	Reading/Decoding & Structural Analysis	Reading/Comprehension	Writing/Grammar	Writing/Composing	Vocab./Spell. & Meaning	Problem-solving	Complete B. Skills Prog.	General B. Skills Content	Workplace Basic Skills	Job-Domain Related	Job Search/Career	E.S.L.	Drill & Practice	Tutorial	Simulation	Games & Puzzles	Apple	I.B.M.	Tandy	Commodore	TRS-80	Macintosh	Publisher/Distributor
Square Pairs	●							●			●								●	●			●			30
States: Geography Study Unit													●							●						37
Success With Writing							●													●	●					30
Survival Reading Series					●						●									●	●					29
TAS																								●		35
Teacher Option Organizer		●																								23
The Body in Focus		●											●							●	●		●			26
The Body Transparent													●						●	●	●		●			13 10 30
The Human Body													●							●	●	●				11
The Human Body - An Overview													●				●			●			●			30
The Human Pump													●							●						34

Index of Workplace & Adult Basic Skills Software

Title	Publisher/Distributor	Macintosh	TRS-80	Commodore	Tandy	I.B.M.	Apple	Games & Puzzles	Simulation	Tutorial	Drill & Practice	E.S.L.	Job Search/Career	Job-Domain Related	Workplace Basic Skills	General B. Skills Content	Complete B. Skills Prog.	Problem-solving	Vocab/Spell. & Meaning	Writing/Composing	Writing/Grammar	Reading/Comprehension	Reading/Decoding & Structural Analysis	Math	Mini-authoring systems	Customize
		System Requirements						**Instruction Method**				**Content**					**Assessment & Skills**								**Teacher/Tutor Tools**	
The Respiratory System A Puff of Air	30 22						●							●												
The Semantic Mapper	36		●				●					●							●						●	
Tic Tac Spell	30						●	●								●			●							●
Time Master	24						●				●					●								●		
Typing Keys to Computer Ease	2					●	●				●			●												
Vocabulary Builder	13 24						●				●					●										●
Vocabulary Challenge	30						●									●			●							●
Vocabulary For the World of Work	13 29	●				●	●			●		●			●				●							
Vocabulary for the World of Work II	13 29	●				●	●			●		●			●				●							
Vocational Construction Trade	3					●	●								●									●		
Vocational Cosmetology	3					●	●								●							●				

Index of Workplace & Adult Basic Skills Software

Software	Teacher/Tutor Tools: Customize	Mini-authoring systems	Math	Reading/Decoding & Structural Analysis	Reading/Comprehension	Writing/Grammar	Writing/Composing	Vocab./Spell. & Meaning	Problem-solving	Complete B. Skills Prog.	General B. Skills Content	Workplace Basic Skills	Job-Domain Related	Job Search/Career	E.S.L.	Drill & Practice	Tutorial	Simulation	Games & Puzzles	Apple	I.B.M.	Tandy	Commodore	TRS-80	Macintosh	Publisher/Distributor
Vocational Math for Automotive Technicians			●									●				●				●	●					1
Vocational Math for Carpenters			●									●				●				●	●					1
Vo. Math for Construction Materials & Costs			●									●				●				●	●					1
Vocational Math for Welders			●									●				●				●	●					1
Vocational Mechanics			●		●							●								●	●					3
Vocational Metal Trades			●									●								●	●					3
Vocational Welding					●							●								●	●					3
Vocational Survival Words - Carpentry Cluster					●			●				●								●	●					3
Vocational Survival Words - Food Service Cluster					●			●				●								●	●					3
Vocational Survival Words - Mechanics Cluster					●			●				●								●	●					3
What do you do with a broken calculator?			●						●		●										●	●				3-4

179

Index of Workplace & Adult Basic Skills Software

Software	Customize	Mini-authoring systems	Math	Reading/Decoding & Structural Analysis	Reading/Comprehension	Writing/Grammar	Writing/Composing	Vocab/Spell. & Meaning	Problem-solving	Complete B. Skills Prog.	General B. Skills Content	Workplace Basic Skills	Job-Domain Related	Job Search/Career	E.S.L.	Drill & Practice	Tutorial	Simulation	Games & Puzzles	Apple	I.B.M.	Tandy	Commodore	TRS-80	Macintosh	Publisher/Distributor
Word Attack Plus!	●							●			●					●			●	●	●		●			9
Wordfind	●							●											●	●						11
Word Machine	●							●			●								●	●						25
WordMatch	●							●			●					●				●						29
Word Parts - Education				●																●						3 14
Wordplay	●							●			●									●						16
Wordsearch	●							●			●								●	●						16 30
Workplace Literacy System										●		●								●						7
Writing Skills Improvement Program						●					●					●					●	●				28

*Numbers in the Publisher/Distributor column refer to the list of publishers on p. 170

Source: © 1989, Institute for the Study of Adult Literacy, Penn State

Appendix 3

The IIP Literacy Training Program Results of Formative Evaluation Research

INTRODUCTION

Over the past 20 years, an individualized instruction-based tutoring curriculum has been developed and implemented by Imperial Corporate Training and Development, an accredited special-function school. Individualized Instructional Programs (IIP) have served over 3,000 individuals, tutored by a faculty of certified teachers utilizing a specially designed curriculum to facilitate the tutorial process. Program offerings have included college and adult academic and vocational programs of study, including academic basic skills improvement (i.e., basic reading and basic math literacy); social-emotional interventions; strategies to mediate the effects of learning disabilities; job-related skills; English as a Second Language (ESL); and foreign language instruction for overseas assignments.

In April 1988 at the annual meeting of the American Educational Research Association (AERA), preliminary research findings were reported on the basic reading skills literacy program. Both skilled and semiskilled workers were enrolled in the literacy classes in a variety of home- and work-based settings.

Individualized Instructional Programs (IIP) were specifically designed for use by a training/administrative team to bring about rapid, verifiable increases in literacy levels. Associated written methods and reporting materials for each IIP enabled the trainers to follow thoughtful, sequential and systematic content presentation, as well as skills practice, with individuals or small groups of no more than five students. Particular attention was given to the inclusion of strategies to increase students' own awareness of their learning, to provide for administrative quality control and to offer formative feedback to company management during the training process.

The IIP curriculum was designed and constantly evaluated to avoid, as much as possible, the duplication of many of the pitfalls of traditional classroom instruction. Many illiterate adults dropped out of school due to personal underachievement and frustration in the classroom. The IIP individual and/or small-group training format takes into account individual differences among the participants and is easily adapted to many different student learning problems.

To facilitate better individualized tutoring across types of subjects, a number of specially crafted curriculum "scripts" were designed to teach student competencies at the introductory, maintenance and/or mastery levels. Over 300 learning descriptors were systematically developed and used to document academic achievement, social-emotional outcomes and selected job-related skills. These learning descriptors were assessed through tutor observations, criterion- and norm-referenced achievement tests and learning/personality profiles.

Assessment results indicated differences in tutoring outcomes across time blocks (1–10 hours, 10–20 hours, 20–30 hours). Program developers initially assumed the differences were due to differences among tutors in allotting time to (1) assess how the tutee approached the learning situation, (2) discover what specific sequential subject-matter skills the tutee lacked, (3) reorganize tutee achievement/study habits, and (4) assess and improve tutee workplace motivators that supported learning.

IIP program developers decided to begin a field-based research project to address two questions. First, what specific effects does the tutoring program have on students' outcome measures of achievement and/or social-emotional functioning? And second, does the number of hours a student is tutored in the program relate significantly to achievement and job performance? Initial research was not designed within the context of an experimental design. Rather, a series of small pilot studies was conducted in an attempt to determine what was happening across naturally occurring time blocks of 10 to 45 hours of tutoring and direct, ongoing research design. The results of these pilot studies are reported here.

PILOT I FINDINGS

A sample of 19 students was selected from existing school records. Students had received tutoring in reading on an average of two hours per week and had been pre- and posttested on alternate forms of the Scott, Foresman Achievement Test in Reading. The test is reported to have a .95 reliability (KR-20). The 90 test items measure vocabulary and comprehension skills, reflected in ability to understand word and phrase, sentence and paragraph meaning.

Either Form A or B was administered by the tutor as a pretest; the alternative form was then administered by the tutor as a posttest. A one-way analysis of variance was applied to the posttest scores on the reading achievement test. The independent variable was the number of hours of tutoring completed by tutees. Three groups were created to follow the natural time blocks in the program: 10–19 hours; 20–29 hours; and 30–45 hours. The analysis of variance (using the Student-Neuman-Keuls procedure to compare group means) indicated that no pair of group means differed significantly ($p = .532$). However, the means and standard deviations for pretest performance by group and posttest performance by group showed substantial gains at 20–29 hours of tutoring. (See Table A.1.)

Out of curiosity, we performed a multiple regression analysis to discover what might be happening between Group 2 and Group 3 effects. The regression results are reported in Table A.2.

Table A.1
Means and Standard Deviation Pilot Data I

	Pretest		Posttest	
	Mean	*S.D.*	*Mean*	*S.D.*
Group 1 (10–19 hours)	45.1	12.7	55.1	17.2
Group 2 (20–29 hours)	59.0	11.4	64.0	11.6
Group 3 (30–45 hours)	68.2	18.4	62.6	16.0

N = 19

Table A.2
Regression Analysis Pilot Data I

Variable	Multiple R	R2	F	Sig F
Groups + pretest	.366	.134	.775	.526
Groups alone	.275	.076	.657	.532
Pretest alone	.341	.116	2.23	.153

Although the overall significance still suggested that the number of hours of tutoring was not having a significant effect on posttest performance, the effect of the pretest as a predictor of posttest performance suggested looking further at the significance of the variables within the regression formula.

The significance of the variables within the regression formula (Beta weights) showed consistently that Group 3 (30–45 hours) influenced the variance in the presence of the pretest (t = .048). When the effects of the pretest were removed, Group 3 was found to be significant (t = .00). However, when the pretest was entered into the regression formula by itself, the pretest also was found to be significant (t = .003).

These pilot data findings raised several concerns. First, the sample size was small. Second, it was possible that the pretest was working as a covariate. The literacy program developers decided to improve their pretest/posttest procedures, continue collecting data but more systematically and increase the sample size.

PILOT II FINDINGS

The sample size was increased to 24; this was recognizedly still a small sample, but the program developers were mostly interested in the effect, if any, of adding to the sample. A one-way analysis of variance was applied again to posttest scores on the reading achievement test. Variables were the number of hours completed by tutees. Once again, three groups of hours were created to follow the natural time blocks in the program: 10–19 hours, 20–29 hours; 30–45 hours.

The analysis of variance (using the Student-Neuman-Keuls procedure to compare group means) indicated that no pair of group means differed significantly (p = .198). Overall, again, the number of hours of tutoring did not appear to make a significant difference in posttest performance. Means and standard deviations for posttest performance by group indicated, again, that greatest gains were made at 20–29 hours of tutoring. (See Table A.3.)

The mean for Group 1 (10–19 hours of tutoring) was below the overall pretest mean (55.96). An earlier meta-analysis of studies of the effects of tutoring indicated an initially high rate of success in a relatively short time (less than 15 hours) in tutoring programs. These initial gains appeared to diminish over time.[1] The means in this pilot study suggested that the greatest increase in reading achievement occurred not in Group 1 but in Group 2 (20–29 hours of tutoring).

A regression analysis was used again to discover what, if any, separate effects were occurring across number of hours of tutoring. A summary of the regression results is presented in Table A.4.

R. T. Putnam reported that the number of hours of tutoring in a reading program appeared to facilitate the development of a "curriculum script" in the student.[2] The IIP curriculum, by its design, already provided a framework for learning that was a curriculum script, providing for specific skills practice and assessment over time. Were some long-term effects due to the format of the program being reflected in the effects on Group 3 (30–45 hours of tutoring)?

The significance of the variables within the regression equation (Beta weights) again showed that Group 3 (30–45 hours of tutoring) influenced the variate in the

Table A.3
Means and Standard Deviations Pilot Data II

| | Pretest | | Posttest | |
	Mean	S.D.	Mean	S.D.
Group 1 (10–19 hours)	45.4	11.8	54.0	15.8
Group 2 (20–29 hours)	62.6	13.1	68.5	18.8
Group 3 (30–45 hours)	68.2	18.4	62.6	16.0

N = 24

Table A.4
Regression Analysis Pilot Data II

Variable	Multiple R	R2	F	Sig F
Groups + pretest	.546	.298	2.83	.064
Groups alone	.377	.143	1.74	.199
Pretest alone	.510	.260	7.73	.011

presence of the pretest (t = .16). When the effects of the pretest were removed, Group 3 was significant (t = .00). When the pretest alone was entered into the regression formula, the pretest was also significant (t = .013). When the pretest and Group 3 were entered into the formula together as covariates, the effects were found to be significant (t = .011). Thus, both performance on the pretest and 30–45 hours of tutoring were significant predictors of posttest performance.

An examination of the correlations among posttest scores (see Table A.5), number of hours of tutoring and pretest scores suggested several points for further inquiry. Posttest and number of hours in Group 2 (20–29 hours of tutoring) correlated positively (.326), and the posttest also correlated positively (.510) with the pretest. Thus, the pretest plus 20–29 hours of tutoring seems to be a good predictor of posttest performance.

Of special interest were the correlations among the groups. Posttest performance in Group 1 (10–19 hours of tutoring) correlated negatively with Group 2 (−.650) and positively with Group 3 (.953). Posttest performance in Group 2 also correlated positively with Group 3 (.964). The findings suggested looking at possible long-term, perhaps cumulative, effects of the literacy training program.

PILOT III FINDINGS

The sample size was increased to 44, and a one-way analysis of variance was applied with posttest scores as the dependent variable. Other variables were the number of hours completed by tutees. Three groups of hours were created to follow the natural time blocks in the program: 10–19 hours; 20–29 hours; and 30–45 hours.

Analysis of variance, using the Student-Neuman-Keuls procedures to compare group means, indicated that no pair of group means differed significantly (p = .9522). Overall, the number of hours of tutoring in reading did not appear to make a significant difference in posttest performance. However, means and standard deviations (see Table A.6) for posttest performance by group indicated greatest variance around the population mean in Group 2 (20–29 hours of tutoring).

The posttest means for both Groups 1 (51.6) and 3 (51.8) were below the population mean (52.6), whereas posttest means for Group 2 (53.8) were above the population mean. The pretest means for Group 2 (48.9) and Group 3 (48.6) were

Table A.5
Correlation Matrix Pilot Data II

	Posttest	Group 1	Group 2	Group 3	Pretest
Posttest	1.0	−.357	.326	−.647	.510
Group 1		1.0	−.650	.953	−.594
Group 2			1.0	.964	.292
Pretest					1.0

Table A.6
Means and Standard Deviations Pilot Data III

| | Pretest | | Posttest | |
	Mean	S.D.	Mean	S.D.
Group 1 (10–19 hours)	44.7	11.4	51.6	16.8
Group 2 (20–29 hours)	48.9	24.3	53.8	23.9
Group 3 (30–45 hours)	48.6	27.7	51.8	22.8
Total population	47.6	21.9	52.6	21.3

N = 44

above the population mean (47.6), whereas the pretest mean for Group 1 (44.7) was below the population mean. Pretest and posttest means raise an important question. Is performance on the posttest related to performance on the pretest?

An examination of the correlations (see Table A.7) among posttest scores, number of hours of tutoring, and pretest scores suggested that this may be the case.

High scores on the pretest appear to be associated with high scores on the posttest. Different individuals had different posttest scores partly because pretest scores differed. There appeared to be little, if any, correlation between the number of hours spent in tutoring in Group 1 (−.031) or Group 2 (.049), although the trend shifted from negative to positive with increased hours in tutoring. With the high positive correlation between the population pretest and posttest scores (.800), questions about the long-term effects of tutoring were raised. What was happening between 25 and 40 hours of tutoring?

Despite the small sample size, a regression analysis was used to look at separate effects, if any, on posttest performance across number of hours of tutoring. A summary of the regression results in presented in Table A.8.

The significance of variables within the regression equation (Beta weights) showed that Group 3 (30–45 hours) influenced the variate in the presence of the pretest (t = .02). When the effects of the pretest were removed, Group 3 was significant (t = .0000). When the pretest alone was entered into the regression formula, the pretest was also significant (t = .0000). When the pretest and Group 3

Table A.7
Correlation Matrix Pilot Data III

	Posttest	Group 1	Group 2	Pretest
Posttest	1.0	−.031	.049	.800
Group 1	−.031	1.0	−.565	−.086
Group 2	.049	−.565	1.0	.053
Pretest	.800	−.086	.053	1.0

Table A.8
Regression Analysis Pilot Data III

Variable	Multiple R	R2	F	Sig F
Groups + pretest	.802	.643	24.0	.0000
Groups alone	.049	.0024	.048	.9522
Pretest alone	.800	.640	74.8	.0000

were entered into the formula together as covariates, the effects were found to be significant ($t = .002$). Both the pretest and extended hours of tutoring (30–45 hours) appear to influence posttest performance.

In an earlier meta-analysis of studies of the effects of tutoring, P. A. Cohen, J. A. Kulik, and C. C. Kulik indicated an initially high rate of success in a relative short time. These initial gains appear to diminish over time.[3] However, in this study, posttest performance tended to increase when pretest performance and increased number of hours of tutoring were considered as covariates.

SUMMARY OF PILOT FINDINGS

In addition to the intriguing quantitative results from the series of small sample pilot studies reported above, qualitative data evaluations (i.e., tutee, tutor and employer evaluations) indicate sustained growth in tutee academic skills, study skills and motivation. Tutees perceived themselves and were perceived as retaining what they had learned. Tutee attitudes toward study, personal motivation and individual achievement showed consistent improvement. Two key motivational factors appear to be delivering the tutoring program near a supportive workplace environment and individual perseverance.

Findings consistently suggested that significant gains were made in reading achievement in this literacy program at 20–29 hours of tutoring, with long-term and possibly cumulative effects surfacing at 30–45 hours. In light of this data, developers of the tutoring program are continuing data collection and analysis in an ongoing research project. Sample size is being increased in an effort to further explain both short- and long-term effects of tutoring. In addition to compiling pre- and posttest results, the authors are systematically compiling employee, employer and peer quantitative and qualitative evaluations of tutoring outcomes.

Future research will focus on comparisons of quantitative and qualitative results across tutees, tutors and employers, together with comparisons of pre- and posttutoring outcomes in experimental conditions where the number of hours, subject matter and tutoring interventions (e.g., academic, job-related, social-emotional) are manipulated. Particular attention will be given to coding types of intervention (e.g., behavioral, cognitive), along with multiple outcome measures across time blocks. Attention will also be given to comparing tutoring outcomes for adult subjects assigned to individual and small-group (3–5) tutoring conditions and to comparing outcome results for those situations where the employer cooperated in the tutoring program versus situations where the employer did not cooperate.

SUGGESTIONS FOR HUMAN RESOURCE DEVELOPERS

What kinds of questions should human resource developers ask of training specialists when considering purchasing literacy training programs?

1. Can you provide statistical data, particularly means and standard deviations across number of hours spent in the training program, to indicate the effects of the program you are offering?
2. Are those data based on comparative pretest and posttest scores on alternate forms of a norm-referenced achievement test?
3. Is the reliability of that achievement test .90 or better?
4. Do you give pretests and posttests at each phase of the training program to indicate effects from number of hours spent in the program?
5. Do you also use criterion-referenced checklists of specific skills to track the individual's skill development through the program?
6. Do the posttest results indicate that effects from the program are cumulative over time?

Questions such as these will provide the human resource developer with information on the reliability and cost-effectiveness of the training program being considered. It is particularly important that pretest and posttest results can be compared across number of hours spent in the program so that you can determine at what point continued training reaches a plateau of effectiveness.

NOTES

1. P. A. Cohen, J. A. Kulik, and C. C. Kulik, "Educational Outcomes of Tutoring: A Meta-Analysis of Findings," *American Educational Research Journal* 19, no. 2 (1982): 237–48.

2. R. T. Putnam, "Structuring and Adjusting Content for Students: A Study of Line and Simulated Tutoring of Addition," *American Educational Research Journal* 24, no. 1 (1987): 13–48.

3. Cohen, Kulik, and Kulik, "Educational Outcomes."

Appendix 4

Reading-Grade Equivalent Basic Skills

What does it mean if a training program claims to raise students' reading test scores by a year or more? Consider the training program data in Table A.9.

It would appear that the percentage gains in posttest raw scores for some students are quite impressive. But even Student A, who gained only 4.3 percent in raw score performance, gained a year in reading-grade equivalent performance. A year's gain is impressive. What does it mean for the individual to gain a year in reading performance? Consider the following changes in reading skills from first-grade to sixth-grade performance:

First Grade

In one-syllable words:

• Recognizes initial and ending consonants

• Decodes by single letters and whole word meanings

Table A.9
Raw Score Pre-Post Test Data Case Example

	Pretest	Posttest	% Gain	G.E.
Student A	22	23	4.3	4.1–5.1
Student B	19	27	29.6	4.1–5.1
Student C	13	24	45.8	3.1–4.1
Student D	11	24	54.2	3.1–4.1
Student E	18	25	28.0	4.4–5.1
Student F	12	15	20.0	2.1–3.1

Note: G.E. = Grade Equivalent

- Implies meaning
- Classifies information through comparison and contrast with what is known
  Second Grade
- Recognizes final consonant
- Recognizes long and short vowels
- Recognizes two-letter blends (e.g., bl, cl)
- Comprehends through single-word meaning
- Uses context clues
  Third Grade
- Recognizes three-letter consonant blends (e.g., thr) and digraphs (e.g., sh, th)
- Recognizes vowel controllers (e.g., awe, fur), digraphs (e.g., ai, ea) and diph-thongs (e.g., oi, ou)
- Recognizes silent letters
- Recognizes accent and syllable patterns
- Comprehends cause-and-effect relationships
- Recalls details
- Recalls character traits
- Reinforces new vocabulary
- Locates information
  Fourth Grade
- Decodes words by prefix, suffix and syllable patterns
- Recognizes main idea
- Predicts outcomes
- Infers sequence of events
- Comprehends through sentence meaning
  Fifth Grade
- Decodes words by root-word patterns
- Recognizes pronouns
- Recognizes verb variations
- Recognizes main ideas and supporting details
- Recognizes description
- Recognizes misplaced events in sequence
- Recognizes fact and fiction
- Interprets simple summaries and follows directions
  Sixth Grade
- Recognizes fact vs. opinion
- Understands persuasion
- Infers messages in diagrams

- Recognizes likenesses and differences
- Infers multiple causes and effects
- Recognizes connectiveness
- Recognizes misplaced phrases
- Compares and contrasts information on a chart
- Reads for details
- Sequences and summarizes events
- Recognizes word meanings from context clues
- Recognizes multiple meanings
- Recognizes analogies and categories
- Recognizes degree of difference in word endings

What do the changes in these skills mean to an employer? First, most technical training manuals are written for sixth-grade or higher reading performance. Second, as an individual gains proficiency in reading, he/she increases in capacity to see and understand patterns in words and sentences. Third, as an individual gains proficiency, he/she increases in capacity to make inferences and recognize subtle differences in literal versus implied meaning. Fourth, with increased proficiency comes a greater ability to process multiple sources of information. Fifth, with increased proficiency comes a greater capacity to sequence, sort and define steps in a process or event. Finally, as reading proficiency increases, so does the individual's ability to decode independently what the printed text means and determine what that meaning implies for the individual's task or decision requirements. In other words, the individual can translate what the printed text requires him/her to do.

Select Bibliography

At the conclusion of each chapter, the reader will find listed many articles, reports, studies, books and research papers cited in the text. However, for the reader's continued study we have compiled a selected bibliography of publications that will broaden your personal perspectives on the related issues of Work Force Education.

Business Council for Effective Literacy. *Job-Related Basic Skills: A Guide for Planners of Employee Programs*. New York: Business Council for Effective Literacy, 1987.

Carnevale, Anthony P.; Gainer, Leila J.; and Meltzer, Ann S. *Workplace Basics: The Skills Employers Want*. Alexandria, Va.: American Society for Training and Development, 1988.

Cook, Wanda. *Adult Literacy Education in the United States*. Newark, Del.: International Reading Association, 1977.

Dertougos, Michael L.; Lester, Richard K.; and Solow, Robert M. *Made in America*. Cambridge, Mass.: MIT Press, 1989.

Eurich, Nell P. *Corporate Classrooms: The Learning Business*. Princeton, N.J.: Carnegie Foundation, 1985.

Graff, Harvey J. *The Legacies of Literacy*. Bloomington: Indiana University Press, 1987.

LiBretto, Ellen V. *High/Low Handbook*. New York: R. R. Bowker, Co., 1985, 1990.

Lund, Leonard, and McGuire, E. Patrick. *Literacy in the Work Force*. New York: Conference Board, 1990.

National Center on Education and the Economy. *America's Choice: High Skills or Low Wages*. Rochester, N.Y.: National Center on Education and the Economy, 1990.

Newman, Anabell Powell, and Beverstock, Caroline. *Adult Literacy*. Newark, Del.: International Reading Association, 1990.

Nothdurft, William E. *School Works*. Washington, D.C.: Brookings Institution, 1989.

Sarmiento, Anthony R., and Kay, Ann. *Worker-Centered Learning: A Union Guide to Workplace Literacy*. Washington, D.C.: AFL-CIO Human Resources Development Institute, 1990.

U.S. Departments of Labor and Education. *The Bottom Line: Basic Skills in the Workplace*. Washington, D.C.: U.S. Department of Labor, U.S. Department of Education, 1988.

Vélis, Jean-Pierre. *Through a Glass, Darkly: Functional Illiteracy in Industrialized Countries*. Paris: UNESCO, 1990.

Index

About the Authors

EDWARD E. GORDON, Ph.D., is President of Imperial Corporate Training and Development and has taught at De Paul and Roosevelt Universities. Dr. Gordon is a widely published author of articles in such journals as the *Training and Development Journal (ASTD)*, *Training Today*, and the *Phi Delta Kappan*. He has also written other books and articles dealing with educational history, school reform and contemporary training and development issues.

JUDITH A. PONTICELL, Ph.D., is Director of the Chicago Area School Effectiveness Council, a school improvement consortium supported by the University of Illinois at Chicago, Center for Urban Educational Research and Development. Her research focuses on adult cognition and educational partnerships. Dr. Ponticell's work has been published by the University of Illinois Press, The Clearinghouse on Teacher Education, and the *Training and Development Journal*.

RONALD R. MORGAN, Ph.D., is an Associate Professor and Director of the School Psychology Program, Loyola University of Chicago. Dr. Morgan is an expert in the psychology of learning and instruction. He is the author of twenty journal articles and the co-author of two textbooks. His publications have been featured in *Educational Psychological Measurement*, *Teaching of Psychology*, and the *Journal of Social Behavior and Personality*.